The
Small Business
Bible

The Small Business Bible

EVERYTHING
YOU NEED TO KNOW
TO SUCCEED IN
YOUR SMALL BUSINESS

STEVEN D. STRAUSS

WILEY

JOHN WILEY & SONS, INC.

For general information on our other products and services please contact our
Customer Care Department within the United States at (800) 762-2974, outside the
United States at (317) 572-3993 or fax (317) 572-4002.

Wiley also publishes its books in a variety of electronic formats. Some content that
appears in print may not be available in electronic books. For more information about
Wiley products, visit our web site at www.Wiley.com.

Library of Congress Cataloging-in-Publication Data:

Strauss, Steven D., 1958–
  The small business bible : everything you need to know to succeed in your
small business / Steven D. Strauss.
       p.   cm.
   ISBN 0-471-68431-7 (pbk.)
  1.   Small business—United States—Management. 2.   Small business—United
States—Finance. 3.   New business enterprises—United States.   I. Title.
   HD62.7.S875   2005
   658.02'2—dc22
2004016912

Printed in the United States of America.

10 9 8 7 6 5 4 3 2 1

*For my sweet, fun, loving, funny, wonderful
family who make it all possible, and worthwhile.*

Preface

Starting, owning, and running a successful small business is one of the great joys in life. No, there are no guarantees, and yes, there are obstacles. But if you do it right, if you start the right small business—one suited to your strengths, one that you are passionate about, one that epitomizes your highest dreams and values, and certainly one that allows you to make a nice profit—then there is no telling how far it can take you.

This book shows you how to get there.

But be forewarned: If what you are looking for is a book that will give you the theoretical underpinnings of small business theory and expository prose about business assumptions, this is the wrong book for you. Put it down. What you will get instead in these pages are tried-and-true, real world business tips, skills, examples, and strategies that have been proven to help small businesses grow, that can help *your* small business grow. Written in a friendly, easy-to-understand manner, chock full of interesting, actual examples, *The Small Business Bible* contains everything you need to know to have a successful, fulfilling, enjoyable entrepreneurial journey.

Covering the simple to the complex, *The Small Business Bible* allows you to easily and quickly get up to speed on any pertinent subject. Would you like to know how to create a memorable brand for your small business? It is in here. Unsure about small business accounting? Read on. Shoestring marketing? Yep, it is here, too. It is all here. *The Small Business Bible* covers everything you need to know, or might need to know, about starting or running a successful and enjoyable small business. It is not called *The Small Business Bible* for nothing.

As the long-time small business columnist for USATODAY.com (www.usatoday.com/money/smallbusiness/front.htm), I have the opportunity to interact with many small business owners. I hear their war stories and learn their secrets, and that is what I want to impart to you in this book: the best tips, hints, and ideas that I have come across. By helping you to avoid mistakes, teaching you important, difference-making business strategies, and sharing what works, *The Small Business Bible* is intended to be your one-stop shop for all things small business. If I have done my job right, it should become an indispensable business partner; a well-used, dog-eared friend that shows you the way. Thanks for taking it along with you on your entrepreneurial journey.

Contents

PART

Genesis

CHAPTER 1

In the Beginning

If one advances in the direction of his dreams, one will meet with success unexpected in common hours.

—HENRY DAVID THOREAU

It is a huge step. Deciding to go into business for yourself is one of the most important decisions you will make in your life. Ranking right up there with picking a partner and buying a home, becoming an entrepreneur is one of those life-altering events that will have repercussions for years to come. No, there are no guarantees, and yes, there will be obstacles. But do you know what? If you do it right, if you start the right small business—one suited to your strengths, one that you are passionate about, one that allows you to make a nice profit—then here is no telling how far it can take you. John Nordstrom, founder of the department store with the eponymous name, said of his roots, "I was not certain what I wanted to do. I started looking around for some small business to get into. Mr. Wallin the shoemaker suggested that we join a partnership and open a shoe store."

ASSESSING YOUR STRENGTHS

Not everyone is cut out to be an entrepreneur. While the common perception of entrepreneurship is that it is exciting, and indeed it is, many other words equally describe the life of the self-made small businessperson: nerve-wracking, liberating, difficult, challenging, time-consuming, overwhelming, fun, joyous, productive, and uncertain—and that's just for starters. Any small businessperson could expand at length about any one of these adjectives, for all come into play to some degree or another in almost every small business, and often in the same day.

So the question is not whether entrepreneurship is right for you, but rather, are you right for entrepreneurship? Can you handle the stress, the freedom, the lack of structure, the uncertainty, and the opportunity that await if you decide to start your own business? This really can't be emphasized enough. While there is no doubt that being in business for yourself can be great, if you are not temperamentally cut out for it, it will be a tough road. There is no shame in this. Some people are artists and others are lawyers, some are vagabonds and others are homebodies, some are entrepreneurs and some are not.

So which are you? Taking the following quiz will help you evaluate your qualifications. The important thing though, as you take the quiz, is to be perfectly honest. There is no point in answering the questions right if they are not true for you.

Test Your Entrepreneurship IQ

1. **Are you a self-starter?**
   a. Yes, I like to think up ideas and implement them. **(5 points)**
   b. If someone helps me get started, I will definitely follow through. **(3 points)**
   c. Frankly, I would rather follow than lead. **(1 point)**

2. **How do you feel about taking risks?**
   a. I really like the feeling of being on the edge a bit. **(5 points)**
   b. Calculated risks are acceptable at times. **(3 points)**
   c. I like the tried and true. **(1 point)**

3. **Are you a leader?**
   a. Yes. **(5 points)**
   b. Yes, when necessary. **(3 points)**
   c. No, not really. **(1 point)**

4. Can you and your family live without a regular paycheck?
   a. Yes, if that is what it takes. **(5 points)**
   b. I would rather not, but understand that may be part of the process. **(3 points)**
   c. I do not like that idea at all. **(1 point)**

5. Could you fire someone who really needed the job your business provided?
   a. Yes. I may not like it, but that is the way it goes sometimes. **(5 points)**
   b. I hope so. **(3 points)**
   c. I really can't see myself doing that. **(1 point)**

6. Are you willing to work 60 hours a week, or more?
   a. Again, if that is what it takes, yes. **(5 points)**
   b. Maybe in the beginning. **(3 points)**
   c. I think many other things are more important than work. **(1 point)**

7. Are you self-confident?
   a. You bet! **(5 points)**
   b. Most of the time. **(3 points)**
   c. Unfortunately, that is not one of my strong suits. **(1 point)**

8. Can you live with uncertainty?
   a. Yes. **(5 points)**
   b. If I have to, but I don't like it. **(3 points)**
   c. No, I like knowing what to expect. **(1 point)**

9. Can you stick with it once you have put your mind to something?
   a. I usually will not let anything get in the way. **(5 points)**
   b. Most of the time, if I like what I am doing. **(3 points)**
   c. Not always. **(1 point)**

10. Are you creative?
   a. Yes, I do get a lot of good ideas. **(5 points)**
   b. I can be. **(3 points)**
   c. No, not really. **(1 point)**

11. Are you competitive?
   a. To a fault sometimes. (5 points)
   b. Sure, mostly. (3 points)
   c. Not really, my nature is more laid-back. (1 point)

12. Do you have a lot of willpower and self-discipline?
   a. Yes. (5 points)
   b. I am self-disciplined when I need to be. (3 points)
   c. Not really. (1 point)

13. Are you individualistic or would you rather go along with the status quo?
   a. I like to think things through myself and do things my way. (5 points)
   b. I am sometimes an original. (3 points)
   c. I think strongly individualistic people are a bit strange. (1 point)

14. Can you live without structure?
   a. Yes. (5 points)
   b. Actually, the idea of living without a regular job makes me nervous. (3 points)
   c. No, I like routine and structure in my life. (1 point)

15. Do you have many business skills?
   a. Yes, I do, and those I don't have, I'll learn. (5 points)
   b. I have some. (3 points)
   c. No, not really. (1 point)

16. Are you flexible and willing to change course when things are not going your way?
   a. Yes. (5 points)
   b. I like to think so, but others may disagree. (3 points)
   c. No, I have a fairly rigid personality. (1 point)

17. **Do you have experience in the business you are thinking of starting?**
    a. Yes. (5 points)
    b. Some. (3 points)
    c. No. (1 point)

18. **Could you competently perform multiple business tasks: accounting, sales, marketing, and so on?**
    a. I sure would like to try! (5 points)
    b. I hope so. (3 points)
    c. That sounds intimidating. (1 point)

19. **Are you willing to really hustle for clients and customers?**
    a. Sure. (5 points)
    b. If I have to. (3 points)
    c. I would rather not. (1 point)

20. **How well do you handle pressure?**
    a. Quite well. (5 points)
    b. It's not my strongest trait, but I can do it. (3 points)
    c. Not well at all. (1 point)

Scoring

80–100: You have both the temperament and the skills to become an entrepreneur.

60–79: You are not a natural entrepreneur, but may become one over time.

Below 60: You would be wise to think of something else to do besides self-employment.

So there you have it. Not only should this quiz help you understand your Entrepreneurship IQ, but it should equally give you some insight into the traits and characteristics of the prototypical successful self-employed businessperson: driven, hard-working, creative, energetic, resourceful, confident, and flexible.

So if this describes you (or a close approximation of you), then the next question is, where do you go from here?

RISK TOLERANCE

The quiz you just took is intended to both help you gauge your Entrepreneurship IQ and show you the traits required to start your own small business. Yes, you will need some business savvy and self-confidence; that is a given. Being creative and hard-working are equally important. But of all the necessary traits, the one that you must have in abundance is a tolerance for risk, because starting your own small business is a risk.

Borrowing money, setting up shop, trying out new ideas—these are things that, while fun and exciting, are also inherently risky. There are no guarantees that your idea and plan will fly. Certainly the goal of this book is to make sure it does, but no matter how much you study and learn, there will always be an element of risk in being an entrepreneur. Would you have it any other way? If your answer is no, then you definitely have the right stuff. If it is not, if the idea of taking a big risk scares more than excites you, then you need to consider carefully whether starting your own business is really for you.

Throughout this book I share with you the traits of exceptional small businesses so that you can see what the best of the best do. Here is the first one, and it is good news: Great small businesses work to reduce their risks as much as possible. They work at covering every angle so that the risks they do take are prudent, calculated ones. That is what you will need to do, too, if you start your own small business—take a prudent, calculated, intelligent risk with a high likelihood of payoff. Just know that even reduced risk will still be present because it is the nature of the game.

THE NEXT STEP

Sometimes the idea of starting your own business can be overwhelming. What kind of business should you start? Where will you get the money? How will you find customers? All are legitimate concerns, and all are addressed in detail. At this point, however, understand that as you drive down the street, almost every business you see is a small business run by someone who, at some point, had never run a business before, either. But they learned how, found the money, found some customers, and are still around. If they did it, so can you. To join their ranks, you must be willing to do your homework.

Education

The next step therefore is to educate yourself. Most people go into business because they love something and want to do it every day: The baker wants her own bakery; the chiropractor wants to start his own practice, and so on. The problem the baker and chiropractor usually have is that while they may know a lot about baking and backs, if they are like most entrepreneurs, they know little about the business and boardrooms; they may know their specialty, but they do not know everything else it takes to start and to run a successful business. And problematically, it is the everything else that will take up *a lot* of their time. Marketing and advertising, sales and income taxes, hiring and firing, and so on have nothing whatsoever to do with backs and bread.

There are several great sites that can teach you a lot about small business:

- www.usatoday.com/money/smallbusiness/front.htm
- www.NASE.org
- www.NFIB.com
- www.SBA.gov
- www.Microsoft.com/smallbusiness
- www.MrAllBiz.com

So the next step is to begin to learn about business in general. Certainly this book should be enormously helpful, and down the road you will see that nothing beats the trial and error of actually running your own venture, but before you can get to that point, you need to get a general idea of how businesses operate.

Even if you passed the preceding Entrepreneur IQ quiz with flying colors, it is probably safe to assume that, while you have an entrepreneurial bent, you likely do not know everything you will need to become successful; that is true for most self-employed people. So the suggestion here is that you begin to brush up on both the subjects that seem interesting to you *and* the ones that scare you. If finances are not your strong suit, then dig in. As a small business owner, you will inevitably wear many hats. It is not uncommon, especially at the beginning, for the founder to be the president, accountant, marketing wizard, and salesperson, all rolled into one. So it helps to get a broad understanding of what it takes to run a business.

It would also be smart to start to read some business magazines every month. Periodicals like *Home Business Magazine*, *Entrepreneur*, and *Inc.* are chock full of easy-to-understand articles intended to make you a success.

Experience

Finally, no education would be complete without some practical, hands-on experience. This can take two forms. First, if you want to open an antiques store, for example, you would be wise to work at one. If you already have that sort of hands-on experience in your chosen industry, then skip the rest of this paragraph. But if you have never actually worked in a business like the one you want to start, you are *strongly advised* to do just that. Your entrepreneurial dream can wait six months while you gain the sort of experience that can make or break your new business. Working in a business like the one you want to create will teach you things that no books can impart. It is a critical step.

Second, you need to find some business owners in your desired field with whom to talk. If you stay in your town, finding entrepreneurs to talk to in your potential industry may be difficult; they will likely view you as a potential competitor (rightly so) and thus be reluctant to share their insights with you. Therefore, it would be much smarter to go to a nearby town, find a few businesses similar to the one you want to start, take the owners out for lunch, and pick their brains. People love to talk about themselves. Find out everything you can about their business:

- What do they like most about it?
- What do they like least?
- How much did it cost to start?
- How much can you expect to make?
- Where do they advertise?
- If they were starting over, what would they do differently?

No one knows this business (whatever it is) like the owners do. You would be hard-pressed to find better, more pertinent information than that from these small business owners who are already doing what you dream of doing.

This informal MBA can reap tremendous benefits. By the time you are ready to start your business, you will have a thorough understanding of the risks and rewards of what you are getting into. Doing this initial research will take time for sure, but if you follow this plan, you can be assured that when you finally do open your doors, you will have reduced your risk to the extent possible, and thus your chances of success will be much greater.

CHAPTER 2

Choosing the Right Business

The road to happiness lies in two simple principles: Find what it is that interests you and that you can do well, and when you find it, put your whole soul into it—every bit of energy and ambition and natural ability you have.

—JOHN D. ROCKEFELLER III

When it comes to choosing a small business, there basically are two types of entrepreneurs. The first is the person who is in love with the idea of starting a very specific business. It may be a gardener who envisions a nursery or a chef who has long dreamed of owning a restaurant. The other potential small businessperson is someone who is also in love, not with a specific idea per se, but with the idea generally of being his or her own boss. As there are both risks and rewards associated with each path, both warrant further discussion.

IF YOU DO WHAT YOU LOVE, WILL THE MONEY REALLY FOLLOW?

There is a saying that goes, Do what you love, the money will follow. While noble and possibly true, there is more to small business success than simply doing what you love. Now, do not get me wrong; doing what you love is indeed the first prerequisite when you are choosing the right business, but it is just that, a first step.

Live with Passion

What do you love? As in the rest of life, we tend to succeed when we are engaged in something that we really enjoy. Your business should be no different. Richard Branson started Virgin Music, not because he thought music would be hot, but because he loved it. Bill Gates started Microsoft because he loved computers. Both companies began as small businesses.

What about you? By now, you know what excites you, what you love most. You know what you like to do, what your passions are, what is fun, and how you like to spend your time. Barbara Winter, in her great book, *Making a Living Without a Job* (Bantam) 1993, says that passion leads to purpose, that once you get in touch with those things you are most passionate about, you can begin to create a business of purpose around them.

So that is your first assignment: deciding exactly which of your passions you love enough to start a business around. Remember, your business will become your baby, and like any other baby, it will require a lot of love, time, money, and attention if it is to grow strong and healthy. Of those, right now, you should be most concerned with time. Your new business will take a lot of it.

Second, once you know what area you love enough to spend all day, every day doing, you then need to figure out what business you could start that relates to that. Say for example that you have a love of plants and gardening and have decided that you want to spend every day doing something related to those things. What are your choices? You could, for instance:

- Start a nursery
- Open a flower shop
- Start a lawn-care business
- Grow organic vegetables
- Buy a farm
- Start a winery

> Stuck for a business that relates to your passion? Open the Yellow Pages and look under your category. You might be surprised to see how many different sorts of businesses other people have created around the same thing.

This is the time for one of those Anything Goes brainstorming sessions. Go for it. Write down any kooky idea you have. No limits! There are few times in life when the stars align themselves just so and one has a chance, not only for a fresh start, but a fresh start completely of one's own choosing. Usually, either money is tight, or the opportunity passes, or something else conspires to interfere with a brand new beginning. But if you are at a place where you are reading this and are ready to start your own business, and you have the wherewithal to do so, *and* you can choose any business you want, then savor this moment for it is rare indeed.

But while it is good and wise to let your mind roam, it is equally shrewd, afterward, to come back to Earth. What if, instead of gardening, your answer is that what you love most is nineteenth century Flemish architecture and that you have decided to become a Flemish architecture consultant? However interesting that may be to you, and while it certainly would scratch your Flemish architecture itch, if there are not people willing to pay you for your expertise, people willing to buy the product or service you want to sell, you do not have a business; you have a bust. So be realistic—there must be a market willing to buy what you plan to offer.

Assuming then that you have decided to pick a business that is a passionate practicality, the last question to be answered is whether you will be able to make sufficient profit in it. There is no sense in starting a business, however much you might love the idea, if you will not be able to make a good living. One reason we go into business for ourselves is the chance to make more money.

Whatever business you want to start then, whatever product or service you decide to sell, you have to be able to sell it at a price high enough to make a profit, but low enough that people will buy it. This is not always an easy balance. Why do so many stores in expensive malls go out of business? Because, even with a great concept, making a profit is mathematically impossible if their overhead is too high. So before jumping into a business, you *have to* crunch some numbers. Do your research. How much does a small business of the type you want to start make? How quickly does it make it? See Chapter 4, *Understanding Your Market*, for more information on how to do this.

Too many new entrepreneurs fall in love with their idea and become convinced that it is the greatest thing since sliced bread. You *Do not make this mistake.* must strive to be as objective as possible. Do other people like your idea as much as you do? Ask around. Get feedback. Crunch your numbers. Be a businessperson. While hunches and intuition are great, you need some objective criteria before making the leap into the land of entrepreneurship.

A Word of Caution

The bad news about starting a new business is that good ideas are not really that hard to come by, but oftentimes not that easy to implement. Every business you see when you drive down the street was once someone's beloved inspiration. But what did it take to turn that great idea into a successful business? How much time, effort, and money were involved? You can bet that the entrepreneur who started that busy business on the corner probably had no idea how difficult it would be to turn his vision into reality.

So finding a good idea is just the beginning; in fact, it is the easy part. The trick is being able to successfully implement that idea. That is much more difficult. As Thomas Edison said, genius is "1 percent inspiration and 99 percent perspiration." That is as true in business as it is in science. So not only must you come up with a good idea, but it must be a good idea that you can move on. That is what you are looking for.

Look around. Are there any similar businesses to the one you want to create? If not, that might tell you something. Maybe your idea is so cutting edge that no one else has thought of it. That can be good, and then again, it might be bad. Innovative businesses have the chance to become the market leader: Amazon.com was first, Yahoo! was first, Post-its and Pampers were first. Being first gives you something called "the first mover's advantage." Simply put, that means that by being first you have the chance to shape the marketplace. The potential profit in such a business is enormous. The problem, as you may have surmised, is that it usually takes a lot of money to successfully create such a business. If you do not have the drive to do so, or the risk tolerance, or the capital, then you would be best advised to follow, and not lead. Later on, once you have more experience and money, you can innovate all you want, but the beginning of your small business journey may not be the best place to boldly go where no entrepreneur has gone before. Now is probably the time to learn, not lead.

So consider picking an idea that others have also successfully implemented. Consider the previous example: Books have been written on how to start a florist shop or a nursery. Books have not been written on how to tap the Flemish architecture market.

Another advantage of being a follower instead of a leader is that you should be able to find plenty of information that can be of great help to you. In our gardening example, besides books, you could go to the Service Corps of Retired Executives (SCORE) and find some retired florists to give you some help, join a nursery association, and read trade magazines. None of these resources would be available to you if you chose to invest your efforts in an obscure, albeit possibly fascinating, business or in a cutting edge business where you will need to teach consumers about your goods or services.

The important thing therefore is that you choose a business that you are not only passionate about, but one that can be successfully implemented.

IN LOVE WITH ENTREPRENEURSHIP

Now we come to the second sort of entrepreneur—the individual who is more concerned with being his own boss than with starting a particular business. Jeff Bezos did not start Amazon.com because he was in love with books. He started it because he discovered that Internet usage in the early 1990s was growing at a whopping 2,300 percent a year. Armed with that valuable insight, he analyzed the marketplace and the opportunity, and concluded that the best way to tap the commercial power of the Net would be through book sales. Because it was not about the books, but rather the opportunity, Bezos is the prototypical second category entrepreneur.

There is no shortage of people who start their own business because, simply put, they want to be their own boss; that is as great a reason as any. The chance to make your own decisions, rise or fall by your own ingenuity and hard work, the opportunity to make more money, and the freedom that comes with being a small businessperson are some of the great joys in life. It is no wonder that many people long to start their own business. When done right, it is special.

In 1986, Roy and Bertrand Sosa emigrated to the United States from Mexico. When they got here, they quickly discovered that they needed a checking account and credit card, yet credit cards were difficult for new immigrants to obtain. Their firsthand market analysis convinced them that there was a huge market waiting to be tapped, and so the brothers started NetSpend, a small business designed to offer traditional financial services to recent immigrants and people with poor credit histories. Using prepaid phone cards as their model, Roy and Bertrand copied and tweaked that model to create a business plan for prepaid debit cards.

Then they had their big break. The brothers Sosa discovered the Small Business Administration's (SBA's) Small Business Investment Companies (SBIC) program. SBICs guarantee the investment made by investors (called venture capitalists, or VCs.) Because the investment is SBA guaranteed, SBIC VCs are induced to invest in projects they might otherwise say no to, like NetSpend. Armed with SBIC VC money, in five years NetSpend went from 0 to 400,000 accounts, and growing. When asked what advice they had for other would-be entrepreneurs, the brothers offered three rules:

1. Figure what pain or need the customer has that you can solve.
2. Create strong, win-win partnerships and relationships.
3. Start with baby steps, but think big.

The question is, what would be the best sort of business to start? If you want to create a great business, a successful business, then here is a critical tip: *Find a business that fulfills a market need.* That sentence should become your mantra. The best businesses find a need, a niche, and fill it. Do that, and almost everything else will fall into place. If you are looking for a business to start, the number one thing to discover is whether that business can sell something people need. "Figure what pain or need the customer has that you can solve."

There are several ways to come to the correct decision and find that great business.

1. *Research, Research, Research, and Then Do Some More Research.* Your first step is to analyze both the marketplace and the opportunities available. Look around, find some businesses doing something that looks good to you, and learn about those businesses. How hard are they to create? How much money do they make? How much money would you need to start a similar business? The options are many and there is no shortage of associations and web sites ready to help you find the right business to start. Among the places you should look are:

   - www.SBA.gov/starting_business/
   - www.Startupjournal.com/
   - www.uschamber.com/sb/business/startup.asp
   - www.FranchiseHandbook.com

   Look for a business that catches your eye, that seems to have great potential for growth, and that is interesting.

2. *Product or Service?* When it comes down to it, your business will provide people either with a product or a service. Service businesses tend to be less expensive to start as there is no inventory to buy. Whereas product businesses mark up prices on scores of products and profit on the difference, service businesses, like those of lawyers, doctors, and consultants, sell time and expertise. An initial decision then is which of these best suits your temperament, skills, and goals.

Business selection do's and don'ts:

- Do be patient. A good selection process takes time and requires knowledge about the industry, marketplace, and competition.
- Do look for opportunity. As hockey great Wayne Gretzky once said, "Go to where the puck is going, not where it is."
- Don't pick a business that is too challenging. You will be challenged enough.
- Don't pick a business that cannot compete. Superstores like Costco, Sam's Club, Target, and Wal-Mart will beat you on price. Find a business, a niche, where you will have an advantage over the competition.

3. *Analyze Your Skills and Experience.*   Suppose you have spent your career doing marketing for major corporations. You then have invaluable skills that should be tapped when deciding what business is right for you. Even if it is not a marketing business, you would be foolhardy not to choose a business that does not somehow tap into your well of knowledge and skill. Now, it may be that you are tired of doing whatever it is you have been doing and that in fact is why you want to start your own business. Understandable, for sure. Just be open to the option of finding a business that gives you a leg up on the competition because of your background.

4. *Consider Your Options.*   You could create a business from scratch. You could buy an existing business. You could start a franchise. You could create a home-based business. The possibilities are many. The important thing is to (1) realize that there are in fact a variety of options when you are choosing a business, and to (2) learn about the pros and cons of each (read those chapters, research the industry, speak with people in those sorts of businesses).

5. *Narrow Your Choices.*   Once you have analyzed the market, the opportunities available, your skills and experience, and your goals, you should be able to narrow your choice down to a few sorts of business. The next step may be the most important. You must—repeat, *must*—go out and find some people who own and run these sorts of businesses. Again, theory and books are great, but nothing beats speaking with someone who lives that business every day.

6. *Start Your Engines.*   Whether you want to start a business because you want to start a business or because you want to spend your time surrounded by your passion, the important thing is to do your homework and find a niche that fills a market need. Do that, and you are well on your way.

CHAPTER 3

Buying an Existing Business

Some regard private enterprise as if it were a predatory tiger to be shot. Others look upon it as a cow that they can milk. Only a handful see it for what it really is—the strong horse that pulls the whole cart.

—WINSTON CHURCHILL

Starting a business from scratch is a daunting task. You must do everything right, from picking the right business and name to finding the right location and lease to getting a business license and insurance—and that is just for starters. It is no wonder then that not a few budding business owners opt to buy an ongoing business.

Doing so has several advantages. First, you will not be starting from scratch; the business already exists. Second, you will not have to create goodwill—a favorable reputation in the community. That important aspect has been handled by the current owner. Third, it is quicker—everything should already be in place for you to hit the ground running. The main benefit though is that buying an existing business reduces your risk. A business risk, a calculated business risk, is one of the things that makes being in business so fun and exciting.

But notice that I said a calculated business risk. Remember, the great entrepreneurs are not gamblers; indeed, they seek to reduce the risk as much as possible. When you buy an established business it has a track record; you can look at the books, see how much money the place made in the past few years, and have a pretty good idea how much it will make next year. You simply do not have that sort of information (and comfort) when you create a business from scratch.

FIRST STEPS

Ideally, you will look for a business in an industry in which either you have some expertise or your skills are transferable. You also need to consider whether you want a business that is retail or wholesale, product or service, large or small, and so forth. As discussed in the previous chapter, the important thing is to find a business that combines your interests with the ability to make a good living. Can you see yourself in this business, every day, and having a good time (mostly)? That is a key consideration.

Where to Find Businesses for Sale

There are four main sources for finding businesses that are being sold.

1. *The classifieds.* The classified ad section of your local paper will have a section called Business Opportunities. That section lists various small businesses for sale, their prices, locations, and so forth. This is a fine place to start.
2. *Magazines.* Trade magazines usually have a section in the back for business owners selling their businesses. As almost every industry has a trade magazine associated with it, it would behoove you to pick up one and scour the ads. If, for example, you wanted to buy a pizza restaurant, *Pizza Today* magazine would be a good place to look.
3. *Online.* If you type "businesses for sale" into your favorite search engine, you will get a list of sites that broker business sales.

A few sites to check out:

- Businessesforsale.com
- Bizquest.com
- Bizbuysell.com
- Mergernetwork.com
- Businessbroker.net

4. *Business brokers.*   While not cheap, business brokers can be an excellent resource when you are searching for a business to buy. A good broker will have access to businesses that you did not know were for sale, and can also be an important sounding board—giving you feedback and background on the pros and cons of the different businesses you are considering.

> It is not surprising why sellers use brokers. A good business broker brings in more qualified prospects, weeds out the phonies, and usually garners a better price for the business.

If you are considering hiring a business broker, be sure to find out the following:

- *The broker's experience.*   The average age of a business broker is 55, and it is not hard to understand why. Good brokers need to understand finances and financing, business valuation, sales, and so forth. You need someone with experience.
- *Whether the broker is certified.*   Look for a broker accredited by the International Business Brokers Association (IBBA) with an accreditation called a Certified Business Intermediary (CBI).
- *The services provided.*   Will the broker value the business for you? Does she only negotiate the deal? A good broker should be a financial advisor for your end of the bargain.

> Need a business broker? Look in the Yellow Pages under Business Brokers or type the name, and your city, into your search engine.

HOW MUCH CAN YOU EXPECT TO MAKE?

You know that you can take your money and make about 10 percent a year by investing it in a mutual fund. If you can earn 10 percent with a passive investment like a mutual fund, then what should you expect to earn from an active investment like an established business? While it is difficult to put a percentage figure on it, it is not unreasonable to assume that you should expect to make enough to cover

- The business' operating expenses.
- Your salary.
- Your loan payments on any credit you needed for the purchase.
- An annual return on your capital.

After that, for any business you are serious about, you need to discover:

- *Why the business is being sold.* It may be that the owner is ready to retire and wants to cash out. That is a good reason. It may be that the place is a dog and the owner wants to sell his problems. That is not. While you can expect the owner to paint the rosiest picture possible, he cannot legally lie, as that is fraudulent and a reason to void a contract. So do your homework. Get some referrals from the owner and call them. Get some trade references and call them. Speak with neighboring businesses in the area. Find out all you can about the business.

> You can get an idea about the business' credit history from Dun and Bradstreet at http://smallbusiness.dnb.com.

- *The competition.* Who are the competitors? Where are they located? How does the current owner deal with them? What would be your competitive advantages if you bought the place?
- *Whether there are nontransferable intangibles.* Some businesses succeed because of the owner—she has fantastic contacts, special skills, an in somewhere, that sort of thing. You must be sure that the business can be run just as successfully when you become the boss.
- *Whether there are any pending changes.* Is the neighborhood stable? Does the government or a potential competitor have any plans for the area?

- *What needs to be changed.*   Are the facilities in good condition? Is the décor dated? How are the plumbing and electricity? You certainly do not want to buy the place and then be stuck with major expenses. For this reason (as with a home purchase) any offer you make should be contingent on a successful inspection of the premises.
- *Profitability.*   The reason you are looking at an established business is because you want to be able to project your profit and return with some accuracy. The only way to do that is to dig into the books with your accountant. Ideally, you want to see an audited set of books, going back at least two years.

> Do you want to buy a business but lack the funds to do so? Then be sure to read Chapter 34, *The Shoestring Entrepreneur.*

Of course, the $64,000 question is the price. How do you know what is a fair price for the business?

BUSINESS VALUATION 101

When it comes to buying a business, there are basically three questions to consider.

1. *What does the business own?*   A business that has invested a lot of money over the years in assets is obviously more valuable than a business that has not. Assets can take many forms: trucks, equipment, contracts, intellectual property rights, goodwill, and plenty more. Sellers tend to overvalue goodwill and buyers tend to undervalue it. The important thing is to realistically analyze the value of the name of the business in the community.
2. *How much does the business earn?*   Again, the same principle applies—a business that makes a profit of $100,000 a year is obviously much more valuable than one that nets $35,000.

3. *Are there any intangibles to consider?* What makes the business unique and profitable? Does it have a great location, a favorable lease, great employees? These are the last things to consider.

The answers to these three questions are then taken into account and used to determine the value of a business. There are three ways to go about calculating that. The first is called *price building*. The second method is called *return on investment*. The third is the *multiplier*.

Price building is a valuation method that simply looks at the hard facts—assets, goodwill, leases, real estate, and so on. Essentially what you do here is list every asset and give it a dollar value. For example, it might look like this:

Bill's Machinery Rentals

- Real estate: $125,000
- Equipment: $40,000
- Inventory: $25,000
- Goodwill: $10,000
- Total: $200,000

$200,000 may or may not be the right price for this business. While it is hard to say, the price builder method indicates that it is (assuming the numbers listed above, of course).

> **Want some help valuing a business? Try visiting www.bizcomps.com and www.bvmarketdata.com.**

Return on investment (ROI) looks at the business profit, per year, to help the buyer see the percentage return on his investment. For example, say that Bill's Machinery Rentals is asking $200,000 for the business. Is that fair? Using the ROI method we would see that

- Net profit is $100,000.
- Business sale price is $200,000.
- Return on investment ($100,000/$200,000) is 50 percent.

Using this method, and these numbers, the buyer would be getting a 50 percent return on his investment in a year. There are few investments out there that allow a 50 percent ROI. Thus, a higher amount for the business is probably in order.

The last method is the multiplier. Here you would again look at the earnings, but you would then multiply them by some factor—it varies depending upon the industry—to get a final price. A factor of 3 would result in a $300,000 asking price. Of course, the battle is what that factor should be.

Yes, all of this is complicated, and that is why hiring a business broker makes a lot of sense. Though you will pay a decent commission, it may be worth it to ensure that you get a good business at a fair price.

GETTING READY TO CLOSE

Aside from poring over the books, your due diligence will take you on a tour of the actual premises. Peek into the nooks and crannies. By this time you should be aware of both the positives and negatives of the business, and you should especially get your questions about the problems answered. Remember that no business will be perfect; your job is to decide whether the benefits outweigh the burdens and if obstacles can be overcome.

Once you have found a business that you really like, your vetting process must include final analysis with your lawyer and accountant, even if you have hired a broker. Leases and financial statements are best left to experts. Speak with customers and suppliers where possible. Once your team has concluded that the business is viable, it is time to negotiate a final price and get set for closing.

As you negotiate the final deal, consider adding these provisions into the contract:

- *Link the sales price to customer retention.*   Much of what you are buying is likely the existing customer base. Yet especially with a service business, the clients may be more committed to the seller than to the business. Therefore, see whether you can link the purchase price to the number of customers who will stay.

- *Have the old owner stay for a while.*   This can help with the transition, as well as assist customer retention. You will pay him or her a consulting fee, but it is usually worth it.

CHAPTER 4

Understanding Your Market

We don't want to push our ideas onto customers; we simply want to make what they want.

—LAURA ASHLEY

This may be the most important chapter in the whole book. Why? Because everything else, from selecting the right business and marketing it
to growing and even eventually selling it hinge on having an accurate understanding of your market. Get this foundation piece wrong and a lot
more *will* go wrong, but get it right and the world can be your oyster.

THE NEED FOR MARKET RESEARCH

You may be anxious to get started, but you cannot start just yet. You
need to sit back, do your research, and think. Maybe your idea is a winner, but maybe not. So analyze your idea, the market, and make sure
you are not the only one who thinks that you have a great business idea.
A hunch simply will not do. You need hard facts.

Sure there are businesses that start without going through this step,
and yes, some may succeed, but if they do, this has more to do with luck
than skill—and one purpose of this book is to take luck out of the small
business success equation as much as possible. The great entrepreneurs
endeavor to reduce their risk as much as possible. Is quitting your job

and starting a business fun and exciting? You bet. But you simply cannot do that without having a fairly accurate idea about what your small business will be, who its customers will be, why they will buy from you and not someone else, and how much money you can reasonably expect to make. Learn that, and quitting your job becomes much less risky.

The bottom line then is that market research is critical. Before you quit your job, before you put your hard-earned money and precious time into an untried business concept, before you risk your and your family's future, it is incumbent that you put in the work to make sure your idea is feasible, and if not, to learn what you need to change.

IS YOUR IDEA FEASIBLE?

The problem for many an entrepreneur is that they so fall in love with their idea, they become so convinced that it can't miss, that they skip the feasibility analysis stage. Rather than thinking, they start executing. More often than not, such endeavors end with a pile of bills and a hill of broken hearts.

The Three Cs

To avoid that unenviable fate, conduct a thorough analysis of the three Cs of your new business: your company, your customers, and your competitors.

- What will your *company* do? What products or services will it be providing? How big or small would it be? Retail or wholesale? Where will it be located? How can you best position yourself?
- Who will your *customers* be? Will you be selling to other businesses or to individuals? Are your customers going to be young or old? Poor or affluent? Men or women? Blue collar or white collar? How big is the market? What do they need? Why would they buy it from you? Will they pay for what they need? How can you get them to change vendors? How can you reach them? What do they read and watch? The more you crystallize your thinking, the more specific you are about whom you are trying to reach, and the more you know about

that market, the greater the chance that you will be able to find and entice customers to your business.

- Who will be your *competitors*? What are they doing right and wrong? What are their strengths and weaknesses? How can you capitalize on their weaknesses? Why would their customers leave and come to you? Can you undersell them; do you want to?

Princeton Creative Research has developed a great checklist for evaluating business ideas. Answer the following questions to evaluate your potential business or a product:

- Have you considered all the advantages or benefits of the idea? Is there a real need for it?
- Have you pinpointed the exact problems or difficulties your idea is expected to solve?
- Is your idea an original, new concept, or is it a new combination or adaptation?
- What immediate or short-range gains or results can be anticipated? Are the projected returns adequate? Are the risk factors acceptable?
- What long-range benefits can be anticipated?
- Have you checked the idea for faults or limitations?
- Are there any problems the idea might create? What are the changes involved?
- How simple or complex will the idea's execution or implementation be?
- Could you work out several variations of the idea? Could you offer alternative ideas?
- Does your idea have a natural sales appeal? Is the market ready for it? Can customers afford it? Will they buy it? Is there a timing factor?
- What, if anything, is your competition doing in this area? Can your company be competitive?
- Have you considered the possibility of user resistance or difficulties?
- Does your idea fill a real need, or does it have to be created through promotional and advertising efforts?
- How soon could the idea be put into operation?

© Princeton Creative Research, Princeton, New Jersey.

There are two possible outcomes of this research. Either you will discover that there is a need for your business, or there is not. All is not lost if it is bad news. It may be that your idea simply needs to be tweaked.

This is what happened to Dave. A computer programmer, Dave decided that he would rather be a small business owner. He looked around, thought about his likes and dislikes, and decided that he wanted to buy a café. He found one he liked and began to research the area, the competition, the clientele—everything. His research led him to the conclusion that this particular café might be a loser because the lease was not long enough and the drive-by traffic not abundant enough. Undeterred, he started over, found a better café with features he liked, bought it, and ended up in a business he not only enjoyed but that provided him with a good living.

Take Two

So before you abandon your idea altogether, see whether you can make it work. Those moments of clarity when great ideas materialize are not to be dismissed lightly. Insights are valuable, and often you need only track down the right research to figure out how the puzzle pieces may fit together.

Therefore, divorce yourself as much as possible from your love of this idea and view it as objectively as possible. Put on your skeptical hat and put away those rose-colored glasses. You need 20–20 vision now.

WHERE TO FIND WHAT YOU NEED TO KNOW

Many resources are available to help you track demographic data, learn about your intended industry, uncover vital info about your potential competition, see whether there is a market for your proposed business, and generally plot your course. Here are your best bets.

Trade Associations

Every industry has a trade association connected to it and these groups have a wealth of information. Find one associated with your idea and contact them. Explain what you are doing and ask about survey data and research reports available. Get copies of their publications. Ask whether they have a startup resource kit available—many do.

Trade Shows

Consider attending the leading association trade show, which will put you in touch with hundreds of like-minded individuals, people who are already successfully doing what you want to do. Meeting them and picking their brain can

- Save you a lot of time.
- Tell exactly who your customers will be.
- Provide experienced feedback about your plans.
- Let you know how much it should cost to start your business.
- Give you a fairly accurate idea about how much you can expect to make.
- Warn you of potential pitfalls.
- Save you from overly-optimistic plans.

Trade Magazines

Each industry usually has one or more trade magazines that may or may not be part of the leading trade association. Find the magazine for your industry and get several back copies. You should be able to notice industry trends, mistakes to avoid, potential costs, and much more.

Web Sites

Aside from the web sites mentioned previously, here are a few more that specifically may be helpful for this stage of your entrepreneurial journey:

- www.Entrepreneur.com/FormNet: This site offers free forms that help you analyze your plans.
- www.census.gov: The U.S. Census Bureau site has a lot of free demographic data.
- www.USChamber.com: Both the national chamber of commerce and your own local chamber of commerce have plenty of resources for the new startup.
- www.TSNN.com: This is a searchable database of trade shows worldwide.
- www.SBA.gov/sbdc: The SBA's Small Business Development Centers offer low-cost help to entrepreneurs. As mentioned previously, www.SCORE.org also is a valuable research resource.
- www.inside.com: The home of *American Demographics*, a monthly magazine that offers information on consumer trends and analysis. This is a pay service.
- www.hoovers.com: Hoover's offers business and industry data as well as sales, marketing, business development, and other information on public and private companies. This is also a fee-for-content site.
- www.marketresearch.com: This site offers more than 50,000 market research articles from more than 350 publishers, categorized by industry.

Interviews and Experiential Research

While reading is great, nothing beats actually talking with people associated with your potential business. There are two groups of people you need to meet and interview:

1. *Potential customers.*   Although finding possible customers for your potential business is not the easiest task in the world, it must be done. You need to find and meet people who would be willing to pay for the product or service you want to provide. Find out what they like and dislike about their present vendor, why they might change, what would cause them to change—lower prices, a better location, more personal service, or what.

> Looking to find and interview potential customers? Consider going to the place of some competition and parking yourself unobtrusively outside. Have a short questionnaire ready and ask people for five minutes of their time.

2. *The competition.* No one knows your potential business better than people who are already running a similar business. Become their customer and shop at their store or use their service. Analyze their strengths, weaknesses, profit potential, and so on.

Hire Some Inexpensive Experts

Find a good MBA program in your area and find out whether it participates in the Small Business Institute program, run by 250 MBA programs nationwide that assigns grad students to intern-type projects like market research. For a nominal fee, or free, you may get a great team to do some quality research for you. For more information, contact the Small Business Advancement National Center at (501) 450-5300.

Libraries

Of course librarians are the keepers of the research key and can show you where to find plenty of free information; that is a given. But here is something extra: *The Internet-Plus Directory of Express Library Services: Research and Document Delivery for Hire* by editors Steve Coffman, Cindy Kehoe, and Pat Wiedensohler lists 500 libraries nationwide that provide low-cost research services that you can tap into.

Create an Online Focus Group

How do Fortune 500 companies and presidential candidates know what commercials to use, products to pitch, or ideas to share? They use focus groups, a group of people who are shown a product or given an idea and asked to comment upon it. Find a listserv discussion group for your industry, subscribe to the list, learn about the group, and then ask your questions. Look for a listserv list at http://tile.net/lists/.

Telemarketing and Phone Research

Telephone research is a fairly inexpensive method, costing about one-third less than personal interviews. Here you would hire a telemarketing firm to conduct a survey of a random sample of respondents. The costs associated with this method include the fee for the telemarketer, phone charges, preparation of the questionnaire, and the analysis of the results.

Here are some tips when using this technique:

- Tell the interviewee up front how important his or her response is and that it will be a short interview (between 5 and 10 minutes).
- Avoid pauses as respondent interest drops.
- Keep the questions short and interesting.
- Make the answer options consistent.

If you get more than 250 interviews, you are nearing a good sample.

Direct Mail

Direct mail questionnaires are also inexpensive when you are using bulk mail prices, but the response rates are usually less than five percent. The main costs of this method relate to printing the cover letter and questionnaire, envelopes, and postage.

To increase your response rate, try these ideas:

- Include a nice letter that explains what you are looking for and why.
- Keep your questions short; limit the length of the questionnaire to two pages.

- Address the letter to a person, not Occupant.
- Address the letters by hand (tiring yes, but also effective).
- Include a self-addressed stamped envelope.

PUTTING IT ALL TOGETHER

After conducting all of this research, sit down, sift through it, and analyze the data. You need to get a clear idea about the strengths and weaknesses of your plan. Either you will conclude that there indeed is a market for your proposed business, or there is not. If not, then go back to the drawing board. Either way, when you so start your business, you will have a much better idea about what it will take to succeed, whom you are going to be selling to, and what they want.

CHAPTER 5

Calculating Your Startup Costs

Nothing splendid has ever been achieved except by those who dared believe that something inside them was superior to circumstance.

—Bruce Barton

Now we get down to the nitty gritty. Having come up with an idea that works for you—financially, creatively, emotionally, intellectually—the next step is to figure out what it will actually cost to start that business, and what sort of sales you will need to achieve to sustain it.

ASSUMPTIONS

Figuring out your startup costs and potential sales is a matter of making educated assumptions. In the preceding chapter, it was suggested that you do a lot of research, much of which should come in handy here. What will it cost to start a business like the one you want? The numbers you input here will help you figure out how much money you need and can make, and will equally apply to the business plan you need to write, as explained in the next chapter. Starting a business from scratch, you will incur many expenses, some of which will not be encountered again—incorporating, security deposits, that sort of thing. Others are ongoing—creating marketing materials, rent, and so on.

Calculating these costs is a four-step process. The first three steps help you understand how much money you will need for initial startup costs, purchasing assets, and for monthly expenses. Step four helps you understand your potential sales and how much money you will need to break even and to earn a profit.

As you calculate these expenses, a word of caution is in order. Be conservative, both with your analysis, and when it actually comes time to purchase these things. Cash is the lifeblood of any business, but especially a new business. And with a new business, there won't be the sales or experience to create a steady cash flow to replace what you will be spending. Don't blow it. Don't spend too much. Buy used. Buy off eBay. Hoard your precious, precious capital.

Step 1: Calculating Startup Expenses

Put a realistic dollar figure next to each category.

1. Creating your legal structure (sole proprietorship, partnership, LLC, or corporation): $
2. Accountant: $
3. Building out the space, decorating, and remodeling: $
4. Licenses and permits from city or county: $
5. Stationery and logos: $
6. Marketing and sales materials: $
7. First month's rent and security deposit: $
8. Insurance: $
9. Telephone and utility deposits: $
10. Signs: $
11. Internet and web site: $
12. Other: $

Total: $

Step 2: Purchasing Assets

What sort of assets will you need to open the doors?

1. Real estate: $
2. Furniture and fixtures: $

3. Equipment and machinery: $
4. Trucks and autos: $
5. Inventory: $
6. Supplies: $
7. Other: $

Total: $

Step 3: Ongoing Monthly Expenses

Keep adding, and yes, these numbers can be daunting. But the fact is, starting a business is usually a fairly expensive proposition. That is why being smart and frugal is so important. In this section, calculate what it is going to cost you to run your business in a typical month.

1. Rent: $
2. Utilities:$
3. Payroll: $
4. Owner's draw: $
5. Supplies: $
6. Insurance: $
7. Transportation: $
8. Shipping: $
9. Legal and accounting: $
10. Advertising and marketing: $
11. Inventory: $
12. Production and distribution: $
13. Taxes: $
14. Debt repayment: $
15. Working capital: $
16. Other: $

Total: $

Now, multiply this last total by six. This will tell you how much money you will need to run the business for six months. Then, add it to the totals in steps one and two. This will tell you how much money you need to open the doors and stay in business for six months. Ideally, having six months' working capital in the bank before you start is a minimum.

Here's an example:

Perry's Pizza Parlor

Step 1: Total startup expenses: $22,000.

Step 2: Assets to be purchased: $15,000.

Step 3: Ongoing monthly expenses: $10,000.

Multiply the monthly expense figure by six (and even that is optimistic as it will likely be more than six months before revenues will be consistent): $60,000. Adding $22,000 and $15,000 to that, we see that Perry's Pizza should ideally have $97,000 to get up and running.

Note that I said "ideally." Not all businesses will have six months' worth of working capital in the bank before they open the doors. Oh well, life is not always ideal, and if you will have less than that, it is still possible to make a go of it; it will just be more difficult. But be forewarned: Starting a new business is challenging enough; having a cash crunch from the get-go makes it that much harder. The six month figure is intended to give you enough of a cushion to get started, open the doors, create some sales, and move forward.

So now the question is, How much pizza will Perry's need to sell to make a profit?

Step 4: Calculate Monthly Sales

Your previous research will tell you how much you can expect to make in this business. The preceding numbers (especially the ongoing monthly expense figure) give you a break-even threshold of sales that you will need to achieve. Perry's Pizza, for example, must gross at least $10,000 a month to break even, $333.33 a day. If an average pizza dinner is, say, $30 a table, then Perry's must serve at least 11 tables a day to break even, and anything above that will be profit.

While 11 tables a day seems eminently doable, it will likely take a while for the restaurant to achieve that. Building a name and reputation take time. It is far more difficult and expensive to create a new customer than to keep an existing one, and the problem is that new businesses have no existing customers, so *all customers* will take effort. With enough money in the bank before you start, you will have the time necessary to build and grow your startup.

Given that, it is reasonable to assume that it will take at least six months before Perry's, or any other business, is making a consistent profit.

FINDING THE MONEY

In our example, Perry's Pizza should have about $100,000 in the bank before the doors open. Where will Perry find that kind of money; where will you find that kind of money? Chapter 6, *Write a Winning Business Plan*, explains how to write a business plan that can get you funded and Chapter 8, *The Money Hunt*, shows you where to shop that plan.

CHAPTER 6

Write a Winning Business Plan

Setting a goal is not the main thing. It is deciding how
you will go about achieving it and staying with that plan.

—TOM LANDRY

Having decided upon a business that seems right, the next step is significant: Draft a business plan. All the research that you did up until this point will now be needed. Maybe you think that you do not want or need a business plan. That is understandable because writing a business plan is a lot of work. In it, you analyze what you are going to do and how you will do it. You crunch the numbers and dissect the competition. You scrutinize risk and ponder reward. It takes a lot of thought and research. So even though business plans are work, and you may in fact be the only person who ever reads yours, if you are going to create a great small business, one that exemplifies your values and earns a fine profit, then writing a business plan is vital.

THE ROAD MAP

A pilot would never fly from Seattle to Miami without a detailed, well-researched flight plan, which helps him figure out how he will get to where he wants to go. It tells him how much fuel he will need, important landmarks to look for, and how long it will take to get there. It is his blueprint for a successful trip.

Your business plan is your version of a flight plan, your blueprint for a successful trip. Creating a business plan forces you to carefully think through your proposed business. It will detail how much money you need to get started and stay aloft. Writing it will sharpen your marketing ideas, help you understand projected costs and sales, help you understand the competition, and much more. By analyzing your business, both the things you know well and some you do not, creating a business plan forces you to really figure out what you are getting into and what it will take to succeed. It is your road map for a prosperous, rewarding journey.

Creating and using a business plan also:

- Helps you avoid pie-in-the-sky projections.
- Allows an investor or lender to analyze whether your proposed business is worth their investment dollars.
- Helps you identify your market and competition.
- Allows you to understand your business better.

> Because the plan projects where the company expects to be for the next few years and how it plans to get there, a business plan also serves as an important tool for established businesses. It lets them know whether they are on or off course. Smart businesses create, use, and revise business plans as necessary.

There are two major downsides to not having a business plan: First, without one, your enterprise will be a gamble. It may succeed, or it may fail. Who knows? Certainly not you without one, so a well-researched business plan reduces the risk of failure. Second, without a plan, you will never attract an investor. If you require outside funding to get your business started, your investor will want to see your business plan. Therefore whether it is a bank, the SBA, an angel investor, your Uncle Larry, or a venture capital firm, a business plan is a prerequisite for getting funded.

BUSINESS PLAN ELEMENTS

So just what exactly is in a business plan? The Appendix contains a complete business plan in full. Generally speaking, here is what you will find in a typical business plan, though not necessarily in this exact order.

Title Page

On the title page should be the name of the business, your logo if you have one, the owner's name, the business address and phone number, e-mail addresses, and the business web site if you have one.

Executive Summary

The executive summary is probably the single most important part of your business plan. It presents the greatest hits of the plan and is vital because it is what investors key in on. If they like the executive summary, they will read more, but if they do not, all your hard work will be for naught. If you do not quickly capture the reader's attention with a dynamic executive summary, you blew it.

Even though your entire business will be described in detail later in the plan, a crisp, three or four page introduction captures the immediate attention of the potential investor or lender. It should explain what your business is, whom your market is, what is different about your business, why this is a good time for this venture, and why this is a unique opportunity. In addition, the amount of money being sought should be addressed.

> Because the executive summary is so important, consider writing it last, after you have thought through the entire plan.

Contents

Next comes a table of contents that lists the section titles and page numbers.

Business Description

Here you describe exactly what your business is going to be and how you see it growing. This section includes a description of the products or services you will be selling, your market niche, and so on. Explain why what you will be offering is different from other options on the market.

Show that the market you are going to tap is large (and hopefully growing). If yours is a local small business, say a pizza restaurant, then explain why there is a demand for this type of restaurant in, say, a 10 square mile radius. If yours will be a national business, or an Internet business, then explain national needs for your services.

Therefore, define accurately the target market for your business. In the case of our pizza restaurant, there may be 20,000 people in the area who would be willing to go to this type of restaurant. This is called its *feasible market*. You must then determine what your share of that feasible market will be. This is called your *market share*.

You will also explain what legal form your business will take—sole proprietorship, partnership, LLC, or corporation.

> Make the business plan yours. Write it in your voice with your passion. Experts can smell a prepackaged, ghost-written business plan a mile away.

Management

It is hard to underestimate just how important your management team is to potential investors. Banks and other lenders take seriously the background and experience of the team you have assembled. Obviously, if yours is going to be a solo small business, then document your own skills and abilities for this type of business. But if you will need others to help you run the business, you better have a good team in place (and if you have not put a team together yet, now is the time to do so).

What sort of team, you ask? Maybe you need a Director of Marketing, an attorney, an accountant, a Director of Operations, and/or a Director of Sales. It all depends on the sort of business you have in mind and what is needed to carry out your vision. But whatever it is, the important thing is to create a team of qualified people who can impress the brass. List your team, their backgrounds, and what their responsibilities will be.

Industry Description

This section is where all of your background research done to date—analyzing your ideas and so forth—can be inserted. The information you received from trade associations and magazines, web sites and books, and interviews and meetings can be used here. Discuss macroeconomic trends and other relevant economic indicators.

> You do not have to draft a business plan from scratch, and it may not even be a good idea to do so. The business plan in the Appendix, provided courtesy of Palo Alto Software/Business Plan Pro, for example, is a very good and very easy program to use. But even if you do use a computer program, be sure to use your own language and make the plan yours as you write it.

Competition

Include all pertinent information about your competition, including the length of time they have been in business, where they are located, and their average annual sales. How will you beat the competition? Will you offer a better location, greater convenience, better prices, later hours, better quality, better service, or what? Analyze:

- What they do right and wrong.
- How customers' needs are and are not being met by your competitors.
- How you will lure their customers away.

Marketing Strategy

How will you position your goods or services in the market? Are you going to cater to an upscale clientele, other businesses, or whom? What will your pricing strategy be? How will you promote your business? What sort of advertising and marketing do you propose? These are the sorts of questions you must answer. Also, if you have contacts or contracts already with clients, mention them here as well.

Sales Forecast

When making a business plan, avoid out-of-the-blue numbers. And make no mistake about it; you will be tempted to throw in some unrealistic numbers. Why? Because one reason for creating a business plan is to get funding, and one way to get funding is to show your potential for explosive growth, so you may be tempted to crank up the numbers.

But it is a mistake to do so, for two reasons. First, sophisticated investors and lenders can see through phony numbers—exposing you as a novice—and novices with bad numbers do not get funded. Second, even if your business plan is for your eyes only, inflated numbers can lead only to unrealistic expectations, which can lead to business failure when you run out of money before you thought you would.

So you have been warned. It is much wiser to deal in reality, especially when making assumptions about your sales. Figure out how much you can expect to sell in the next few years. Even though you will be making some assumptions, when doing so, err on the side of caution. Be conservative. If you sell more, great; if not, at least your plan served its purpose and warned you. Your honest sales forecast will contain:

- Monthly forecast for the coming year, both in dollars and units sold
- Annual forecast for the following two-to-four years, both in dollars and units sold
- The assumptions upon which you base your forecast

Where do you get this information? Time for more research! Analyze potential competitors. Consider their sales, traffic patterns, hours of operation, busy periods, prices, quality of their goods and services, and so forth. If possible, talk to customers and sales staff. Estimate as specifically as possible what they make in a given month. Your sales forecast can be based upon the average monthly sales of a similar-sized business operating in a similar market. Second, tap your trade associations and magazines to get an idea about what a typical business in your new industry can expect to make.

Estimate your sales, but estimate conservatively. Yours is not an established business, but a new startup. It is highly unlikely that your sales will be as robust as an established competitor for at least a few years.

Finally, include your sales strategy (sales objectives, target customers, sales tools, sales support), distribution plan (direct to public, wholesale, retail), and pricing structure (markups, margins, break-even point).

Financial Analysis

Use your previous analyses to explain how much it will cost to get your business up and running, and how much it will cost to keep it going. Explain how much money you are asking for and how it will be spent. The basis of this section are several financial spreadsheets—balance sheets, profit and loss statements, and cash-flow projections. Here again you will be making financial assumptions, which can make or break your business. If you do not understand financial planning, you need either to learn it or to hire a professional to help you. It is that important.

This financial analysis is often the most difficult part of a business plan for small businesspeople. It is easy to wax poetic about your great idea and how it will make the gang rich, but actually putting real numbers to those projections is hard work. Even so, you have to do it, crunch some realistic numbers to go along with your realistic plan.

Computer programs can be of great assistance when it comes time to analyze your business' finances. Microsoft's accounting software, as well as Intuit's QuickBooks are good places to start.

Start with an *income and expense statement*. It is what it sounds like—a projection of income and expenses. It includes an opening balance sheet, detailed income projections, operating expenses, and a financial forecast for the next year of operation and for the following two years. It also includes a cash flow forecast of inflow and outflow on a monthly basis for the next year.

Where do you get this information? The usual suspects: competitors, suppliers, trade associations, chambers of commerce, web sites, and trade publications.

Next, you will need to include a *profit and loss statement*. This is a summary of your projected business transactions over a period of time. It explains the difference between your income and expenses.

Café Coffee
Projected Profit and Loss Statement

Projected Income, Fiscal Year 1	**$187,900**

Projected Expenses

Cost of Goods Sold	$76,300
Labor	$33,700
Bank fees	$ 250
Equipment	$4,900
Insurance	$2,800
Marketing	$6,200
Postage/FedEx	$1,200
Phone	$2,400
Printing	$1,900
Supplies	$7,200
Taxes	$6,800
Projected Total Expenses	$143,650
Projected Net Profit	**$44,250**

A Profit and Loss Statement is also known as a P&L Statement or an Income Statement.

The *balance sheet* of the business is a snapshot of the venture on a given date. It should include a projection of assets and liabilities.

The *cash flow statement* shows how much cash your business will need, and when and where it will come from. For example, how much inventory will be required and what will that cost every month? The cash flow statement is important because it forces you to realistically look at the bottom line and see if you are going to make enough money (i.e., enough "cash flow") to handle your debts.

The financial section of your business plan will also analyze the use of any loan proceeds you are seeking, including the amount of the loan and the term. Finally, disclose your financial situation and how much you will personally be contributing to the venture.

Exit Strategy

Conclude with your proposed exit strategy, which may be a sale of the business or eventual retirement.

Appendix

This section will contain:

- Substantiation documentation and articles of interest
- Names and contact information of your references
- Name of present bank
- Names of your lawyer and accountant
- Personal net worth statement
- Letters of intent (possible orders, letters of support)
- Insurance coverage (policies, type, and amount of coverage)

THE BOTTOM LINE

Writing is re-writing. Your business plan is no different, so write it and re-write it. It is a healthy process that will enable you to have a much better understanding of your business, what it will take to succeed, and what risks to expect. Although it will be a lot of work, it should be worth it. Either you will get funded, or, at a minimum, you will have learned a great deal about how to make your business fly. Either way, you win.

CHAPTER 7

Structuring Your Business

The first thing we do, let's kill all the lawyers.

—WILLIAM SHAKESPEARE

As you begin to put the foundation for your small business in place, you need to quickly decide the legal form your business will take. You have four options: It can be a sole proprietorship, a partnership, a limited liability company (LLC), or some type of corporation. This chapter should help you make that important decision. However, as each business form has different legal and financial ramifications, and although you can theoretically make a choice based on your supposition about what is right for your business, it is best to do so in conjunction with your lawyer and accountant.

SOLE PROPRIETORSHIP

A sole proprietorship is the cheapest and easiest form of business you can start. All you need to do is name the business, get a business license from your city or county, publish a fictitious business name statement in a local newspaper, open a checking account, open your doors, and you are, quite literally, in business. It should cost about $100 to start a sole proprietorship.

According to the Small Business Administration, roughly 17 million of the 23 million small businesses in the United States are sole proprietorships.

While the good news about sole proprietorships is that they are inexpensive and easy to create, the bad news is not insignificant. The main problem is that, legally speaking, you and the business are one and the same. If something goes wrong down at the shop, you are personally on the hook. Say, for instance, that you open a pizza parlor as a sole proprietor and that one day one of your delivery boys is drunk and kills a pedestrian while the boy is attempting to deliver a pizza. Because he was drunk, your insurance will not cover him. Because he worked for you and was trying to perform a work-related duty, your business will be liable for his actions. And because your business is a sole proprietorship, you personally, and your personal assets (cars, home, retirement, and so on) could be tapped to pay the damages from the resulting lawsuit. Obviously, therefore, starting a business as a sole proprietor is probably not a good idea, legally speaking.*

Aside from putting yourself in legal and financial jeopardy by starting your business as a sole proprietorship, another problem with this form of business is that it often means you will be working alone. It is not called a sole proprietorship for nothing. You will have no partners around to work with or bounce ideas off. Maybe a partnership is the way to go then, you say? Let's see.

PARTNERSHIPS AND LIMITED PARTNERSHIPS

A business partnership is a lot like a marriage. Because you will be spending an inordinate amount of time together, making decisions to-

---

*Throughout this book I give legal tips. As I am an attorney, please understand that such tips are based on my real-world experience as a business lawyer. Also know, however, that legal tips such as these are not legal advice and are no substitute for conferring in person with an attorney familiar with your business and situation.

gether, making individual decisions that will affect the whole, and being together in both good times and bad, think very carefully about (1) whether you really want a partner, and if so (2) who fits the bill.

General Partnerships

Legally speaking, a general partnership is even more precarious than a sole proprietorship, if that is possible. Why? Because not only are the partners individually liable for the business debts, just as a sole proprietor is, but *either partner* can get the whole partnership into debt. When that happens, both partners are legally liable for the debt. So the danger is that your partner can make some dumb decisions, sign a bad contract or some such thing, get the partnership into debt, and you will be personally responsible for that debt.

Another thing to consider is the emotional aspect of having a partner. Do you want one? Can you share the power? One nice thing about being a sole proprietor is that you alone are the boss; you have no one to answer to except yourself. But having a partner means, well, you will have a partner. You will need to listen to your partner, respect her, defer to her judgment when necessary, and be willing to share responsibility for all decisions and actions. And remember, partnerships do not always work out—best friends who become partners do not always stay best friends.

Conversely though, there is plenty to be said for having a partner. The first benefit is significant, namely, a partner gives you someone to work with, to share ideas and brainstorm with, to bounce ideas off. Also, a partner shares the workload. One bad thing about working alone is that there are too many hats to wear: CEO, head of sales, marketing director, and too often, receptionist and secretary. Partners help alleviate that. Finally, a business partner is someone who should share the financial commitments of the business, and that should be a relief.

So consider carefully these pros and cons of having a partner, and then, if you decide that the benefits outweigh the burdens, find someone with whom you could work well. Even if you get along swimmingly, be sure to check out your potential partner's background, credit history, and so on. Get some references and call. This is a very important decision, so act accordingly.

Finally, if you do decide to go the partnership route, you are strongly advised to get a partnership agreement, preferably drafted by an attorney. This agreement should spell out who contributed what, who will do what, and if the partnership ends, who will get what. It is really a very important document.

> If you have someone in mind for a partner, it is a good idea to start out working on a project or two together first. See if your styles are complementary, and whether you have more fun than issues. After all, one reason you start your own business is to enjoy your work more, and your potential partner should add to that.

Limited Partnerships

Whereas in a general partnership, all partners are equal (each can incur obligations on behalf of the partnership and each has unlimited liability for the debts of that partnership), in a limited partnership things are different. Usually, there is only one person running the show, the general partner. The other partners are called "limited partners," who also have limited liability and limited input. They cannot incur obligations on behalf of the partnership and do not participate in its daily operations. A limited partner is essentially a passive investor.

A limited partner's liability is limited to the amount of his or her financial contribution to the partnership, while the general partner has unlimited liability, to go along with his power. This structure allows the general partner the freedom to run the business unfettered and gives the limited partners limited liability if things go wrong. Another key benefit of the limited partnership, aside from the diminished liability of the limited partners and freedom of the general partner, is that it pays no income tax. Income and losses are attributed proportionally to each partner and accounted for on their individual tax returns. A limited partnership is often the structure of choice for real estate and stock investment groups.

CORPORATIONS AND LIMITED LIABILITY COMPANIES (LLCs)

As you now know, the problem with general partnerships and sole proprietorships is the personal liability that accompanies business debts and other liabilities; these entities do not shield you from legal responsibility. Not so for corporate entities. In fact, one of the main reasons to incorporate is to legally shield your personal assets from business debts. Consider our pizza parlor fiasco. If you had incorporated and one of your drivers had negligently killed someone, it would have been the business assets at risk. While still unpleasant, it sure beats having your personal assets at risk. Creditors are limited to the assets of the corporation only for payment and may not collect directly from the shareholders.

Pros and Cons of Incorporating

Pros

- The corporate shield protects you from legal responsibility and personal liability.
- Corporations are theoretically infinite—they can last in perpetuity. Sole proprietorships and partnerships usually end upon death, retirement, disability, or bankruptcy of the sole proprietor or partner.
- As the corporation grows, owners can continue to share in the profit as shareholders but do not have to stay and run the business. This is not normally true for sole proprietorships and partnerships.
- You may be taken more seriously if your business has an "Inc." behind the name.
- There are many tax advantages to having a corporation, as well as pension and profit-sharing options.

Cons

- Creating a corporation is not inexpensive.
- Shareholders have little say in day-to-day operations.
- Corporations are subject to greater governmental regulation and scrutiny.
- The tax code as it relates to corporations is complex, not easy to understand, and will likely require the yearly assistance of a lawyer or accountant.

S and C Corporations

There are several types of corporations. The main two are the *S corporation* and *C corporation* (S and C are subsections of the IRS Code). While there are several differences between the S and C corporations, there are two main ones.

The first is that C corporations are taxed twice: once when profits are realized, and a second time when those profits are passed on to the shareholders. The advantage of the S corporation is it does not pay a corporate tax at all; instead, its shareholders report profits and losses on their personal tax returns, and therefore, profits are taxed only once.

Another difference between the two has to do with size. For the most part, C corporations are large, publicly traded businesses. When you see a business whose shares are bought and sold on the New York Stock Exchange, that is a C corporation. In fact, the ability to freely sell shares is one of the main advantages of a C corporation. People who start businesses with an exit strategy of going public start C corporations. While most large businesses are C corporations, some small businesses choose this form of structure as well for one very good reason: C corporations can deduct 100 percent of the health insurance costs for its employees (including you).

The double-taxation whammy of the C corporation pushes many small business owners toward S corporations, which are, generally speaking, intended for and used by smaller businesses. There are certainly more pros than cons to starting your small business as an S corporation:

- S corporations offer limited personal liability.
- S corporations pay no corporate taxes. Again, profits and losses flow through to your individual tax return.
- A sole owner of an S corporation does not have to pay the FICA tax—Medicare and the self-employment tax, which are roughly 15 percent on the first $75,000 you earn.
- The bad news is that there are restrictions on S corporations: You can have no more than 75 shareholders, and you cannot have any preferred stock.

Whether to incorporate as an S corporation or a C corporation is something you should decide in conjunction with your attorney.

Another sort of corporation is called the *professional corporation*. This type is for the professionally licensed small business owner only, and that professional can be the only shareholder. The type of professional who can take part in this plan varies by state, but usually includes lawyers, doctors, dentists, accountants, and psychologists. It is important to understand that this sort of corporation cannot normally shield you from a malpractice award.

Limited Liability Companies

Limited liability companies (or LLCs) are a hybrid, combining the best of corporations, sole proprietorships, and partnerships, and have become very popular for good reason among new entrepreneurs.

First, and best, like S and C corporations, LLCs protect their owners (called "members") from personal liability for business indebtedness. Second, like partnerships and sole proprietorships, LLCs are fairly informal. A nice thing about sole proprietorships and partnerships is that they are less structured than corporations, especially with regard to taxes. The tax code is full of detailed rules applicable to corporations. These complicated rules and tax rates create a lot of bookkeeping and legal issues for corporations. Sole proprietorships and partnerships on the other hand simply have business profits and losses "flow through" to the individual taxes of the owners. Because it's much simpler, the second main advantage of the LLC is that its members can choose to be taxed as sole proprietorships and partnerships are, or they can choose a corporate tax structure if that is more advantageous.

By combining the best of corporations (the so-called "corporate shield") and the best of sole proprietorships and partnerships (so-called "flow through" taxation), the LLC has become the business form of choice for many a small business.

LLCs are easy to create, inexpensive (the filing fee with your state will be far less than if you started a corporation), and can be formed

Comparing Business Entities

	Protection from Personal Liability	Formalities	Transfer of Ownership	Perpetual Existence	Tax Benefits	Ease of Creation	Cost	Used by Small Businesses
Sole Proprietorship	No	Few	Easy	No	None	Easy	Minimal	Often
General Partnership	No	Few	Difficult (Need partner's approval)	No	None	Moderate (A partnership agreement is advisable)	Minimal	Fairly Often
Limited Partnership	Limited Partners Only	Need Partnership Agreement	Yes	No	Some	Medium	Moderate	Rarely
C Corporation	Yes	Many	Easy	Yes	Many	Difficult (Usually requires a lawyer)	Expensive	Rarely
S Corporation	Yes	Many	Moderate (Must find a buyer)	Yes	Many	Difficult (Usually requires a lawyer)	Expensive	Fairly Often
Professional Corporation	Yes	Many	No	No	Many	Difficult (Usually requires a lawyer)	Expensive	Sometimes
LLC	Yes	Moderate	Easy	Yes	Many	Moderate (May require a lawyer)	Moderate	Often

with only one member (unlike a corporation, which requires officers and a board of directors). Members can use capital or property to buy into the LLC and will get a percentage share of the business to reflect their contributions. When profits are distributed, the member will usually get an amount commensurate with his or her ownership share (again, because LLCs are so flexible, you can even decide to distribute profits unequally if you so choose).

There are two types of LLCs. The first is called "member managed." In this type, all the owners (there is no limit on the number, but it is usually a half dozen or less) actively run the business. The second is called "manager managed." Here, the owners have managers running the business. Typically, only members get a right to vote on company issues.

LLC laws are state specific, and each state has different requirements. Generally speaking though, to create an LLC, file a document called either "articles of organization" or a "certificate of formation" with the proper state office, and pay the fee. How much? Roughly $75 or so in most states. After you file the proper documents, draft your "operating agreement." In it, detail how much each member has contributed, what their percentage of ownership is, how you will run the business, how you will handle distributions, and so on.

Nolo Press puts out some great do-it-yourself LLC books. In particular, I recommend the *Legal Guide to Starting and Running a Small Business* by Fred Steingold, and *Your Limited Liability Company: An Operating Manual* by Anthony Mancuso.

Once formed, an LLC can protect you from business liabilities, create an easy structure for running the business, and make tax time easier. All in all, it's usually a good idea for most small businesses.

CHAPTER **8**

The Money Hunt

If you would know the value of money, go and try to borrow some.

—BENJAMIN FRANKLIN

The previous few chapters are intended to help you put the foundation of your business in place: Coming up with your best idea, figuring out what it will cost to create a business out of that idea, drafting a business plan, and choosing the right legal structure are the basic building blocks of any successful small business. Now you can build upon that solid foundation, starting with this chapter. Getting the money to realize your dream can happen only if you have that solid foundation in place; any lender or investor will want to see that those pieces are set. And even if you are going to self-fund the business, either through savings, credit cards, or some other plan, this foundation is no less important, as it is the basis for creating a small business that lasts.

Therefore, if you did the work suggested in the previous few chapters, you know exactly how much money you need to get started and stay open, which puts you far ahead of most new small business entrepreneurs who have only some vague idea about how much money they need. So the $64,000 question, maybe literally, is where will you find the money to start your business?

There are many, many sources (listed later), which is good because it is highly unlikely that you will secure all of your required funding from one place. Maybe you will combine personal savings and credit cards with an SBA loan and a gift from an uncle. Who knows? While finding the money to fund the dream is always a challenge for the entrepreneur, it is part of the job. Yes, it will likely be tough, you may get discouraged, and you may not raise as much as you want, but remember: Countless new business owners have found the money to start their businesses, and if they did you can, too. Stick with it. If you have a good idea and a solid plan, you can do it.

THE USUAL SUSPECTS

The vast majority of small businesses are started using funds, at least partly, from the entrepreneur himself. Indeed, even if you are looking to outside investors, most will want to see that you are sharing some of the financial risk. Yes, tapping your savings for a new, untried venture is a scary thought, but remember, an entrepreneur is a person willing to take a risk with money to make money. So risking some money, then, is part of the job description.

Where do you find that money? If you have savings, you will need to use at least some. If you may be getting an inheritance down the road, see if you can get an advance on it. Many new small business owners use their IRAs or 401(k) funds; damn the penalties, full steam ahead. If you have a stock portfolio, consider selling it. You will have to be creative and a bit bold, but that is what will likely be needed if you are going to make your dream come true.

"The moment one definitely commits oneself, the Providence moves too. All sorts of things occur to help one that would have never otherwise have occurred . . . I have learned a deep respect for one of Goethe's couplets: 'Whatever you can, or dream you can, begin it. Boldness has genius, power and magic in it.'" W.H. Murray, *The Scottish Himalayan Expedition* (J.M. Dent & Sons, Ltd., 1951.)

Another option that I like far less is using home equity. Yes, people do it all the time, but no, it is not wise, and it should be avoided if it can be. Why? A home equity loan (or something similar) is a loan secured by your house, as you well know. If your bet doesn't pay off, if the business does not fly, you have put your home at risk. If the business does not pan out and funds get tight, how are you going to pay back that home equity loan, and what will happen if you can't? Recall what we said earlier—smart entrepreneurs do their best to reduce their risk as much as possible. Risking your home may be too much to ask.

CREDIT CARDS

Another very popular option for funding a startup company is the credit card. According to one study, almost half of all businesses use credit cards to help with the startup. Again, it is easy to see why. Credit cards are readily available and can be paid back in installments. But the problem is, it is very easy to get in over your head with credit card debt. So before you go running up the cards, charging that new computer and office furniture, some words of warning might be in order.

The Credit Card Trap

Excessive credit card debt is one of the most common debt issues that small businesspeople face, and it can be a major factor leading to small business failure. Many of us have learned the hard way about the credit card trap. You know what it is too, right? Charging or taking cash advances, getting stuck with a huge bill, paying the minimum, watching the interest grow every month, and thus ensuring that the balance is never paid off. It is a trap because you are caught in a predicament that is difficult to get out of, and it ensures that your small business will likely remain a bit out of kilter.

For example, let's say that you charge $7,000 to help get your new business off the ground. Reasonable, no? Let's further assume that you have an interest rate of 17 percent (this is a credit card, after all). How long do you think it will take you to pay off that balance paying a minimum payment of 2 percent? Three years? Let's do a little math. A monthly interest payment of 17 percent on $7,000 is $104. Adding that to your balance means that you will have a new balance in month two of $7,104. Two percent of that is $142; that is your minimum payment. So, if you just paid the minimum, it would take (get ready for this) more than 40 years to pay off the entire card. Don't worry; it gets worse. You would also end up paying almost $14,000 on your $7,000 balance.

Credit Card Smarts

So getting stuck with excessive credit card debt is one of the worst things that can happen to your new small business. If you need to use credit cards to help fund your startup, you absolutely have to get those balances down as quickly as possible. Here's how:

- *Pay more than the minimum.*   The first way to reduce credit card debt is to pay more than the minimum payment due; as much more as you can afford. In the preceding $7,000 example, the 2 percent minimum payment amount goes down every month as the principal decreases. However, if you keep paying the original minimum payment of $142 instead of the new, lower minimum, you will decrease the time it takes to reduce your credit card debt from 40 years to just about 5 years.
- *Do the balance transfer dance.*   One of the easiest, and best, methods of lowering both your monthly credit card payments as well as your company's overall credit card indebtedness is to transfer the balance on your cards with a high interest rate to a card or cards with a much lower rate, something like 4.9 percent. Look for introductory teaser rates.

Credit cards, while useful and convenient, can kill even the best small businesses. Use them if you must to fund your startup, but do so with a plan to pay them off as soon as possible.

Using a card with a zero balance and timing your purchase correctly can mean that you will never have to pay interest again. Here's how: Let's say that you need a cash advance, you are billed on the first of the month, and your payment is due on the twenty-fifth. That means that you have 25 days to repay the debt without getting charged interest (the "grace period"). Now, if you take that advance on the second of the month, you won't even receive a bill until the first of the following month. You then won't be charged interest until the twenty-fifth of that month. Thus, just by timing your card use, you can avoid all interest payments and still have almost two months to pay them off.

THE FRIENDS AND FAMILY PLAN

The next most common method of funding your startup is to find friends and family members who believe in you and your vision and would be willing to invest in your new company. Again, this is where your business plan will be necessary. If you can show potential investors a plan that makes sense, the chance of getting them to invest greatly increases. A great thing about this option is that friends and family tend to lend or invest either interest-free or at a very low interest rate, which makes your job much easier. Especially at the beginning of your venture, capital is precious and must be, if not hoarded, at least highly respected. Keep your overhead as low as possible. Low interest on debts helps with that and is why this can be an attractive option.

When Scott Haney and Chris Abbot came up with the idea for a new board game, they were two unemployed journalists with little more than a novel idea. They drafted a business plan and then started talking to everyone they knew about investing in the fledgling company. Finally, they pestered 32 friends, relatives, and former colleagues into investing in the business, raising about $60,000 in the process for their new game—Trivial Pursuit.

The danger, of course, is that most small businesses are not business home runs like *Trivial Pursuit*. Far more likely is that you will create a successful business that makes a nice profit and that affords you some freedom and a good standard of living. But if that does not happen, if the business does not fly, owing money to friends and relatives for a failed business venture is not a pleasant experience. You have been warned.

BANKS AND CREDIT UNIONS

Of all investments a bank or credit union can make, loaning money to an untried, brand new startup is about the most risky. Home loans are secured by collateral, as are car loans. Loans to existing businesses offer some security, as the business has a track record or assets. But the new startup has none of those things, so getting a conventional bank loan for a new business is not always easy. Sure, it can be done, but it usually means either putting your home up as collateral or signing a personal guarantee for the loan. The problem with a personal guarantee is that incorporating to reduce your personal liability will be a waste of time if you sign a personal guarantee for a bank loan. Then again, entrepreneurs have been known to do almost anything to get the show on the road, and that may be the price you have to pay.

Is there a better solution? Indeed. The United States Small Business Administration (SBA) is one of the best friends your new business can have. The SBA has plenty of ways to help your business (many others of which are recounted later in this book), and can help you get that loan.

Here's how: The U.S. government knows how important small business is to the American economy. As such, it created and funds the SBA, whose mission is to help the country's small businesses succeed. One main way the SBA accomplishes that goal is by guaranteeing certain loans made by lenders to small businesses. By acting as a guarantor, the SBA reduces the risk to the lender, and so many more small business loans are made. So find a bank or credit union that deals with SBA guaranteed loans.

The Reconstruction Finance Corporation (RFC) was a loan program created by President Herbert Hoover to help businesses hurt by the Great Depression. When Franklin D. Roosevelt was elected in 1932, he adopted and expanded the program. However, during World War II, many small businesses were unable to compete against large corporations and their large government contracts, so Congress created the Smaller War Plants Corporation (SWPC) in 1942. Similar to its governmental cousin the RFC, the SWPC provided loans to entrepreneurs and business. After the war, the SWPC was dissolved and the Commerce Department's Office of Small Business assumed some of its responsibilities. Finally, in 1952, President Dwight D. Eisenhower signed legislation to create a full-time, peacetime small business agency—the Small Business Administration.

There are many loans and many programs. Here are the main ones.

7(a) Loan Guaranty

This is the granddaddy of them all, the SBA's bread and butter loan program. Not only can a 7(a) loan be used for startup purposes, but it is flexible enough to be used for working capital, equipment, furniture, and real estate. The length of the loan can be anywhere from 10 to 25 years. For more information, go to www.sba.gov/financing/sbaloan/7a.htm.

7(m) Microloan Program

This program is smaller, the term of the loans are shorter, and the amounts you can borrow are less. Here you can get up to $35,000 for working capital or for the purchase of furniture, supplies, inventory, fixtures, or equipment. You cannot buy real estate with these funds, nor are loans made through traditional lenders. Instead various non-profit organizations who have experience lending and who can offer business assistance make the microloans. For more information, go to www.sba.gov/financing/sbaloan/microloans.htm.

504 Certified Development Company (CDC) Loan Program

This program offers long-term, fixed-rate loans for real estate and machinery purchases, or for modernization and expansion. The usual 504 deal requires that the small business contribute at least 10 percent of the funds, a private lender will fund approximately 50 percent, and the 504 loan secured from a CDC covers 40 percent. The 504 share of the deal can go up to $1.3 million in some cases. For more information, go to www.sba.gov/financing/sbaloan /cdc504.htm.

> The SBA has one other program that you should know about if you are looking for startup capital. The Loan Prequalification program will analyze your loan package (up to $250,000) before you take it to a lender. An SBA-designated liaison will review your application, offer suggestions, help make corrections, and generally strengthen your submission.

ANGEL INVESTORS

Angel investors are, as the name implies, people who help businesses with either startup or expansion capital. Typically, angels are individuals who have made a lot of money and are looking to invest in new startups. Usually, they have made their money in a particular industry and prefer to reinvest their money into that industry.

Where do you find angels? Usually they are found through networking. Speak with your lawyer and accountant. Check also with stockbrokers, real estate agents, bankers, customers, sales reps, and industry colleagues. Be persistent, as you never know where that angel may come from. It is also possible to find angels online. Two of the sites you should check out are:

1. www.vfinance.com
2. www.capital-connection.com

Of course, finding an angel is probably not going to be easy, but it is possible. If and when you do find one, here are three steps that can help you get a deal:

1. *Prepare Your Elevator Pitch.* An "elevator pitch" is business jargon for a proposal that can be explained in about 30 seconds or so; the length of time you might be in an elevator with an investor. Your elevator pitch must be intriguing, intelligent, short, and powerful, and should motivate someone into wanting to know more. (See also Chapter 23, Marketing Muscle). Since the first thing you will do when approaching any potential angels is to pitch your idea, have a snappy one ready.

2. *Do Your Homework.* If your pitch works or you otherwise get a meeting, come prepared. Of course your business plan must be flawless; that is a given. Equally important, though, is having some background knowledge about the potential investors. How did they make their money? What is their background? What else have they funded? Learn all you can about the investors before going to the meeting. Pique their interest, show potential, and create rapport. Be enthusiastic and know your business plan inside out.

> Many angels like being mentors and may be willing to use their own contacts to help you find additional funding or other assistance. Ask.

3. *Follow Up.* If the meeting goes well, make sure to get some references from the angel for other deals he has done. Call up the references and make sure the angel is easy to work with and legitimate. If everything checks out, then congratulations are in order.

VENTURE CAPITAL

An angel investor is an individual with a lot of money, but a venture capital fund is a group of similar people with even more money. Venture capital (VC) firms could be made up of family members, investment

banking firms, professional investors, or some other group that is looking to invest in small businesses with big potential. But understand
that most VCs are interested in businesses that need at least $250,000,
and even then, the possibility of landing VC money is remote at best. A
VC firm may receive more than 1,000 proposals a year, and the vast
majority are rejected. The major things VC firms look for are unique-
ness, growth potential, and a strong management team. Unless yours is
a small business with huge potential, you would be best advised looking for funding elsewhere.

> If VC money is what you want, check out VC firms associated with the SBA,
> called SBICs (Small Business Investment Company). As the SBA model of guar-
> anteeing part of the investments applies here as well, SBIC firms are especially
> attractive for the small business because they fund many small businesses that
> otherwise might not attract VC funding. Go to www.sba.gov/INV.

DEALING WITH INVESTORS

When a business wants to bring in an investor, whether it is a family
member, an angel investor, or whomever, there are several ways to
structure the deal, depending upon the legal structure of the business.

Sole Proprietorships and Partnerships

If your business is a sole proprietorship or a partnership, the investment
money could be considered a loan that will be paid back by an agreed-to
time and at an agreed-to interest rate. Alternatively, you could say that
the investor is buying a part of the business and will get a percentage of
the profits every month. This is something to be negotiated.

Corporations

When a company is a corporation (either an S or a C), the two basic
methods for raising revenue are the sale of debt and the sale of equity.

The sale of debt is, essentially, a deal whereby the invested money is considered a loan. These are called "debt securities." Some investors like debt securities because they take precedence over equity securities. That is, in a risky startup, if something were to go wrong, your investor's loan (his debt securities) is legally protected and given higher legal priority than your ownership interest.

One reason you might want his investment to be a debt security is taxes. If you were to simply sell this investor stock, when he is repaid, it would likely be considered a dividend. When your business pays someone a dividend, it is not deductible on the business' taxes. However, if you structure the deal as a sale of debt (a loan), your repayments are considered interest payments, and thus are deductible on the business' taxes. By structuring the deal as a loan then, your business would pay fewer taxes.

The second method for structuring the deal is to simply sell your investor's shares of the corporation, called "a sale of equity" or "a sale of securities." Many investors like this option because it gives them an actual ownership interest in the businesses. The sale of common stock to an investor carries with it both the right to participate in earnings and a right to vote on the board of directors. This is the most common type of corporate financing arrangement. Know too that the sale of stock means the Federal Trade Commission (FTC) may have oversight duties.

How much stock should the investor get? It is impossible to say. It depends upon the size of your business, the amount of money he is investing, how much authority you want him to have, and so on. Discuss this with your lawyer.

LLCs

If you own a limited liability company (an LLC), things are a bit different. LLCs do not have shares of stock as a corporation does. Instead, its owners are called "members," and you sell membership shares. If you want to sell your investor shares of your LLC, you are certainly free to do so. However, if you do, it may change the structure of your LLC. Recall that there are two types of LLCs. Most are "member managed": The owners, the members, manage and run the business.

The other management structure is called "manager managed." This means that the owners have managers who help run the business. The nonmanaging owners (presumably your new investor) would simply share in LLC profits.

The important thing to understand is that in a manager-managed LLC, only the named managers get to vote on management decisions and to act as agents of the LLC. Your investor would be like a shareholder in the corporation, except that he wouldn't have a right to help pick a board of directors, nor could he sit on the board. Why? Because LLCs don't have boards of directors.

PART

Setting Up Shop

CHAPTER **9**

Location, Location, Location

Nothing focuses the mind better than the constant sight of
a competitor who wants to wipe you off the map.

—WAYNE CALLOWAY

Now comes the fun stuff. While the matters discussed in the previous
section—drafting a business plan, finding the money, and so on—are a
necessary prerequisite to starting a successful small business, they really cannot be described as fun. But the things you will do now should
be quite enjoyable. From finding the right location to outfitting the office or shop, you should take pleasure in the actual process of physically
creating a business.

NOT ALL LOCATIONS ARE CREATED EQUAL

Not every business needs a great location. It depends upon the type
of business you have, the brand you are creating, the amount of
foot traffic you require, and the amount of money you have to spend.
A business where you will be going to your customers' locations,
rather than vice versa, certainly does not need a terrific location—
house cleaning or pool care businesses, for example. Wholesale businesses, warehouses, and factories also do not need great locations.
An out-of-the-way location can be a great, inexpensive choice for

many businesses. Opening in a redevelopment area, for example, may afford you tax breaks.

The first consideration, then, is how important traffic will be to your business. If your business will be a retail store catering to the public, if there will be a lot of spur-of-the-moment drop-in customers, then a high-profile, high-traffic location is vital. A convenience store needs a great location with a lot of traffic, but a chiropractor does not.

Location Checklist

Consider the following when looking for a good location:

Population.   Are there enough people in the immediate area and broader region to support your sort of business? What has been the fate of similar businesses in the area?

Traffic.   If your business will depend upon drive-by traffic, then locate on the way to or from, or at, a center of activity. Also, is the location served by public transportation? Is it on a major thoroughfare?

Competition.   Where is the competition in relation to the store? Having too many competitors nearby can definitely be a problem.

Visibility.   The location probably needs to be visible from the highway and not set back or otherwise easily missed.

Signs.   As good signs can make a big difference, make sure that there are neither legal nor lease restrictions precluding you from erecting a noticeable sign.

Facilities.   What are the facilities like? Is there enough parking? Is there a bathroom for the public, for your staff? What about outdoor lighting and landscaping?

The landlord.   Get some references. Is the landlord responsive and easy to work with, or is he impossible?

History.   Avoid locations with bad reputations because you will have to spend a lot of time overcoming preconceived notions about the space.

Rent.   Rent, while obviously a concern, should not be the sole and deciding factor. Yes, you need to keep your overhead low, but locating your business in a cheap, bad location is also a path to failure.

Finally, whatever location you choose, be sure that it is zoned for your type of business. Other things you might want to consider are:

- Can employees and suppliers get there easily?
- Is there an adequate shipping and receiving area?
- Are there any environmental issues to consider?
- Is it wired for the Internet?
- Is there room to expand?

My dad was a retailer and always liked locating his stores across the street from major malls. He figured he would get the benefit of the mall's advertising and pull without having to pay mall rent.

NEGOTIATING THE LEASE

Negotiating a lease with a landlord is like any other negotiation. The important thing is to know going in what you want and what you can afford. Remember *everything is negotiable*. If you are negotiating over lease terms, then understand that you are a valuable commodity to a landlord. It is no easy task for a landlord to find a qualified commercial tenant. He probably wants you as much as you want the space. Accordingly, you may be in more of a power position than you think when negotiating a lease and thus can ask the landlord for concessions and changes to the lease, if required.

To negotiate a good deal on your lease requires that you know the rental history for the area. What are similar spaces renting for? What is the vacancy rate in the area? If it is high, you can negotiate a good deal because the landlord really needs you. If the space has been empty for a while, you need to find out how long and why. The more you know, the better deal you may be able to negotiate.

When presented with a lease, go over it with your lawyer. The lease was drafted by the landlord's lawyer for the landlord's benefit, so you need your attorney to figure out what is fair and what is not. While you might be presented with a preprinted lease that seems like it cannot be changed, it can. The essence of contract law is that both sides must agree to all conditions. That, in fact, is why a contract is also called an agreement. If you find areas that you and your lawyer do not like, negotiate to change them. Always remember the rule: *Everything Is Negotiable*.

> Any oral promises made by the landlord *must* be made part of the written lease or they will be unenforceable.

IMPORTANT LEASE ISSUES

When you are analyzing the lease and the space, the first issue to consider is the square footage listed in the lease. Because your rent is normally tied to the location's square footage, you might want to have an architect measure the usable space you will be renting because it often is less than what the landlord says or the lease indicates. The landlord will typically include things like closets, bathrooms, and halls as part of the square footage, yet these are spaces that are not "office space." Other issues to consider:

Rent.   When negotiating a long-term lease, ask for a few months' free rent.

Length.   The length of the lease must be long enough to establish your business, but not so long that you cannot move or close the doors if things do not work out there. A year or two, with an option for a renewal is probably about right for starters.

Assignments and subleases.   Negotiate for the right to assign or sublet your space, so that if you need to get out, you can. With an assignment, the new tenant would be totally responsible for the rest of the term, whereas a sublet keeps you financially on the hook until it is over. Either way, the landlord will probably want the right to review (or refuse) the person you pick, and that is a reasonable request.

Gross or net?   A gross lease is one where the landlord pays the insurance, taxes, utilities, and so forth. If it is a net lease, you must be very clear about what is, and is not, included. Who pays for heating and air conditioning? Who pays for security, cleaning, and parking? Who pays for repairs?

> A "triple net lease" is one where the renter also pays, in addition to rent, all operating costs and expenses for the property, such as security, maintenance, taxes, and insurance.

Escalation charges.   Be sure also to restrict any "escalation charges" for later years. Escalation charges are expenses incurred by the landlord for things like increased property taxes, property and business insurance, and so on. Although you will be asked, you *do not* have to agree to share these costs.

Signs.   Broach the subject of signs early, long before you sign any agreement. Signage issues can be deal breakers.

Utilities.   Under some leases, the small businessperson must purchase the utilities from the landlord. Be sure that the lease grants you the right to audit his utility bill so you can make sure he is not defrauding you.

Renovations.   Your landlord may agree to help or otherwise contribute to renovations you require before move-in. Why? Because doing so increases the value of his building and also helps lock you into a several-year lease.

Restrictive covenant.   You may require a restrictive covenant to prevent competitors from opening similar businesses nearby. For example, if you are in a mall, you might want to restrict the landlord from renting to another business like yours.

It is imperative that you review the proposed lease with your lawyer. Above all, try to cultivate a good working relationship with your landlord. That will go further toward working out problems than a dozen letters from your lawyer.

CHAPTER 10

Branding 101

Customers must recognize that you stand for something.

—HOWARD SCHULTZ, STARBUCKS

Gene Simmons, lead man of the rock band Kiss once remarked that while he liked being in a rock and roll band, he loved being in a rock and roll *brand*. What did he mean by that? Think about Kiss for a moment. What images and feelings come to mind? Probably that distinctive Kiss logo, the white makeup, the outrageous shows, the wild stories. Kiss carefully cultivated that billion dollar bad boy brand and it's worth a fortune to them. That is what Simmons meant; having a band is great, but it's the brand that pays the bills.

BRAND NEW

What do you think of when you think about Rolls Royce, or Nike, or Apple Computer? Each business evokes very clear thoughts, feelings, and images. All have a strong corporate identity, or *brand*, associated with their names, and it is no accident. These companies have spent a lot of money getting you to conjure up specific images and feelings when you think about their businesses, which begs the question: What is it you want people to think of when they think about your small business? The idea of creating a brand for your small business is really quite important. Maybe you are thinking that doing so is beyond your reach, that branding is a concept for the Big Boys. Think again. Branding is something you can and should do, too.

Branding Background

You could not have picked a better time to start or to own a small business because a variety of factors have coalesced to make this a new era for small business, an exciting new era full of potential. Big business used to have the inside track over small business because of their greater resources. Bigger used to be better, but no longer. Little is the new big. Three things have changed the landscape in your favor:

1. *A change in thought.*   What the business world has come to see is that smaller is quicker, more innovative, more entrepreneurial, and better able to adapt to increasing change. Bigger can be slower, plodding, boring, and bureaucratic. More and more, big business sees the power of small.

2. *The information/computer/technological revolution.*   This revolution means that small businesses can look much bigger than they actually are, and no one need know. Between computers, laser printers, cell phones, PDAs, faxes, and great software, any small business can look big.

3. *A growing market.*   More and more, big businesses are seeing the power and market potential of small businesses and are catering to that market. As such, ideas and tools once considered the private domain of large businesses are being offered to, and used by, small businesses. Evidence: Staples, a plethora of small business software, and Kinko's.

There are roughly 23 million businesses in the United States. Of those, according to the U.S. Census Bureau, only 6 million have a payroll, and 99 percent of those are small businesses with less than 100 employees (and most of those have less than 10).

So the era of little has arrived, and branding is but the first of several ideas in which you will see that strategies once confined to the corporate boardroom can equally be applied on Main Street.

CREATING YOUR BRAND

If you want to succeed in business, you, too, will need to create an identifiable brand. Boiled down to its basics, a brand is the essence of what makes your business unique. It combines your name, logo, and purpose into an identifiable whole. It is your image, based on reality. Your brand is your business identity, your unique position in the market. Are you the upscale restaurant, the holistic market, the geeky computer consultant, or what? Without a brand, you may find that instead of being all things to all people, you are nothing to no one. A brand is a hook to hang your hat on so that people remember you. Nike? That swoosh and Just Do It come to mind. That is the gold standard that we are aiming for.

You begin to create a brand by carefully thinking about what your business is, what makes it unique, who your customers are, and what they want. Deciding upon a brand is vital because many other decisions will hinge on this one. Your name, logo, slogan, even the location you choose and your pricing structure depend on the brand you are trying to create. A discount motorcycle warehouse will put things together far differently from a Harley showroom.

Here are the elements of your brand.

Your Name

For the small business, what you name your business will have as much to do with extending your brand as anything else. Because you will not have the sort of budget required to create brand awareness in the general public as large companies do, one of your best chances of creating a favorable image is with your name when people first hear it. If you are creating a restaurant, Aunt Suzy's Food Emporium creates a much different image from Susan's Brasserie.

When naming your business, you have two choices. Either choose a name that explains exactly what the business is and what benefits it offers, or choose a name that has nothing to do with the business at all. The latter category includes names like Xerox, Amazon.com, and Kodak. While interesting, the problem of course is that if you don't have enough money to get people to remember the name of your business, instead of a memorable, quirky name, all you are left with is a quirky name.

The other option is almost always preferable for the small business. This process involves coming up with the benefits your business offers the public, and naming the business after that. Examples here include Jiffy Lube, Baja Fresh, or Quickee Mart. Choosing a name that creates awareness of your business benefits can go a long way to creating a brand that people remember.

So there are two important things to consider when naming your business. The first is the image and brand you want to create. The thing about a successful brand is that there is consistency across the board—the image and colors and location and logo and pricing all reinforce one another. If you are creating an upscale, Italian furniture store, you need a location, prices, *and a name* that reflect the image you are trying to create. Maria's Discount Italy probably won't cut it, but Maria's Casa d'Italia might. See?

The second factor, aside from the name, is, as indicated, the benefit someone would get by patronizing your business. The best name would be one that combines the image you want to create with a perceived benefit: NetFlix, or Discount Warehouse, or Speedy Linguine.

Your Logo

A graphic image that reinforces the name builds the brand. Ideally, it says who you are and what you do. A logo can be a symbol (the Target target), a graphic interpretation of your business name (USA TODAY), or both. Either way, it needs to concisely convey the image you want to present to the world. Here is my logo:

When choosing a logo, therefore, the essential thing is that it graphically represents to the world who you are and what is unique. Accordingly, choosing a logo is akin to naming your business: You want a logo that is distinctive, memorable, and benefit-laden.

When creating a logo, you again have two options: You can do it yourself, or hire someone to do it for you. Doing it yourself probably requires that you use a graphics program (like Microsoft Publisher) that offers clipart, pictures, and photographs. It is important that you not use in your logo design any material that is copyrighted or trademarked.

> You can find some free logo generators online. One good site is www .cooltext.com.

If you can hire someone to create a logo for you, do it. Prices vary—you could pay anywhere from $100 for a student to $10,000 for a professional. You might be surprised at the great quality and affordable prices you will get from a graphic arts student.

One way to add even more value to your logo is to incorporate a slogan with it. You want your catchphrase to reinforce your desired image, and the benefits you offer should be part of that catchphrase as part of your overall branding strategy. If you are sensing a theme here, you're right. For example:

- IBM: Think
- Carpet World: Elegance Underfoot
- BMW: The Ultimate Driving Machine

These three things, your name, logo, and catchphrase, are the holy trinity of your brand, and all are equally essential.

Next, you want to pick colors and fonts that reinforce your emerging brand. A computer consultant would be fine using a `computer-looking font` but would be unwise to use an 𝕺𝖑𝖉 𝕰𝖓𝖌𝖑𝖎𝖘𝖍 𝖋𝖔𝖓𝖙. Self-evident for sure, but important to remember, nonetheless. The font you choose and color you pick will then be used to represent your name, logo, and slogan in all of your printed materials. This tapestry of decisions should create a unified, interwoven theme that reinforces the brand you are working to create.

Once you have your name, logo, slogan, font, and color ready, it is time to get the word out. All are combined to create your graphic materials. Your name, logo, and slogan should be on your stationery, business cards, envelopes, mailing labels, signs, invoices, receipts, everything.

BRANDING SECRETS

Okay, so you get the idea. You want to create a consistent theme that reinforces the image you intend to create. But branding goes even beyond that. Since your brand is based both on how you want to be perceived and how you are in fact perceived, it follows that the other half of brand building is creating positive perceptions based on substance as well as style. How?

Do What You Do Best Again and Again

A brand is a promise that essentially boils down to: "If you buy this product, you know what you will be getting because our company stands for X, Y, or Z," that is, Volvos are safe, Nordstrom's offers great customer service, that sort of thing. This kind of branding takes time, and derives from a company doing what it does best and then making sure that everything else they do supports that value proposition. Consistency is key.

Offer Superior Customer Service

This is a theme that is discussed in more detail later in the book, but suffice it to say that all your hard work creating that cool brand will be a waste of time and money if it isn't reinforced by happy customers. Customers should find it easy to work with you or buy from you.

Be a Mench

Mench is a Yiddish word that basically means "a good person." If your business practices mench ethics, your brand grows. While good looks may get you a date, being a mench will get you a mate. So, too, your business. Flash may bring people in the door once, but caring for them, and your employees, and your vendors, gets people to stick with you for the long haul. Pay invoices on time. Do more than asked of you. Do things when not asked. Help out in the community. That really builds your brand.

> You cannot get by on brand alone. That is the lesson of the dotcom boom and bust. Take the now-defunct Pets.com for example. That high-flying startup burned through multiples of millions of dollars, mostly because it focused far more on branding than it did on business. Its once-famous sock puppet was interviewed by *People* magazine and was on *Good Morning America*, but the company soon learned that creating an identifiable brand is not the same as creating a valuable business.

The bottom line is that you want to constantly reinforce the image you are creating with actions. Remember, the two keys to establishing a strong brand are developing a specific identity, and then communicating that identity consistently. Do that and your brand has begun.

CHAPTER 11

Products and Inventory

Products are made in the factory, but brands are created in the mind.

—WALTER LANDOR

Needless to say, the type, quality, and style of the products you stock go hand in hand with the brand you create. The question now is where to find those products and how to best keep them on hand. While stocking the store may initially seem like a needle in a haystack chore, it need not be. With a bit of investigation, you can find the right suppliers.

IT IS ALL IN THE BUYING

Jon owns a very successful antique shop in California. In fact, it is so successful that he works only about six hours a day, four days a week, and he still makes a six-figure income. His store is usually busy and it is not hard to see why. It is full of fascinating, old knickknacks, doodads, odds and ends, and other stuff that he buys from a variety of sources: Dealers, antique shows, garage sales, classified ads, and estate sales are the most common.

When asked what the secret of his success is, Jon answers quickly, "It's all in the buying." Jon loves shopping for things to put in his shop, but won't buy anything, no matter how cool it is, unless he can get it for the right price. He knows that if he pays too much, no matter how interesting the item, it will take up valuable space in his store, space that could be used by products that sell. He also knows that if he can get the right item for the right price, selling it won't be a problem. Jon is convinced that the reason for his success is not how well he sells, but how smart he buys.

It's all in the buying could be the motto for this chapter. It is as sound a small business principle as you will hear. So your caveat is this: As you start to make the decisions that will build your brand, don't forget that the name of the game is making a profit. Buy low and sell high. The key now is to find the right suppliers who will help you buy low.

FINDING THE RIGHT SUPPLIERS

There are many existing channels for buying merchandise; you just need to tap into them. Here are your best bets.

Referrals

The problem with speaking with people in your community who have a business similar to the one you have or want to start is that they may very well view you as a competitor and therefore be reluctant to help you. It is probably wiser, then, to find someone in a neighboring area and speak with them. They can tell you who their suppliers are and the names of the suppliers' representatives. Call the reps and have them come to your home or store to show you their line. Internet discussion groups can also be a good place to get referrals.

Trade Shows

Trade shows are maybe the best place to find products and suppliers for your business. Trade shows are presented by people in the business for people in the business. By attending, you will make invaluable contacts,

Manufacturers, wholesalers, and distributors have traveling agents and representatives who sell their products. Some of these sales reps represent a single company while others rep several companies who sell similar products. A sales rep for the gift industry, for example, may rep the lines of many different manufacturers who create products that might interest a gift store: stationery, cards, candles, picture frames, soaps, magnets, and so on. Sales reps travel with their wares and visit the shops of potential and current clients. They will suggest new products, show samples and catalogs, take orders, and even help install specialty equipment or displays. By some estimates, there are more independent sales reps than any other type of home based businesses.

see the latest trends, meet potential suppliers, learn the lingo, and essentially get a crash course in your industry. By wandering the aisles, finding the products you like, and then talking with the rep in each booth, you will begin to establish yourself. To find a trade show in your industry log on to http://www2.tsnn.com.

Trade Magazines

Pick up a copy of the trade magazine(s) for your business and look at the ads. Call the companies whose products you like, and again, get them to send out a rep to meet with you.

Trade Associations

One of the nice things about contacting your trade association is that they may have a list of overseas contacts who sell what you are looking for, and those products likely will cost less.

Go Online

Here's a great way to get a list of possible manufacturers of products for your store. Go to the online version of the *Thomas Register* and type in the products you are looking for at www.thomasregister.com.

Go to the Source

If you know what product you want and who makes it, then go online and get the company's contact information. Call them up and ask for the sales department. Explain who you are, what you are doing, and that you would like to meet with the rep in your area.

MEET THE REPS

If you already have an established business, then meeting with the rep should be simple. They know that you know the program. But if yours is a new business, the challenge is to get the rep to take you seriously, to see you as a viable contact. Most reps are overworked and don't have much time to waste, so be sure to present yourself professionally. If you are new to business, maybe the company or the rep will want to see letters of credit, references, or something similar. They will want to be sure that you will be able to pay for what you order, in full and on time. Of course the vendor wants your business, but business is business. Therefore, finding vendors is a matter of relationships as much as anything else, and you need to establish relationships with your potential vendors and their representatives.

Sometimes, without any trade references, getting your foot in the door and proving your mettle is difficult. This is especially true if you are trying to establish trade credit and to get the vendor to sell to you net 30. If you find the big manufacturers difficult, you can start with a smaller company, or a local company. If you start small, establish yourself, and build up some trade credit and trade references, then you can expand and attract the bigger manufacturers.

> Net 30: Paying for items 30 days after the invoice comes in.

When meeting with company representatives or independent sales agents, make sure to get samples of what they are offering. Sometimes these will be free and sometimes not. Pay if necessary. Take the samples and make sure that they are the quality and style you want. The important thing is that you find products that

- You can afford.
- Customers will want.
- Build your brand.

Remember: *It's all in the buying*!

> If you don't have enough money to buy all the product you want or need, be sure to check out Part VIII, Business on a Shoestring, which offers several ways of stocking the shelves with little or no money.

INVENTORY CONTROL

Order enough stock in enough variety to respond to the needs of the many different types of customers who will be coming into your store. Remember that cars come in all shapes, sizes, and price ranges for a reason. It takes all kinds of people to make the world go 'round. If you stock your store only with items you like, then you are losing the chance to sell to people unlike you, and rest assured, there are plenty of those out there. You may not like stuffed kitty cats, but someone does.

How much product do you need? First, the shelves must look full. Second, while it might sound trite, you need enough product to meet the normal demands of your business. A store with a track record can look to previous years, but a new startup must use the figures used in the business plan (I told you it was important!). Once you know how much you need, you should order that amount, and a bit more, maybe even 10 percent more. This is enough of a cushion if a vendor delivers late, or there is some force majeure (act of God) that causes your shipments to arrive late.

This leads us to reorders. After a while, you will get a rhythm for your business and you will know how long it takes supplier X to deliver product Y, and you will order accordingly. But especially in the beginning, you need to be all over this. If you have 50 stuffed kitties, and sell 5 a week (a 10-week supply), and if it takes two weeks to get them delivered, you need to reorder them when you have three weeks' worth of product left so that you never run out. Running out of inventory is an amateurish mistake and one that can be easily avoided with just a little bit of planning.

New York Pizza is a restaurant whose affable owner Ed hails from Brooklyn. He says they make the best pizza west of the Mississippi, and he may be right. But sales didn't match his skill, so Ed hired a public relations firm to get the word out. Before long, the local paper interviewed Ed and planned a big story for the next Friday. The story came out—a glowing review of the restaurant. That night, the place was inundated with new customers. By 9:30, though, New York Pizza had run out of dough and by 10:00, cheese. Excited new customers were turned away at the door, and Ed missed a golden opportunity, all because he hadn't bought enough inventory.

The flip side of a lack of inventory is having too much inventory. This can be an especially nasty problem if you sell perishable goods or seasonal items. Excess inventory slows your cash flow and costs you money by taking up space for items that would otherwise be selling.

What do you do when you have too much product on hand? The time-honored thing to do is to have a sale. "Sale" is one of the two most powerful words in business ("free" being the other). The good thing about sales is that they bring people in the door for the sale items who just may stick around and buy other items not on sale. The bad news is that you are losing money on sale items that you need to move because you didn't practice smart inventory management.

Cash Flow and Inventory Control

One of the most important concepts in business is the 80–20 rule: Eighty percent of your sales will come from 20 percent of your customers. Know who those customers are, treat them right, and your continued success is almost assured.

The 80–20 rule applies to inventory as well. Eighty percent of your sales will likely come from 20 percent of your products. They probably aren't your most expensive items. Rather they probably are the less expensive items that have been turned over again and again that will account for your 80 percent of sales. Those vital 20 percent products are the lifeblood of your business, accounting for much of your cash flow. Obviously, if you don't always have enough of whatever those 20 percent products are, you will be severely hampering your cash flow.

Certainly you may not be able to afford everything you want for the store when you want it. But if you know which products account for 80 percent of your sales, you will be able to prioritize accordingly.

Tracking Inventory

Depending upon how much inventory you stock, you may need an inventory control system. Such a system can tell you what you need to order, what sells best, and whether an employee may be stealing from you. Although your system might be manual, these days it is far more common (and smarter) to have a computerized system. Accounting programs like QuickBooks have inventory tracking control systems as part of their standard functions.

> With a manual inventory control system, each item in the store is tagged, the tag is removed when it sells, the used tags are itemized (so you know what sells), and then checked against the physical inventory (to see if anything is missing.)

A sophisticated inventory control system will allow you to know exactly what sells, how it compares to what else sells, lets you know when to reorder, and helps you figure out which products are the most profitable. Another option is to invest in a point-of-sale system (POS). POS software creates up-to-the-minute inventory records from the point of purchase.

> You may want to check with your trade association to see whether there are industry-specific accounting and inventory systems that you could purchase. Most industries have these now. While more expensive, because they are industry-specific, they make a lot of sense for your individual business. In that regard they can sometimes be better than off-the-shelf options.

Whatever system you choose, software today is very powerful and can give you much more than a mere recitation of what sold and what did not. Now you can get sophisticated reports that help you analyze sales data, chart sales by month, compare sales by price (or any other variable for that matter), keep track of accounts receivables, calculate sales taxes, and generally run your business very effectively.

If you buy the right products at the right price, and keep track of what you need when, your small business should remain profitable. And always remember—*It's all in the buying.*

CHAPTER 12

Successful Pricing Strategies

If you really put a small value upon yourself, rest assured
that the world will not raise your price.

—ANONYMOUS

How much should you charge for your products or services? This is a
question that vexes many an entrepreneur. Of course you want to
charge enough to make a healthy profit, but not so much that you drive
customers away. Moreover, the price you charge is an important aspect
of your brand. Thus, you may need to tinker a bit before you find that
perfect price.

THE PSYCHOLOGY OF PRICE

You expect to pay more for a BMW than a Volkswagen because of the
brands they have created (among other reasons). BMW aims to sell
fewer products at a higher price to a wealthier and maybe more dis-
criminating audience. VW goes for high volume and less profit-per-sale.
Both are valid strategies, and both work.

So the price of your product carries with it great psychological
impact. When you pay more, you expect more; you expect more from
a car that costs $50,000 than you do from one that costs $20,000.
That there is a direct correlation between price and quality in the

minds of consumers is no secret. Your task is to use that mind-set to your advantage.

For example, products with an even-numbered price are generally considered of higher quality than those with an odd-numbered price. A stereo selling for $200 is thought of as better and of higher quality than one that sells for $179.99. If you are seeking to sell high-end items then, consider pricing them with an even number. If you are looking to be the low-cost leader in your area, then use $.99 to your advantage. So the first thing to consider when pricing is the type of consumer you are trying to reach, which relates to the brand you want to create.

> Peculiar numbers work, too. One study found that merchandise sold better in lots of 3 for $5.31 ($1.77 apiece) than for $1.69 each. A price of $3.33 might also catch someone's eye.

Determining Your Optimum Price

Your optimum price is the one that affords you the most sales at the greatest profit and that fits the brand you are creating. Determining that optimum price is a five-step process.

1. *Figure out your minimum price.*   If you are selling widgets, you need to know what it costs you to sell one widget. This includes your actual cost to buy or manufacture that widget, plus a proportional cost of your overhead—rent, labor, shipping, insurance, and so on. Once you know what it actually costs you to buy and sell a widget, then you will know the minimum price you must ask for that item. Anything less and you will go out of business. Anything more is profit.

2. *What is the focus of your brand?*   Is yours the gourmet, boutique market or the produce warehouse? The gourmet store can charge more, but the produce warehouse will sell more. You can sell a lot for less at a lower profit, less for a lot at a higher profit, or something in the middle.

3. *Analyze your competitors.* Comparative price is not the only factor consumers look at when making purchasing decisions, but it is a factor. You absolutely have to know what your competitors are charging and take that into account. Maybe you want to undercut them, which works. Maybe you want to match them while offering some different incentive. That works, too. Either way remember that capitalism is cutthroat. You have to be cognizant of what your competitors are doing and offer something better—price, service, location, something—if you are going to succeed.

   When analyzing competitors' prices, be sure to note whether your products are superior, inferior, or similar. Which of your competitors seems to be doing the best? Ask yourself whether price is the reason. If not, what is? Can you beat them on price? If so, that's good.

4. *Set a price.* Knowing the minimum you must charge, knowing what your competitors do charge, and knowing the image you want to portray allow you to set your prices accordingly.

5. *Test, test, test.* Your first price is not your last price. Especially at the beginning you will need to tinker a bit. If you have a product that you are selling through other stores for example, test one price in one store and another price in another store. Try an ad in one paper at one price and an ad in a similar paper at a different price. Compare the results.

> Even small business owners who have been in business for a long time should occasionally test new prices for old products. You never know, there may be a hidden gold mine in your store, simply awaiting your discovery.

Product pricing is part art, part skill, and all perception. A person will pay a price for your product if he perceives that it is worth that price. If not, you will never make a sale. Why do Ralph Lauren Polo shirts cost almost $100 when a similar shirt without the polo pony costs $25? Perceived value. Why can't you sell a rotten tomato, even for a dime? Perceived value. You need to find that magic equilibrium point where customers perceive value and you perceive dollars.

Too many small businesses are afraid to raise prices for fear of losing customers. That is probably a mistake. Inflation is real. What it cost you to produce and distribute a product five years ago is less than it is today if for no other reason than inflation has made your dollar worth less. Raise your prices and see what happens. The worst thing is that you lose some sales and have to drop your prices again. The best thing is that extra revenue begins to come in the door.

GAS WAR!

Some people reading this book will remember a time when gas stations at the same intersection would have a Gas War! One station would drop its price per gallon to, say, 29.9¢ and the station across the street would go down to 28.9¢. This would go on for a while, and people would flock to the stations to get cheap gas.

The problem with the gas war mentality is that all of your hard work—coming up with a great idea, drafting that darned business plan, finding just the right spot, building a brand, all of it—is reduced to selling your stuff for less. Unless you can really compete on price, and want to, don't make the mistake of thinking that you can simply charge what your competitors charge (or less) and all will be fine. McDonald's is the cheapest because they can afford to be and that is their business plan, ditto Wal-Mart. Is that your business plan?

Customers look at a variety of factors when deciding where to buy. Sure, price is a big factor, but it is not the only one, and often not the dispositive one. Think about when you buy something. How often do you buy solely because you found it for less? Probably not all that often. Starbucks is certainly not the cheapest place to get a cup of coffee, but it is the most popular. Its customers have reasons beyond price for frequenting that establishment. What do your customers want? Give them that, and then worry about price.

Let's say that you are a lawyer with a wills and trusts practice. Yes, you can charge what the trust mill across town charges, but you probably don't want to, and you certainly don't have to. All sorts of consumers are shopping for a wills and trusts lawyer. The ones who go to the will mill probably have fewer assets and fewer issues. But if you open up shop in a nicer part of town and charge more, if the brand you are trying to create is excellence and quality legal work, then you can charge more. Perception creates price. If consumers perceive you as a great lawyer who does good work, you can charge commensurate fees. You will attract better clients with interesting issues who have more resources to pay higher fees. Price is not what they are worried about; finding someone who can save potential estate taxes is. Entering into a gas war, then, in this scenario means that you will get stuck with a lesser practice.

If you offer rush orders or emergency services, be sure to charge extra.

There are several other reasons why competing on price is probably a bad idea.

- *You will not make enough money.* This is especially true for a service business. It takes time and costs money to maintain your office, travel to see clients, buy insurance, and so forth. You simply have to be able to charge enough to cover your monthly nut and earn a profit to boot. Remember, too, that it is unlikely that you will bill 40 hours a week; you simply can't if you are going to run the business, too. You have to charge enough to make a good living.
- *You will attract customers who care only about price.* If that is the sort of customer or client you want, fine, but if it isn't, then avoid the gas war.
- *You will not get good customers.* The flip side of the previous fact is that by being the cheapest, you will drive away quality customers who care about more than just price.

Of course you want to be competitive, but offering a fair, reasonable price is different from offering the lowest price, much different. But what if the price you think is fair differs from what a customer or client thinks is fair? Should you negotiate your fees or prices? It depends. If you have a sofa in your furniture gallery that has been there for a year, you would be silly not to negotiate down the price and move the merchandise. On the other hand, you don't want to get into the habit of negotiating every time you quote a fee or name a price. The best advice, then, is to be judicious, avoid negotiating if possible, but do so if you must. It is probably better to get less and secure the sale than to be rigid and get nothing.

How to get customers to pay more for your services:

- *Offer a flat fee.*   Customers like knowing exactly what they will pay and will often pay more for that peace of mind.
- *Offer a free consultation.*   A half hour free builds rapport, and rapport means work. If you get the gig, you can always build the free half hour back into your fee (or not).
- *Start small.*   Offer to do a smaller project first to build confidence. Once they like you and your work, you can charge more.
- *Guarantee your work.*   Guarantees build confidence, and confidence means higher fees.

THE LOSS LEADER

The loss leader is a tried-and-true pricing strategy that can keep old customers, attract new ones, and increase sales. Sound good? You bet, but it comes with a price—if done incorrectly, you can lose a lot of money.

The loss leader is a pricing strategy that attracts consumers to your business by offering them sharp discounts on specific items or services, goods or services that you sell at, or close to, a loss. Often, the sales price will not even cover the costs of your advertising, overhead, cost of the goods, and the product itself. The idea is that by taking a loss on the sale (hence "loss leader") you are leading people into your store with the intent of having them buy not only the bargain, but other things that are not discounted.

When you see an ad for a great sale somewhere, that store is using the loss leader strategy. They are hoping to lead you into their establishment with the discounted ad price, and then sell you something more expensive. Customers may buy the discounted item, or they may not. The important thing is that they are visiting the business.

Once they get there, the rest is up to you. It is when they buy other things from you that you make up for the loss you are taking on the sale item. For example, say that you own a book store. By advertising a best-seller cheap, you might attract your clientele back into your store. Once they come in and locate that book, they might find alongside it a compatible book, or some CDs, or some other item that could compensate for loss on the best-seller. The loss leads to a bigger sale.

Other than bringing customers in the door, a loss leader is also used for the following.

Moving Unwanted Merchandise

If you have stock that is not moving or that you otherwise want to get rid of, a loss leader can move it. People love a bargain.

Attracting New Customers

New customers can learn about your business when they hear about the sale. For example, the book store could buy a lot of teen novels, discount them, and thereby attract the always-desirable younger shopper with disposable income.

Building Your Brand

Earlier I said that if you do not want yours to be known as a discount shop, do not compete on price. However, now the opposite is true. If you would like to be known as the "low-cost leader," then a loss leader strategy will help associate your business with that phrase. It is important, though, that you not sell junk at a discount. That is probably not the sort of brand you want to create.

Create Repeat Customers

Once people find your store and see how well they are treated, what good prices you have, and the friendly staff that waits on them, they will likely come back again and again.

The loss leader is a time-honored business strategy that works, but to make sure it works for you, two precautions are necessary. First, make sure that the lost profit can be countered by the sales of other goods or services. If you price something too low, and people don't buy anything else, the loss leads nowhere. It's no longer a loss leader, it's just a loss. Second, be sure that you actually have the discounted item for sale, and at the price you advertised it. Not having it (unless you sell out), or not having it at the price you mentioned in the ad, is fraud and is illegal.

As long as you do not price the item too low (and thereby take too large a hit in the process), the loss leader can be a very smart pricing policy. Use it to build your customer base and your reputation.

CHAPTER **13**

Small Business Technology

Any sufficiently advanced technology is indistinguishable from magic.

—ARTHUR C. CLARKE

The computer-Internet-information-technology revolution that has occurred over the past 20 years has radically transformed business generally and small business in particular. Indeed, if there has been one event in the past generation that has changed small business, the computer revolution is it. Today, small businesses have the tools and technology to look and act big, while maintaining the nimbleness and entrepreneurial spirit that makes them unique.

However, technology is changing so rapidly that it would be impossible to discuss what is being offered today without its being out of date tomorrow. Rather, this chapter examines the trends in small business technology, so that you can see that the options small businesses have today are not your father's Oldsmobile.

THE INTERCONNECTED OFFICE

One of the best new features of the small business office is that you can now run your business from anywhere—from home on the weekends or while on a business trip in Cincinnati. Computer technology has made it so that you can access vital info on your computers wherever you are, and share it with members of your team, wherever they are. This is done in one of two ways.

First, for the smaller small business the latest version of Microsoft Windows allows for the creation of a remote connection to other computers. By properly configuring your home computer, for instance, you can remotely access your computer desktop at the office.

Second, we all know that a server has something to do with the Net, but what exactly? When two or more computers log into the same Internet site, that site sits on a server, sort of a master hub that connects other computers. For a business, you might want to think of it as the central nervous system; the place through which all business information can flow, and more importantly, can be shared within the business. Most offices these days have information stored on various computers. Key contacts might be on your computer, while important e-mail addresses might be on your secretary's, and your client list sits on the computer of your VP of Sales. No, it's not the most efficient system, but it is how many small businesses work.

Imagine now that instead, you had a master computer to house and store all of your vital company information, a computer that can be accessed equally by everyone in your office, from wherever they may be in the world. This is your server. A small business server is a centralized place to store business information, keep you better organized, and keep your staff better informed.

THE WIRELESS OFFICE

Beyond networking your computers, another great advancement in the field of small business technology is wireless fidelity, or Wi-Fi. Checking e-mail, surfing the Net, or connecting to your desktop from your laptop while sitting at Starbucks or at an airport makes running your small business easier, and more fun. Even more important is that wireless networks allow your employees to be connected while on the go. Without having to wait until they get back into the office or get to the hotel to plug in allows them to get more work done in real time. Be-

Dr. Arthur Lavin is a pediatrician who owns Advanced Pediatrics in Beachwood, Ohio. With two doctors, some nurses and support staff, Advanced Pediatrics is the prototypical small business. When he opened the doors to his clinic, Dr. Lavin installed a Microsoft Small Business Server and is quite happy with the results. Because his computer desktop sits on his server, and not his desktop computer, he can access his virtual desktop from anywhere. Thus, for example, if he gets a call one night from a parent of a sick child, he can log onto his home computer, access his office computer (the interface looks exactly the same as if he were on his office computer, by the way), and read the child's chart, knowing instantly the child's medical history, medications, and so on.

Dr. Lavin also installed an intranet. This is an internal webpage that only staff can access. It can, for instance, announce the next staff meeting, list the vacation schedule, publicize important events, and so on. Dr. Lavin told me that he loves this network because "it ties the team together." He estimated that the business has saved the practice between $40,000 and $60,000 this year because the technology allowed him to hire less staff.

cause wireless networks use radio signals (as opposed to wires and cables) to connect to a Local Area Network, or LAN, you have the ability to get connected from a wide variety of places.

Wireless networks are growing quickly, and as sales increase, price drops. So going wireless has never been easier or more affordable. If you would like to create a wireless LAN for your small business, keep these tips in mind:

- *Understand the need.* Today's small business is much different from those in days of yore. The new small business should be a fairly high tech, computer driven workplace. Moreover, the days when employees come in at 9 and leave at 5 are also gone. Between job sharing, flex-time, changing schedules, and increased mobility, many employees work at times and places other than the old norm. According to Microsoft.com/smallbusiness, small business employees are at their desks only 30 percent of the time. As such, wireless networks can make your employees more productive. Between meetings, they can catch up on e-mail, or work on that presentation, for instance. Furthermore, by using laptops, personal digital assistants (PDAs), or even their phones, employees are able to access the network. If however, yours is a business that is more traditional, then a wireless network is probably not necessary.

- *Find a vendor that specializes in small business.*   Yes, you may get a better deal from a smaller company, but in cutting-edge technology especially, it is smart to buy from established veterans who have the infrastructure in place to help you make your wireless network succeed.
- *Hire an expert.*   The larger your network (that is, the more users), the more complicated it is to create and maintain a wireless network. It is smart to hire an Information Technology (IT) expert to set up your network properly from the get-go.

MOBILITY TOOLS

Wireless is just the latest of the many (and ever-increasing) tools in the arsenal of the mobile business warrior.

Laptops

As laptop computers become lighter and less expensive, and as e-mail and Internet use are always increasing, the tool of choice for many mobile small businesspeople is the laptop. What is making laptop use even more attractive these days is that not only has battery life increased, but wireless cards enable users to log on almost anywhere.

> A recent variation on the standard laptop is the Tablet PC. These devices use handwriting recognition software to allow users to enter information in longhand. Tablet PCs have proven especially handy for use in meetings.

A word of warning: More than half a million laptops are stolen every year. It is therefore important to protect yours. First, always keep it near you, especially at airports where thieves look for laptop cases briefly unattended. Especially in airport restrooms, be sure to keep your laptop case close by. (More than a few businesspeople have had their laptops stolen, snatched by the strap while they were, well, indisposed.) Consider also insuring your laptop. A policy can be bought for less than $100. Moreover, as damage to your laptop is more likely than theft, that such policies cover most damage makes buying one even smarter. Finally, you can purchase software that tracks your laptop to its new Internet connection if it is ever stolen.

> Absolute Software's software tracks stolen computers: www.absolute.com.

PDAs/Cell Phones

It used to be that PDAs (personal digital assistants like a PalmPilot) and cell phones would be treated as separate entities: Cell phones made phone calls and PDAs kept you organized. But no longer. One of the best changes in mobile technology is the advent of an all-in-one device that allows you to handle all of these chores, and more, in one nifty device. Products like RIM's Blackberry, HP's iPAQ, Handspring's Treo, and a host of so-called "smartphones" and pocket PCs will let you make calls, send and receive e-mails, take pictures, work, and of course, play games.

Global Positioning Systems (GPS)

Many of the aforementioned devices, as well as standalone products, offer Global Positioning Systems, or GPS. This allows you to always know where you are and practically never get lost. That's especially good if you are on the road a lot. Your exact location is plotted via a 24-satellite navigational system that orbits, and continuously sends signals back to, Earth.

Videoconferencing

Another tool you may want to check out is videoconferencing. Especially after September 11, videoconferencing has taken off. While traditional videoconferencing was done with video cameras and tele-phones, this technology is being challenged and changed (as is every-thing else) by the Web. Internet videoconferencing allows you to meet with people remotely on a prearranged web page, or via web-cam, share PowerPoint presentations, and conduct a virtual meeting. It is much less expensive than the traditional model, and can also be done via laptop while you are on the road.

INTRANET

Another trend in business is the use of an intranet to facilitate commu-nication among you and your staff. An intranet is a web-based network available only to you, your employees, and possibly selected partners and customers.

Having an intranet makes a lot of sense for many small businesses. First, if you have people who are not always working at the place of business (for example, you have a virtual company, or partners on the road, or telecommuters, or traveling salespeople, and so on), communi-cation is always an issue. An intranet allows you to instantly communi-cate the same message to everyone. On it (that is, on your internal company web site), you can post important updates, sales reports, memos, policies, meeting times, vacation schedules, PDF files of im-portant forms, and other information everyone needs to know.

An intranet can also build camaraderie. By offering chat boards and instant messaging, your intranet can become the twenty-first century water cooler—the place where employees can get to know one another, exchange ideas, and chat about work. More importantly, on the in-tranet, people can work on, and share, the same documents and files. Accordingly, the most up-to-date version of that file will always be avail-able and in a place where everyone knows where it can be located.

You can hire an expert to create an intranet for you, or you can buy an off-the-shelf solution. Some of the more popular ones are Instant Intranet Builder, IntraSmart, Intranet Suite, and InfoStreet. The cost should be a few hundred dollars a year.

COMPUTER SECURITY

To avoid losing time, documents, customer lists, or worse, here are some simple steps you can take to ensure the safety of your computer or network.

> We hear a lot about computer worms and viruses. What are they, exactly? A *virus* is a program that destroys data. A *worm* is a program that sends copies of itself to people in your e-mail address book.

Get a Firewall

A *firewall* is a program that does two things. First, it hides your computer from the Internet at large so that hackers and viruses can't see you. Second, if a virus does infect your computer, the firewall warns you and lets you stop it from transmitting to other computers via the Net. As the name implies, it is a wall between your computer and the outside world. Zonealarm.com has a great free firewall you can download.

Get an Antivirus Program

Although a firewall is intended to protect you from unwanted infiltration, it does occur. Antivirus software is your next line of defense. A good antivirus program is a must, as it both warns you of potential problems and then rids you of actual ones. Symantec and McAfee make very good antivirus programs.

> New viruses come out all the time. Therefore, it is vital that you get an antivirus program that can be updated via the Web, and that you update it every month or so.

Protect Yourself from Spyware

Spyware are programs that infect and slow down your system with un-wanted and unnecessary "spy" programs. You must run anti-spyware software on a fairly regular basis to keep your machines running fast. Check out lavasoftusa.com/software/adaware/ and spybot.com for down-loadable free anti-spyware programs.

Back up Your System

Losing data to a virus is a very bad experience (try losing four chapters of a book!). It is quite important then to back up your data fairly regu-larly. Saving critical documents onto a CD or a DVD is easy.

CHAPTER 14

Small Business Software

Buying the right computer and getting it to work properly is no more complicated than building a nuclear reactor from wristwatch parts in a darkened room using only your teeth.

—DAVE BARRY

The point of software is to make your business more effective. Although it is supposed to save you time and make things run more smoothly, we all know that is not always the case. With the tons of software available, both pre-installed and commercially available, it is sometimes hard to separate the wheat from the chaff. So in this chapter we look at what software your small business really needs and give you an idea about your options.

A caveat: There is so much software on the market today that it would be impossible to analyze every product available. A good web search will allow you to compare scores of products and prices. Instead, I want to give you an idea about which products are the market leaders and how these leaders compare. This is not to say they are the only products available because they are not. However, I have found that when a few products dominate a field, it is for a good reason—they are usually the best.

You can compare prices for business software at www.mysimon.com.

OFFICE SUITES

Almost all computers now come preinstalled with some sort of basic office suite that allows you to draft simple documents and so on. While these are nice products, if you are serious about running a successful small business you will likely need to upgrade to something more robust. A good office suite should be an integrated program that allows you to create documents and spreadsheets, produce marketing materials, manage e-mail and contacts, and much more. As your office suite will become your basic, essential daily tool for organizing and running your business, you should not shy away from buying a good one. This is not a place to skimp.

Microsoft Office Small Business Edition

Microsoft has been putting out a small business edition of its ubiquitous Office suite for several years, and it is worth checking out. It really is designed with the small business owner in mind. As with regular editions of Office, Office Small Business is a bundle of essential programs: Word (word processing), Excel (spreadsheets), Outlook (contacts, calendar, and e-mail), and Publisher (graphics). It also now comes with PowerPoint (presentations), and a new product called Business Contact Manager, which allows you to track leads and help turn them into sales. It is the leader.

Corel WordPerfect Office

Microsoft Office or Corel WordPerfect Office are your two main choices when it comes to office suites. The Corel program comes with WordPerfect (word processing), Quattro Pro (spreadsheets), Corel Presentations (presentations), and Corel Central (appointments and e-mail). Like Microsoft Office, this is an excellent product for handling your daily office tasks. The question really is whether you want to work in a Microsoft environment or a Corel environment.

Microsoft Works

This is a program designed for home and student use as most businesses will need Excel and PowerPoint, and Works does not come with those. However, for a small home-based business, Works may do the trick, and it is hard to beat the price (about $100). Here you get simple spreadsheets, a calendar, address book, word processing program, and some extra goodies (mapping software, finance program, and so on).

CONTACT MANAGEMENT SOFTWARE

Contact management software is intended to keep track of clients, leads, and prospects and to help turn those leads into customers. A good contact management program should be able to import contacts from other programs and integrate with e-mail programs.

ACT!

Like other similar programs, ACT! (which has been around for quite some time) allows you to

- Manage contact information in one place, including names, business names, phone numbers, addresses, and so on.
- Manage leads, customers, and vendors.
- Track each relationship.
- Create sales forecasting models.

ACT! can be shared, thereby keeping everyone's notes about customers and vendors in a central location. However, some people have a hard time integrating ACT! with Outlook.

Goldmine

Another granddaddy in this field, Goldmine is a popular choice. Its interface is similar to Microsoft Outlook, with taskbar and menu options, including the ability to create custom taskbars. The program easily integrates with Outlook, Microsoft Exchange, Lotus Notes, and Lotus CC:Mail. Goldmine's contact management tools are powerful. For instance, when you create and send a letter, fax, or e-mail, the program automatically records your interactions with the contact. You can also forecast sales, complete transactions, assign quotas for employees, and easily create reports and charts analyzing sales data.

Microsoft Business Contact Manager (BCM)

BCM allows you to manage your customer and sales opportunities very efficiently. What are the prospects of making that sale—80 percent? Plug that into BCM, sort your highest potential sales, set a call back date, and presto! Your prospects with the highest probability of being sold are now part of your calendar. BCM also allows you to create any one of 20 custom reports that can then be exported to Excel or Word. Note, however, that when integrated with Outlook, both BCM and Outlook take quite a while to load.

ACCOUNTING SOFTWARE

A good accounting software program is also probably a must for a small business with employees. If your small business is just you, you can probably get by with a basic money management program like Quicken. But if your business is bigger, or is going to get bigger, then a program like the ones listed next is required. All of these programs offer similar tools: budgeting, accounts receivable management, payroll, inventory control, and so on. The key, then, is to find a program that offers the extra bells and whistles you want and the functionality you like.

QuickBooks

QuickBooks is the standard in the field. It has an easy-to-use, intuitive interface and powerful tools which should please both the new and seasoned entrepreneur alike. Sure it handles all of your basic accounting needs, but it also has more sophisticated functions like loan management, cash flow forecasting, tracking of fixed assets, and vehicle mileage tracking.

Peachtree Complete Accounting

Peachtree is another solid choice. It is especially good at handling e-commerce, and has a host of usable financial features. Some of the best options are the inventory control function, which lets you track product based on size or color, and the Daily Register Report, which is a snapshot of your daily activity.

MYOB Plus

This is a simpler, less expensive program, which does not offer advanced options like cash flow projections. The newer versions of this product allow you to process credit card payments and direct deposit paychecks into employee accounts.

Simply Accounting

This program is easy to use and inexpensive, good for the small business that has basic accounting needs and a tight budget.

BUSINESS PLANNING SOFTWARE

Business plans are not just for startups in need of capital. They are essential tools for anyone running a small business who wants to think strategically, plot a course of action, and then follow up to see how well the plan is being followed. A good business planning program will walk you through the steps necessary to create a usable, powerful business plan.

Business Plan Pro

The best-selling business planning software for a reason, Business Plan Pro is useful to the novice and experienced businessperson alike. It easily helps you work through each category in the plan (e.g., Executive

Summary, Sales Forecasts, etc.), and contains more than 400 sample plans. The business plan in the appendix of this book comes from Business Plan Pro. With excellent templates, charts, and graphs the program is also easy to use. An excellent choice.

> Palo Alto Software, the makers of Business Plan Pro, also has a great product that can help you create a marketing plan, called Marketing Plan Pro.

Business Plan Writer

This program interviews you and then helps shape your answers cogently. It offers examples for each stage along the way, has hundreds of sample plans, and helps you through the process.

ANTIVIRUS AND ANTI-SPAM SOFTWARE

The twin technological plagues of the modern era—computer viruses and e-mail spam—must be controlled if you are to be at all productive at work. As a virus can ruin your computer and spam can slow work to a crawl, containing these problems is vital. As discussed in the previous chapter, Symantec and McAfee make excellent antivirus programs. And while spam control is being built into many office suites nowadays, you still may need extra help.

McAfee SpamKiller

Unwanted e-mails can be greatly reduced with this program. Using filters, lists, and reports, SpamKiller blocks plenty of spam, monitors your e-mail, and quarantines what does get through.

Mailwasher

Another excellent program, and—even better—*free*. Go to mailwasher .net. The makers of this product, PanicWare Software, also offer a very good pop-up blocker, also free.

Norton AntiSpam

The makers of Norton Anti-Virus have a similarly effective tool for the spam menace. Very effective.

> Also install an anti-spyware program. Check out www.lavasoftusa.com/software /adaware/ or www.spybot.com.

E-COMMERCE SOLUTIONS

Almost any small business needs a Web presence today, for obvious reasons. Whereas creating a web site used to be a fairly complicated matter requiring a webmaster, and although more sophisticated sites will still require expert help, simple off-the-shelf solutions are available for those small businesses that just need a basic web site. These programs will help you design and publish a fine site, shopping cart included.

Macromedia Dreamweaver

A very popular program among professionals, Dreamweaver has a powerful array of layout tools, applications, and other services to create and implement web sites. "Easy to use," says one expert.

Microsoft FrontPage

FrontPage is another easy-to-use product that allows you to intuitively create web sites, especially if you are used to the Microsoft Office environment, as FrontPage uses the same sort of interface as, say, Word. FrontPage works well for both beginners and those more experienced with web design. Note that your web host will need FrontPage extensions installed on their server for your site to work.

NetObjects Fusion

This easy-to-use design program helps you build a site with WYSIWYG (what you see is what you get) technology while offering shopping carts, credit card processing, and other e-commerce solutions.

Yahoo!

Yahoo! Small Business offers very easy, affordable merchant solutions. Starting at about $50 a month you can get online and start selling. Go to http://smallbusiness.yahoo.com.

The preceding categories should give you a basic understanding of the types of software most small businesses use and your options within each category. Maybe you will need additional software, such as point-of-purchase programs, but as a general rule, these programs will give you a solid foundation.

PART

III

Money

CHAPTER 15

Accounting Ease

There's no business like show business, but there are several businesses like accounting.

DAVID LETTERMAN

Business accounting is a way to keep score. If one purpose of business is to make a profit, then proper business accounting helps you know how well you are doing. No, it is not glamorous, and yes, it is important. Remember: There are two parts to your business: doing the things you love and doing the things you must. Accounting falls into the latter group (unless, of course, you are an accountant).

ACCOUNTING BASICS

Accounting is the general process of tracking your income and expenses and then using that data to examine the financial status of your business. Your basic accounting tool is the *general ledger*. It is the place where you keep track of all the business' financial transactions. That information is then used to create financial statements such as *balance sheets* and *income statements*. An *accounting period* is a set amount of time where a business' financial reports can be compared with one another; they can be months, quarters, or years. One year in a company's financial life is called a *fiscal year*.

The general ledger is made up of four basic categories: assets, liabilities, income, and expenses. All general ledger entries are double entries. Debits are kept on the left and credits on the right, and for every financial transaction in your business the debits and credits flow from one side of the ledger to another. When you sell something for instance, you record a sale (credit) on one side, but you also have to debit your inventory on the other. For every debit, there should be an equal and offsetting credit. When debits and credits are unequal, your books don't balance. All debits and credits either increase or decrease an account balance.

> Double-entry, general ledger accounting dates back to the fifteenth century. The first written description comes from a 1458 manuscript by Benedetto Cotrugli, and Franciscan monk Luca Pacioli included it in his seminal work, *Summa de Arithmetica, Geometria, Proportioni et Proportionalita*, printed in Venice, Italy, (on a Gutenberg press) in 1494.

Each area that feeds the general ledger is also its own subledger containing details about what is going on. For example, daily sales and payments are recorded in the accounts payable and receivable subledgers, and correspondingly increase cash and decrease inventory in the general ledger. In the previous chapter several different accounting programs that you can buy are listed. It is much easier to understand how a general ledger works if you buy a program like QuickBooks, since it will walk you through the process and do much of the work for you.

> When you are organizing the accounting department of your small business, although one person often handles everything, it is optimum to hire two. The problem with a single accounts payable and receivable person is that having one person write checks, and then reconcile the checking account, is asking for trouble.

Your ledger will be the basis of your basic financial reports, that either your software or your accountant will create. Financial reports, like profit and loss statements, are important because they are a snapshot of the financial health of your business. For instance, your income ledger will tell you how much money you brought in this month, but you will know your profit only when it is compared to your expense ledger. Your accounts receivables will tell you whether your customers are paying on time, and whether you have enough coming in to pay your accounts payable. Therefore, financial reports give you the overall picture of the fiscal condition of your business.

BUDGETING

Would you ever get into your car with a bag over your head and drive away? Of course not. How would you know if you had enough gas, or were headed in the right direction, or had an emergency red light flashing? Your eyes and the car give you the feedback necessary to help you safely get to where you want to go. In financial terms, running your business without a budget is like driving a car with a bag over your head. How will you know if you have enough money to expand? How can you tell if you are on track to accomplish your sales goals this year? Can you afford another employee? Your budget will tell you. Without a budget, you can't really see if you are headed where you planned on going.

Indeed, all too often small businesspeople have no clear financial idea of how they will get where they want to go, and it is not hard to see why. Most of us view budgets as a necessary evil at best and something to be avoided at worst. The traditional view is that a budget is a restrictive plan forcing you to deprive yourself of what you want. The good news is that a budget can be much different.

It helps to rethink the word. Instead of the word "budget" substitute "plan." A good plan is a guide, not a noose. A reasonable, intelligent plan is a business tool that allows you to allocate your resources to your greatest benefit. Creating a plan lets you control your business's cash flow, instead of it controlling you.

Creating a budget need not be a complicated or time-consuming task. The key is to figure out how much you will have to spend and where you want to spend it. It is a matter of digging through your records to see how much comes in, where it has been going, and then deciding *where you would rather have it go*. That really is all a budget is—a business plan that allows you to put your money where it can best be used.

Your budget will have two categories: projected income, and expenses (again, any good accounting program will walk you through this). In the income category, conservatively estimate how much you can expect to make next year from all sales and other sources of income. Look at what you made last year, and extrapolate from that. If you are new to business, what does your business plan say? Be realistic. If you paint too rosy a picture, then you can easily get in over your head and spend money that never materializes. If you make more than your projected income, great. But if you make less, watch out!

As far as expenses go, consider every expense you have: Advertising, auto, insurance, lease payments, taxes, phone, utilities, inventory, equipment, payroll—any and all expenses that you anticipate—will be borne by the business next year.

Once you see your projected income and expenses on paper, you will know exactly how much you really need to make every month to keep things afloat and how much you have left over. You will be far less tempted to indulge in business expenses that are not part of the plan. By having a budget, you will ensure that your expenses are not more than your income, and that your money goes where you think it can best be used.

CASH FLOW

Cash flow is your business oxygen. Without it, your business will suffocate and die. One more reason, then, to create a budget is to ensure that you will have adequate cash flow. I can't say this any more plainly: Without consistent, sufficient cash flow to buy inventory, pay bills, handle payroll, and pay yourself, you will go out of business. Preserving and defending your cash flow, therefore, is critical.

Aside from creating a budget, there are three more ways to control your cash flow.

1. *Live by the rule: Without your business oxygen, your business will suffocate and die.*
2. *Create cash flow projections.*   You need to know what will come in and when. Realistic cash flow projections are key. The question is: What do you expect your cash balance to be in six months? Always know that number. Think ahead.
3. *Keep the pipeline open.*   A client or customer you create today may hire you, but it may be a few months before you finish the work and send out a bill, and it may be another month or two before they pay. You have to keep creating clients and doing work *today* to keep the cash flow spigot open.

> When it comes to cash flow always project three to six months ahead. If you will need money in six months, you *must* create new business within the next three months. That way you can do the work or sell the product, bill it, and get it paid within six months.

A cash flow crunch is usually the result of poor planning. All businesses have business cycles and they must be planned for. Starbucks knows that coffee sales go up in the winter and down in the summer. In the summer then, they introduce cooler drinks to keep the cash flowing. The same should be true for you. You must know your business cycle, know when times should be good and bad, and plan accordingly.

If you do run into a cash crunch, there are two things you can do. First, receive your receivables. Allowing clients to pay Net 30 is common business practice. But anything more than that is bad business. If you consistently have outstanding invoices, change your terms. Always remember that accounts receivables (AR) are the lifeblood of your business, representing your business' cash flow and liquidity. Getting your receivables current, therefore, can bring in immediate cash.

Here is how to get those tardy accounts receivables up to date:

- Assign an employee the task of contacting all AR over 30 days old, and get a specific date as to when the debt will be paid. Have the employee call again that day if the money is not received. Once an AR is more than 60 days old, you have a real problem. If you are a sole proprietor, you must prioritize this task.
- Institute a new policy on 30 days notice that a surcharge of at least 10 percent interest will be due on all AR over 30 days old.
- Inform your customers that all outstanding balances must be made current before any new product will be sent out.
- If necessary, hire a lawyer or a collection agency to commence collection activities.
- As a last resort, you can always sell the debt. The money owed to you is a commodity and can be sold like one. Collection agencies buy bad debt every day, for a sharply discounted price.

Your other option for dealing with a cash crunch, ironically, is to get a loan. Sometimes you simply need a short-term infusion of cash to keep things going until business picks up again. A prudent loan with a plan to pay it back can be a smart solution to a short-term cash crunch.

HIRING AN ACCOUNTANT OR BOOKKEEPER

Many small businesspeople have a hard time dealing with the financial aspect of their business. They may be great innovators, have plenty of enthusiasm, and be the best salesperson around, but ask them to create a balance sheet and watch their eyes glaze over. Even the most powerful accounting software is useless if you cannot input or understand the data. So sometimes, nay often, hiring an accountant or bookkeeper is smart business.

Duties of an Accountant

While accountants cannot guarantee your success, they can be an important adjunct to your business. Their basic services include keeping track of how much your business owes, how much it is owed, creating financial statements (such as balance sheets, income statements, and cash flow statements), and reconciling bank statements. Beyond that, a CPA might

- *Handle taxes.*   A good accountant can save your business thousands of dollars through proper tax planning.
- *Do your payroll.*   Payroll is often outsourced.
- *Handle audits.*   An accountant might prepare an audit for a small business whose potential investors require audited books.
- *Deal with the IRS.*   The other sort of audit, the unwelcome one, is another place where accountants can come in quite handy.
- *Offer business and financial planning.*   A CPA can help with succession and estate planning, or help value the business for sale purposes.

So where do you find a good one? Referrals are the best source. If you know someone who has a good accountant, get their name. Get referrals from friends, business associates, your banker, your attorney, or from other entrepreneurs whom you know. After you get a few names, set up some appointments. Interview a few and find out

- *Their experience.*   You want someone who deals with small businesses, especially in your field.
- *Whether timely service is delivered.*   Numbers are constantly coming in from your business, so make sure that you will get reports at least monthly.
- *Who will service the account?*   Will it be the person you are meeting, or some junior accountant you do not know?
- *What services can you expect beyond reporting?*   Will they handle your taxes, payroll, or what?

- *Will you get business consulting as well?* A good accountant or bookkeeper should become a valuable member of your team, helping you in areas where you are weak.
- *How much will it cost?* You should know fairly accurately how much time they will put in each month and what you should expect to pay.

> Fiducial is the leader in small business tax, financial, and accounting consulting. Go to www.fiducial.com.

Again, as this person should become a dependable business advisor, you want someone whom you can trust and with whom you get along well and feel comfortable. Independent accountants or small accounting firms can provide personalized service, while a Big Five firm offers more services and can lend prestige to your company. This in turn may help you raise capital, establish credit, and open doors.

Cutting Costs

Accountants are professionals and their fees are not inexpensive. Even so, there are a few ways to keep your accounting costs down.

- *Keep great records.* Keep receipts organized. Have your ledger legible and up-to-date. Have your records automated if possible.
- *Handle the small stuff.* The stuff that you can do, do.
- *Use a bookkeeper.* If all you need is someone to do the books, a bookkeeper is much less expensive.

CHAPTER 16

Making a Profit

It is no secret that organized crime in America takes in over forty billion dollars a year. This is quite a profitable sum, especially when one considers that the Mafia spends very little for office supplies.

—WOODY ALLEN

The name of the game, of course, is making a profit, and many things go into the equation: overhead, markup, and what the competition is doing, for starters. In this chapter we examine how to make a consistent profit and what to do if you are not.

COMPUTING YOUR PROFITABILITY

As a concept, profit is easy to understand. It is the difference between what it costs you to make or buy your product and what you earn when you sell it. But it is when you break this seemingly simple concept down that things get a little complicated. When it comes to profit, there are four subconcepts to understand: Gross and net profit, your profit margin, and markup.

Gross and Net Profit

The *gross profit* on a product sold, or service rendered, is computed as the money you brought in from the sale, less the cost of the goods sold (COGS). *Net profit* is your gross profit less taxes and interest. Net profit is the same thing as *earnings* or *net income*.

> Your COGS is the cost you actually incur in making the product or service. For a product, it will include raw materials, labor, and other directly associated costs. For a product you sell, it is your wholesale costs.

Computing Your Profit

Keeping a running tab on profitability helps you stay focused and can be an early warning sign of trouble ahead. Let's say you run a child care center. To compute your profit, you must figure out your total costs to take care of each child, such as:

- Rent
- Labor
- Food
- Insurance
- Utilities
- Advertising
- Auto
- Other

Let's assume that your total overhead every month is $5,000. If you have 10 children, then, obviously, your expenses per child would be $5,000 divided by 10, or $500 per child. That is your break-even point per child per month. Let's further assume that you gross $8,000 a month, meaning that you charge $800 a month per child ($800 × 10 children = $8,000). Your gross profit therefore, per child, is $300, and your total gross profit is $3,000. Is that good or bad? It depends on your *profit margin*.

Profit Margin

While your gross profit is expressed as a dollar amount ($3,000), your gross profit margin is a percentage, computed as follows: Gross Profit divided by Sales equals Gross Profit Margin. In the preceding example, the gross profit would be $3,000 divided by $8,000, or 37 percent. That is good. Any business that makes 37 percent profit is doing something right. Again, some good accounting software will help you calculate these numbers quite quickly.

Markup

Knowing your markup is critical to understanding your profitability. Like your gross profit margin, your markup is also expressed as a percentage: Sales Price minus Cost to Produce divided by Cost to Produce. In the case of the childcare center it would look like this:

$$\$8,000 \text{ (sales price)} - \$5,000 \text{ (cost to produce)} = \$3,000$$
$$\$3,000 \div \$5,000 = 60\%$$

So the markup for each child is 60 percent, again, quite impressive, which begs the question: How much should you be charging for your goods or services?

PRICING

Just how important is selecting the right price? It could mean the difference between success and failure. The wrong price can put you out of business. Finding that magic number requires careful thought and planning. In the previous example, we know that you must charge at least $500 per child to break even. The trick is to come up with a price more than what gives you a good profit while still attracting customers.

There are basically two schools of thought when it comes to pricing your product or service (above your break-even point): If you are more interested in growing rapidly and capturing a share of the market

> The money aspect of running a small business is often confusing. There are classes at your local community colleges that can teach you more. Other places to look for continuing adult education business classes are chambers of commerce, web sites, and private seminar companies.

(called, of course, your *market share*), then you need to price your goods as low as possible because the laws of economics dictate that a lower price will attract more customers. Volkswagen sells far more cars than Mercedes, but Mercedes makes more money, per car. If you are going for a broad customer base, then you need to figure out, often by trial and error, what price people will consider a bargain and what still allows you to make a profit.

However, if dominating the field is not your business model, if you are more interested in increasing profits, then you need to go with a higher price. It has to be near what the competition is charging yet high enough for you to live on. No, it's not always easy to figure out and yes, it takes time.

Add into this equation the brand you are attempting to create. As discussed, a big part of how people perceive your business is based on what you charge. Two lawyers may do the exact same sort of work, but the one who charges $350 an hour will be perceived as better than the one who charges $150 an hour. Yes, she will get fewer clients, but they probably are better clients.

Here is the analysis to go through to determine your fees and prices:

1. *Determine your break-even point.*   Use the formula given to calculate your break-even point and start there.
2. *Identify your customers and brand.*   Are your customers middle class or wealthy? Is your brand upscale, or not? Do customers want bargains or is quality more important?

3. *What is the competition doing?*   Again, people look for bargains. If you can afford to beat the competition, all other things being equal, you *will* get business.
4. *Don't set your price too low.*   The best source of cash for growth is a healthy gross profit margin.
5. *Test, test, and test some more.*   Finding the right price will require trial and error. Tinker.

INCREASING YOUR PROFIT

There are three ways for you to improve your profits. First, you can sell more. Second, you can increase your prices. Third, you can reduce your overhead. That's it.

Selling More

Of course, the best way to increase your profit is to sell more. Easier said than done, you say? Maybe, but the entire next section of this book is devoted to giving you many different ways to grow your business. You probably sell more today than you did five years ago. The trick is to duplicate what you have done right, continue to do that, be sure to add some new profit centers, and read Part IV, Growing Your Business.

Increase Prices

Many small business owners are afraid to raise their prices because they fear that they will drive away customers. That may or may not be true. When you use price as the primary gauge for your services, then other, maybe more important factors, get left out of the equation—things like quality, personal service, convenience, or speed. McDonald's and Wal-Mart emphasize low prices because that is their business model, and unless it is yours, too, then constantly worrying about fees and prices is likely a mistake.

Because you are your own boss, you set the prices. When is the last time you raised your prices? While you should be justly concerned that you may drive away clients if you do, it is still worth a shot. If your fears are valid, you can always lower your prices again. But if your fears are ungrounded, you will be giving yourself a well-deserved raise.

> If yours is a service business, consider testing a price increase on a few customers first. If they do not balk, then you can roll out your price increases across the board, and if customers do, you can always change your mind.

Reduce Your Overhead

The tried-and-true way to increase profit margin is to decrease costs. When a Fortune 500 company lays off 5,000 employees, they are utilizing this strategy. Of course the risk is that by cutting costs you may cut into the very thing that brings in business. That is a real danger. And that is why firing people usually is not the answer. What is?

You have to figure out a way to reduce your overhead, and more importantly, to have employees care about keeping costs down, because it is often your employees who hold the key to cost overruns. If you can get them committed to saving, then staying consistently profitable is much more likely. How do you do that? Ask Jack Stack.

Stack is an entrepreneur who runs a company called the Springfield Remanufacturing Corporation. SRC began like many a small business—in debt and struggling. Within five years however, Stack had created a new way of doing business, and soon his business was worth millions. How did he do it?

Stack taught his employees about business. He helped them understand how the finances and overhead worked, how reducing waste for example made a big difference, and then gave them a stake in the outcome by instituting profit sharing. Stack's employees became part-owners of the business and thereby had a stake in the outcome. By teaching them how their department's finances ran, and how they could help the company and themselves make a profit, SRC reduced overhead dramatically and increased profits correspondingly. The system came to be called "open book management" (OBM) because the company opened its books to employees. Now, this is probably a fairly sacreligious thought to most small business owners. Most want their profits or losses to remain secret. While understandable, the thing to know is that there is another way, and the other way works.

By opening the books, by giving his employees the knowledge that what they do makes a big difference to the bottom line, and by giving them an ownership interest in that bottom line, Stack created, in essence, a workforce of small business owners; and we all know how motivated small business owners are.

> If you would like to know more about open book management, pick up *A Stake in the Outcome: Building a Culture of Ownership for the Long-Term Success of Your Business*, by Jack Stack (Currency, 2003).

Aside from adopting a business strategy like OBM, there are many other practical ways to reduce your overhead:

Cut back on available supplies. One of the things employees love about being employees is that they can nab pens and send FedExes without paying for them. However, if costs are an issue in your workplace, you simply must stop excess waste in this area.

Rent out space. If you have unused workspace, you may be able to rent it out to another small business.

Give incentives. Because employees are on the front lines, they may see waste that you do not. Rewarding them for suggesting cost saving measures that you implement is a smart strategy.

Buy in bulk. Sam's Club, Costco, and the like are savings bonanzas for the small businessperson. Costco's executive membership costs about $100 a year, allows you to shop earlier, and offers you the chance to buy low-cost insurance, telephone service, lines of credit, and much more.

Buy used. Instead of new furniture for instance, buy used.

Use the United States Postal Service.   Instead of spending $15 to overnight a package, think ahead, and use the USPS priority service (2–3 days for delivery) for about $4.

The postal service has many services geared for the small businessperson. Go to http://www.usps.com/smallbiz.

Rethink phone service.   There are so many carriers with so many great deals, you better not be paying retail any more.

Review insurance coverage.   The coverage you bought a few years ago may be outdated and overly expensive. Call your broker and get him to give you new quotes from several different insurers. Non-smoker and good driver discounts should be explored.

Utilize videoconferencing.   Online videoconferencing is a great way to reduce travel costs.

Request proposals.   Your tried and true vendors may have gotten a little lazy, taking your account for granted. Shop your needs to some new vendors and see if they can save you some money.

Read Part VIII of this book, "Business on a Shoestring."   Scores of other ways to save money are offered.

These are just a start; of course there are many other ways to reduce overhead without affecting the bottom line.

PAYING YOURSELF

A question many small business owners have vis-à-vis profitability is how much they should be paying themselves. The most important thing to consider is your business' financial condition. Before you can decide how much money you can safely pull out of the business each month, first figure out how much money your small business needs, because its needs come first. If you bite the hand that feeds you, it will bite you back. Calculate your break-even point and go from there. Knowing how much comes in and goes out allows you to figure out how much you can realistically afford to pay yourself. How much is that? Only you can say for sure after seeing your budget, but as you begin to formulate that number, keep the following three things in mind:

1. *Your business structure often determines when, and how, to pay yourself.* There are five forms your business can take: C corporation, S corporation, limited liability company (LLC), partnership, or sole proprietorship. Only owners who have set their businesses up as C corporations are legally considered "employees" of the business. If your business is a C corporation, then you can pay yourself as you would every other employee—as part of normal payroll.

> Beware of paying yourself too much, because it can trigger a tax audit. Let's say that you own a C corporation with $600,000 in profits, that is, taxable income. You might decide that a hefty, six-figure bonus to yourself makes sense. While probably deserved, if the amount of your yearly income is significantly more than what similar CEOs get for the industry, the IRS may conclude that the bonus was a sham transaction intended to reduce corporate profits and pay less taxes. As a general rule, salaries of less than $500,000 are not challenged, but those that are more, are.

Many small businesses start as sole proprietorships or partnerships. Sole proprietors can pay themselves whatever they want; it depends almost entirely on how much profit you make, how much money your business needs, and thus what you can afford to pay yourself. Partners must consider the desires of each other when determining how much they will be paid.

The same is true for LLCs that have more than one owner, with one caveat: You can make a distribution of profits legally, *only if* doing so does not impair the solvency of the business.

2. *Avoid paying yourself as the money comes in.* Many small business owners make this mistake. If they have a good month, they take

the extra out of the business; if they have a bad month, they don't. Not only does this violate the aforementioned Rule of the Budgets, but it doesn't account for potential business emergencies. It is imperative that your business checking account always has enough money in it so that if something goes wrong, you can afford to fix it. If you pay yourself whatever comes in every month, saving for a rainy day will be impossible. The smarter thing to do then is to come up with a figure to pay yourself that your business can live with, and pay that amount to yourself on a consistent basis.

3. *Consider the tax consequences.*   If you have a C corporation, when you pay yourself, the business is responsible for payroll taxes on the amount you get paid. In the case of a sole proprietor and partnership, whatever profits the business makes flows through onto your personal income tax—your business' profits or losses are considered your personal profits or losses. Partners and sole proprietors are also responsible for the self-employment tax, which runs about 15 percent.

Remaining profitable takes constant attention to detail. Keeping track of your margins and then increasing business or reducing costs as necessary is what is required.

CHAPTER 17

Getting and Extending Credit

There are three great friends: An old wife, an old dog, and
ready money.

—BENJAMIN FRANKLIN

The world runs on credit, and if you are going to run a successful small business, you need to know how to get it and when to give it. Whether it is obtaining a loan to open a new store or extending credit to a new customer, understanding the world of credit is a must.

BUSINESS LOANS

You never know when you might need a business loan. You may be chugging along, making a tidy profit every month, doing just fine, and then suddenly you get sick and are unable to work. You have to hire additional help to make up for the time you are away. Or maybe everything is going along just fine when a great opportunity arises, but to take advantage of it requires capital you don't have. Whatever the case, the time will come when you will probably need a business loan. To get one, think like a banker.

When lenders look to extend credit, what they are most concerned with are the four Cs of Credit.

1. Capacity. Will you have the ability to repay the loan? A bank will want to see that your business has sufficient cash flow to service the loan, and thus will ask you for your financial statements to justify and prove-up your capacity to repay. It is for this reason that banks are much more apt to loan to a business that has been around for a while and has a track record. New startups, with little history, fail this test. Because of this, the new business (and certainly more estab- lished ones, too) should consider a loan guaranteed by the SBA (see chart).

2. Collateral. Can you secure the loan with some sort of collateral? If the answer is yes, then the likelihood of getting a loan is much greater. Just as banks do not make home loans without securing the loan by get- ting a deed of trust on the property, so, too, do they usually require some sort of collateral to secure a business loan. If you do not have col- lateral, you will likely need a cosigner who does.

What sort of collateral do you need? Here is a chart provided by the Small Business Administration, examining how different types of collateral are valued by both a bank and by the SBA for its loan guar- antee programs.

Collateral Type	Bank	SBA
House	Market value × .75 – Mortgage balance	Market value × .80 – Mortgage balance
Car	nothing	nothing
Truck & heavy equipment	Depreciated value × .50	same
Office equipment	nothing	nothing
Furniture & fixtures	Depreciated value × .50	same
Inventory perishables	nothing	nothing
Jewelry	nothing	nothing
Other	10%–50%	10%–50%

Receivables	Under 90 days × .75	Under 90 days × .50
Stocks & Bonds	50%–90%	50%–90%
Mutual Funds	nothing	nothing
IRA	nothing	nothing
CD	100%	100%

3. Character. Does your business have a history of repaying loans on time? Do you have a history of paying on time? Because you will likely be asked to sign a personal guarantee for any business loan you get, your personal credit history is important. So before you apply for any loan, you better know what is in your credit report. Start by getting a copy of your credit reports. There are three.

Equifax	*Experian*	*TransUnion*
P.O. Box 740241	P.O. Box 2002	P.O. Box 1000
Atlanta, GA 30374	Allen, TX 75013	Chester, PA 19022
1-800-685-1111	1-888-397-3742	1-800-888-4213
www.Equifax.com	www.Experian.com	www.Transunion.com.

> You can get a copy of your business' credit history from Dun & Bradstreet: 1-866-472-7362, http://smallbusiness.dnb.com.

If you have paid an account on time, that will be there. If you have been late, that will be there, too. A late payment here or there will not affect your ability to get a business loan, but a pattern of late payments will. Charge-offs, judgments, and bankruptcies certainly hurt your cause.

Next, check for errors and outdated information. Anything (aside from a bankruptcy) that is more than seven years old should no longer be on your credit report. More importantly, credit reports are rife with factual errors. One billion pieces of credit are reported every month, and along the way, incorrect information ends up on far too many credit reports. The good news is that the Fair Credit Reporting Act mandates that *any* wrong info on your credit report must be removed once you draw the credit reporting agency's attention to the mistake. Usually this takes a few months, so well before you are going to apply for a business loan, you are advised to get a copy of your credit report and challenge anything that looks fishy.

> The Fair Credit Reporting Act 15 U.S.C. §1681 (2002) is a powerful tool that you should use. It mandates that incorrect information *must* be deleted from your credit report if *any* part of an account is incorrect. As such, if a legitimately late account *also* has some wrong piece of information attached to it (your name is spelled wrong, an account number is incorrect), and you challenge it, it must be deleted from your report. This is how people "clean up their credit."

4. Capital. How much money do you need, and why do you need it? You have to come into the bank with financial statements, a business plan, and a solid reason for asking for the exact amount you want, how it will be used, and when it will be paid back.

Aside from the four Cs, banks may also look at two additional factors when determining whether to give you a loan (called "underwriting"). Let's call these the two Es:

1. **Equity.** When you buy a home and begin to pay it down, you build equity. If the house is worth $100,000 and you owe $75,000, then you have $25,000 in equity. It is your actual cash value of the property. Well, the same is true for your business. Ironically of course, one way to get a business loan is to prove that you don't need one, and the way to do that is to have equity built up in your business. This can be done by retaining earnings or through a cash injection from an owner. Most banks like to see that your debt is no more than four times your equity. You need equity to make sure your ratios pencil out.

> The amount your business owes versus the amount it is worth is called its "debt to equity ratio." Your balance sheet will help you determine this.

2. **Experience.** More relevant to a new startup, your experience in the business, and your experience in the area that the loan is going toward, is a final factor a banker will look at when conducting a lending analysis.

So, do you qualify for a business loan? Let's find out.

1. Do you have a good credit history? ( ) Yes ( ) No
2. Are your taxes-up-to date? ( ) Yes ( ) No
3. Can the business repay the loan? ( ) Yes ( ) No
4. Does the business have equity? ( ) Yes ( ) No
5. Does the business not have a lot of debt? ( ) Yes ( ) No
6. Do you, the owner, have your own money invested in the business? ( ) Yes ( ) No
7. Does the business have collateral? ( ) Yes ( ) No
8. Would you be willing to personally guarantee the loan? ( ) Yes ( ) No
9. Do you have a solid management team? ( ) Yes ( ) No
10. Do you have a business plan? ( ) Yes ( ) No

Scoring: Unless you answered yes to all questions, you may have a hard time getting a conventional bank loan.

(Courtesy of the Small Business Administration)

SBA LOANS

The U.S. government and its arm the Small Business Administration want you to succeed, and one way they help you do so is through the SBA's various loan guarantee programs. Again, the SBA does not make the loans, but by guaranteeing loans made by selected banks, the SBA expands the pool of small businesses that are able to qualify for debt financing. This chart explains the different loans available.

Loan Type	Amount	Length	Discussion
7(a)	Up to $2 million	7 years	The SBA's basic loan program
SBA Express	Up to $2 million	7 years	Answers in 36 hours
Microloan	Up to $35,000	6 years	Often used for small startups
Disaster Recovery	Varies	Varies	Disaster relief loans
CDC/504	$1 million	5–10 years	Long-term investment for fixed-asset purchases
Low Doc	Up to $150,000	5–10 years	Answers within 36 hours
CapLines	Up to $2 million	Up to 5 years	For short-term and cyclical working-capital needs
Community Express	Up to $250,000	7 years	Applicable for low and moderate income areas
Export Express (See also SBA Export Working Capital loans.)	Up to $250,000	5–25 years	For companies that export
International trade	Up to $1.25 million	Up to 25 years	For companies engaged in or hurt by international trade

EQUITY FINANCING

Going into debt, or *debt financing*, is one way to fund expansion. The other is called *equity financing*. Many growth-stage small businesses use equity financing to fund expansion plans. As its name implies, equity financing occurs when you sell part of the business in exchange for capital. The deal can take many forms, from the sale of shares in a corporation to adding a partner to adding members to your LLC. As in the startup stage, equity financing often comes from nonprofessional investors such as family members, friends, business associates, or industry colleagues.

The other form of equity funding comes from professional investors known as venture capitalists (VCs) and angel investors. VCs are typically groups of wealthy individuals or financial institutions and most specialize in a few industries that the members know well. In the Silicon Valley for example, the lion's share of VCs are former computer executives who want to invest in new high-tech startups. Angels are individuals who want to invest in growth-opportunity businesses.

VCs, while certainly on the lookout for the Next Big Thing, more often look to invest in companies that are three-to-five-years old that have a solid plan and sound management team in place able to execute that plan. VCs will look at and listen to hundreds of pitches and plans before investing in the cream of the crop.

EXTENDING CREDIT TO CUSTOMERS

The flip side of getting credit is extending credit. Offering terms of Net 30 or 60 is common (Net 30 should be your maximum), but should not be undertaken lightly. If you do extend credit, you will need to create an accounts receivable plan, send out invoices monthly, and then keep track of who has paid and who has not. It takes time.

While you likely will need to extend credit to get business, you do not have to extend it to everyone. The important thing when extending credit to customers is to limit your risk by investigating the creditworthiness of the customer. And remember this rule: If a customer can't or won't pay when he or she wants to hire you—*when they need you most*—they probably won't pay later. You do not need every customer that comes in the door. Be picky about whom you work with; it will prevent problems later.

Here is what a credit application should look like.

Business name:

Other names of the business:

Name of owner(s):

Legal structure of business:

Address:

Phone and Fax:

Taxpayer ID number or Social Security number:

Number of years in business:

Trade references:

1.
2.
3.

Bank references:

1.
2.

Credit amount requested: $

The undersigned authorizes inquiry as to credit information and acknowledges that credit privileges, if offered, can be withdrawn at any time for any reason.

Dated: _____ Signed: _____

You then need to filter this information though a credit reporting bureau like Equifax or TransUnion.

Michael Gerber, author of the best-selling small business book, *The E-Myth*, says there are six reasons why businesses fail:

1. Lack of management systems
2. Lack of vision
3. Poor financial planning
4. Not understanding your market
5. Competition
6. Underfunding

CREDIT CARDS AND CHECKS

It is a proven fact that accepting credit cards means you will sell more. It allows customers to make impulse buys and pay for things when they don't have cash. The downside is that it is not inexpensive to take credit cards. Expect to pay:

- The discount rate: From 1.5 percent to 3 percent, the amount you pay per transaction.
- Equipment costs: You either lease or purchase equipment.
- Monthly fees for your merchant account.

To accept credit cards, you need to establish a merchant account with each of the credit card companies whose card you want to accept. You can do this through your own bank. If you have a hard time setting up a merchant account at your bank (for credit reasons) look online or in the Yellow Pages for independent credit card processing companies. They are more expensive, but are more flexible, too. After your merchant account is set up, you will receive a startup kit and instructions, explaining how to swipe cards and get authorization.

Finally, the same prudence that goes into extending credit also must go into the acceptance of checks. Of course, you need to see proper ID when taking a check from a customer, but beyond that, keep two tips in mind: First, don't accept new checks. Checks without a name imprinted on them, or numbered 1–500 indicate new accounts, and new accounts are the ones most likely to bounce checks. Second, wait for any check to clear before giving a refund.

CHAPTER 18

Insurance

Insurance: An ingenious modern game of chance in which the player is permitted to enjoy the comfortable conviction that he is beating the man who keeps the table.

—Ambrose Bierce

September 11, 2001 had profound effects on business, one of which is that it made business owners take a second look at their insurance policies and needs. Yet insurance is fairly oxymoronic—you buy something you hope you never need. But even so, you sure are glad it is there when you do need it.

TYPES OF INSURANCE

When you own a small business, the array of potential insurance products can be overwhelming. Which types of insurance are really important?

Health

Employees consistently rank health benefits among the most important benefits of employment. Because it is so important, and complicated, this issue is dealt with extensively in Chapter 27, *Employee Benefits Demystified*.

Business Owner

Business owner insurance is also known as "catch-all" coverage. It is a basic policy that provides protection from fire and other mishaps, as well as some liability protection (see next item).

Property/Casualty

Just as you insure your house against property loss, so, too, must you insure your business for the same. Property insurance protects your business against physical damage or loss of business assets. It is used when troubles like fire, theft, explosion, or vandalism damage or destroy your equipment, inventory, or buildings. Consider insuring the following:

- Buildings and structures, whether leased or owned
- Equipment, whether leased or owned
- Inventory
- Machinery
- Cars and trucks
- Computers, printers, fax and phone equipment
- Furniture and supplies
- Money and securities
- Important papers, books, and documents
- Signs, fences, and other outdoor property
- Intangible property like goodwill

How much should you expect to pay for property insurance? It depends upon your claims history, the insurer, what you want insured, the type of structure, whether you have any protective safety measures, and the location of your property vis-à-vis high-risk areas. As with the rest of your insurance needs, you need to shop around, as rates can vary widely.

Liability

Also known as "comprehensive general liability," or CGL insurance, this is a policy that has two functions. First, if someone is injured because of the negligence of you or your employees, the policy pays the claim. Second, if you are sued for damages relating to the policy, it will pay the cost of your attorney. Needless to say, in this litigious society of ours, liability insurance is almost a must.

Worker's Compensation

Worker's compensation insurance is required in every state except Texas. Note, however, that not every employer is required to carry it; in some states, small businesses with few employees (typically less than five) are not required to carry worker's comp insurance. Check with your state insurance commissioner's office.

Like CGL insurance, worker's comp does two things. First, it covers medical bills and lost wages for injured employees. Second, if an employee is injured or killed, it protects the owner against claims by the injured employee's family. Additionally, you can buy extra coverage that protects you from claims of sexual harassment or discrimination.

Rates for worker's comp depend upon how long you have been in business, your state, and the number of claims you have. Rates are usually set for three years, after which the insurer compares the number of claims you submitted against other similar businesses. If you have less, some insurance companies give you a refund. One way then to reduce your premiums is by having a good safety record. Your insurer may require that you follow Occupational Health and Safety Administration (OSHA) guidelines, or classify your employees, since insurers base premiums, at least in part, on the risk of injury for various job classifications.

It is sometimes difficult for small businesses to get affordable worker's compensation insurance. In response, some states have created risk-sharing pools for those companies. Do not expect to find many discounts if forced into this option, however, as this is the insurance of last resort.

Errors and Omissions (E and O)

E and O insurance is for the service businesses, and offers protection if you neglect to do something causing a customer or client damage. For example, a physician's medical malpractice insurance is a type of E and O coverage.

Business Interruption

Business interruption insurance (BII) is designed to cover the loss of income if normal business operations are disrupted by damage due to fire, flood, or other disaster. The important thing to understand here is that BII is intended to cover loss of income directly related to loss of physical property. Thus, if your location is vital to your ability to make money, then business interruption insurance is important. A service business would probably not need BII as they can perform their services most anywhere, but a factory would definitely need business interruption insurance.

Key Man

Like the name indicates, this sort of policy insures your business against the death of a key employee, be it the CEO, Vice President of Sales, or whomever. Think about it: What would happen to your business if a key employee died? For some small businesses, the company would die too. The important things to understand about Key Man insurance is:

- If your top management is thin, if one or two people are responsible for keeping the ship afloat, then Key Man is key.
- Buy as much as your business can afford. Accurately estimate what it would cost the company if the key men or women were to vanish and buy a policy for that amount if you can afford it.

Auto

If your business makes deliveries or if you provide employees with company cars, then auto insurance is a must. While you may be tempted to purchase the minimum coverage required by your state, that is not enough since the point of insurance is to protect your business. If your driver kills someone in an auto accident, a minimal $25,000 policy will equal bankruptcy. For an established business, $1 million in liability coverage is probably right. A better way to keep premiums down is to increase your deductible.

Life

Why are you in business for yourself? One reason surely is that you want to create financial stability for your family. Well, what if something happens to you, what becomes of the dream then? Without adequate life insurance, it probably will turn into a nightmare. Beyond that, many banks require that the owner of the business have life insurance before the bank will loan the business money.

When shopping for life insurance, you will be faced with a decision: Term or a whole life policy? Whole life is like buying a house; as you pay the premium, you build equity in the policy. Term is like renting—it is cheaper, but you build no equity. In this case, renting is probably better than buying as rates for term life insurance are amazingly affordable. Even though you will not be building equity, the money you save is usually better spent in other areas of your business.

> Premiums for business insurance are tax deductible as a business expense, although life and Key Man insurance premiums are not deductible if the business is the beneficiary of the policies.

BUYING INSURANCE

The preceding list of potential insurance is a bit daunting, and no one is telling you that you must buy all of it. Sure it would be nice, but just as in the rest of your business, choosing what sort of insurance you really need is a matter of weighing the risks and rewards. There is a finite limit on what you can realistically do, and sometimes you simply must marshal your resources to the best of your ability and hope for the best.

To save as much as you can, then, on your insurance costs it is important to know the difference between an insurance agent and an insurance broker, because it is a distinction that can save you money. An agent is an agent for a single company. He or she may be able to get you a good deal, but only within the company that they represent. A broker on the other hand represents many different insurers and thus has the ability to shop your needs around to many different insurers and find you the best deal out there.

The second way to reduce the cost of your premiums is to take the highest deductible that you can reasonably afford. Needless to say, it has to be an amount that you can actually afford. There is no point in taking a $5,000 deductible if your small business will be unable to absorb the difference.

Another way to make the payments more manageable is to create a payment plan that works for your budget. Fortunately, insurance companies are quite flexible when it comes to payment of the premiums. You can pay every month, or quarterly, or yearly for that matter. So find yourself a good insurance broker and go over your needs. He or she will be able to guide you to making the right decisions and to obtaining the coverage that is right for your business.

Exclusions

Whatever policy you look at, be sure that you understand what the exclusions will be. *Exclusions* are those things that the policy does not

---

There are four basic parts to any insurance policy:

1. *The declarations page.* This names the policy holder, explains what is insured, and lists the maximum payout by the insurer.
2. *Insurance agreement.* This section sets out the responsibilities of both sides under the insurance contract.
3. *Conditions.* This section details exactly what is covered and under what circumstances.
4. *Exclusions.* This area details what is covered and what is not.

cover, and every policy will have some. Some policies will have many, and there are not many things businesswise worse than having a loss, thinking you are covered, and then discovering that the type of loss you suffered was specifically excluded in the fine print of your policy. For example, a property loss policy will likely exclude losses due to the theft by an employee. So be sure you know before you sign what is covered and what is not.

MAKING A CLAIM

The time may come when you suffer a loss and need to make a claim against your carrier. Insurance companies are sticklers for details, and if you do not follow procedures to the letter, you may find that they will deny your claim, and legitimately. So follow these tips to ensure that your insurance works for you.

Before Making a Claim. Be sure you have excellent records and that they are kept in a safe, secure spot, preferably off site. All receipts, backups of important files, and backups of computer data should be readily accessible so that you can get to them easily. Similarly, it is a good practice to make a video of your premises and property every year. Spend some time going around and documenting what you have where. Then put the tape with your other vital records in your secure location. It will be invaluable if you ever need it.

> A main reason for keeping good records is that it speeds up the claims process. The longer it takes you to gather the information that your insurer needs, the longer it will take to process your claim, and the longer it takes to process your claim, the longer it will take to get that check.

After a Loss. Follow these steps when making a claim.

1. *Report the incident immediately.* Tell your agent or carrier about the problem as soon as you can. Some policies require notification

within a set time limit and can deny coverage if notice comes in too late.

2. *Protect your property from further damage.* If it is a property loss claim, such policies often require that damaged property be kept safe from further damage.

3. *Provide documentation.* If you have receipts, copy and provide them. If you made that videotape, get it out.

4. *Communicate and cooperate.* The easier you make it for the adjuster, the easier it will be for you.

CHAPTER 19

Get a Handle on Taxes

To you taxpayers out there, let me say this: Even though income taxes can be a pain in the neck, the folks at the IRS are regular people just like you, except that they can destroy your life.

—DAVE BARRY

Taxes are one of those areas in which almost every entrepreneur hates dealing. So I will make you the same deal I make with the readers of my weekly *USA TODAY* column (www.usatoday.com/money/small business /front.htm) whenever I write about taxes (twice a year—April and December): Give me just a bit of your time, and I will make this as painless as possible, and hopefully save you some money in the process.

TAX BASICS

The amount you or your business will pay in annual taxes depends on several factors: the legal form of your business, how much money it made that year, what your expenses were, how sharp your accountant is, and how much you personally know about the tax system. Here is what you need to know about taxes if you run a small business.

Deductions

You already know that you can deduct "ordinary and necessary" business expenses to reduce your taxable income; that's the easy part. Travel, supplies, inventory, labor costs—all are deductible from your federal income taxes. The real question is, Are there any loopholes you can use?

Entertainment. While you used to deduct up to 80 percent of all legitimate entertainment expenses, the limit now is 50 percent. The good news is that almost any entertainment activity that relates to business can be deducted: a round of golf, important dinners, taking a client to a game or a concert, or even a day on a boat. Keep good records, all receipts, and be able to prove that the expense was actually related to business. Write on the receipt whom you were with before filing it away.

> If you throw a party, picnic, or some other entertainment event for your staff and their families, those expenses are 100 percent deductible.

Travel. As you know, travel expenses you incur for business are 100 percent deductible. However, if your family joins you for your business trip to Orlando, their expenses are not deductible. But the loophole is that if you stay over for a night or two to get a discounted airfare, your extra hotel and meals are deductible.

Automobile. There are two methods for calculating your vehicle deduction. The "standard mileage" method allows you to deduct 36 cents per mile when you drive the car for business, as well as business-related tolls and parking expenses.

The "actual expense" method permits you to deduct your total expenses for gas and repairs, plus depreciation. Then, multiply your expenses by your percentage of business use. For example, if your total auto expenses are $10,000, and you use the car 40 percent for personal use and 60 percent for business use, your deductible auto expenses would be $6,000. Keep a log of when the car is driven for which purpose.

Business Losses. These can be deducted against your personal income. If the amount your business lost is more than your personal income, the extra loss can be applied to future income taxes.

Loans and Credit Cards. Interest on the loans, purchases, or advances can be deducted as a business expense.

> Professional association fees are deductible. You can deduct up to $25 per business gift given. Bank charges, magazines and books, losses due to theft, commissions paid, web site development, parking and tolls, seminars, and even bus fare are deductible.

Charity. Sole proprietors, partnerships, LLCs, and S corporations can have charitable contributions passed through and deducted on the owner's personal tax return. C corporations claim any charitable deduction for themselves.

Taxes. Sales taxes on items you buy for the business are deductible. Fuel and excise taxes are often overlooked deductions. Property tax and local assessments are deductible as are employment taxes you pay, although the self-employment tax paid by individuals is not deductible, and neither is federal income tax paid.

> Small businesses lose audits when they have poor records, so keep all receipts, cancelled checks, credit card statements, and so forth. If you do keep good records, and if you are ever audited, your chances of success—of not getting hit with an extra assessment and fine—will be much greater. Keep good records!

OTHER TAX BASICS

Employees and taxes go hand-in-hand. When hired, your employees need to fill out a federal W-4 form and an Immigration and Naturalization

Service Form I-9. As you begin to pay them, you deduct a variety of taxes from their paychecks.

- *Social Security.* Social security taxes (also known as FICA) must be withheld from an employee's pay. Match the amount withheld and pay it to the federal government.
- *Medicare.* Medicare must also be withheld. Match and pay this amount, too.
- *Unemployment tax.* You need to withhold, match and pay this tax, too.
- *State income taxes.* These, too, are withheld.

Because payroll and employee withholding is such a complicated area, you are strongly advised to hire a payroll service like ADP, Paychex, or something similar.

Sales Taxes

Unless you live in one of the five states that have no sales tax (parts of Alaska, Delaware, Montana, New Hampshire, and Oregon), and if you sell a product, you will owe your state tax money. What you will owe varies greatly; not only does the amount vary by state, but some states tax services as well as products. Check with your state tax board to see whether the rules apply to you. If your service or product is subject to your state's sales tax, register with your state's tax department, track taxable and nontaxable sales, and then include that information with your state tax return.

There are two exceptions to the sales tax rules (which essentially amount to *pay tax on anything sold to anyone*). The first is resellers—such as wholesalers and retailers with a resale license—who do not owe sales tax. Also, you owe no sales tax on sales to tax-exempt organizations like public schools and churches.

Deadlines

When you own your own small business, be aware of tax deadlines beyond April 15:

- Corporations must file their returns within two and a half months after the end of their fiscal year.
- Quarterly estimated taxes are due four times a year: April 15, June 15, September 15, and January 15.
- Sales taxes. Sales taxes are due quarterly or monthly, depending upon what state you are in.
- Employee taxes. Employee taxes may be due weekly, monthly, or quarterly, depending upon the number of employees you have.

> Quarterlies should be paid by any small business that expects to pay at least $500 in taxes for the year. You are supposed to pay either 90 percent of the tax you will owe or 100 percent of the previous year's tax.

Property Taxes

If your business owns real estate, it will owe property taxes. Moreover, if you lease property, your lease may require you to pay the property taxes. In some leases, the owner pays the "base year taxes" (an amount equal to the amount owed the year before the lease was signed) and the lessee (you) owe any increases. In most places, the tax rate on commercial property is significantly higher than on residential property.

TAX TIPS

All small business owners want to save on their taxes. The question is, How? There are many different strategies you can adopt to help you reduce your tax bite. Do not wait until December 31 before deciding to take action. Some preplanning can go a long way to reducing Uncle Sam's take come tax time.

Set Up a Retirement Account

The self-employed have the opportunity to divert pretax dollars into different types of retirement savings accounts and thereby reduce their yearly taxable income.

Keogh Plans. A Keogh retirement plan allows self-employed taxpayers to contribute significant sums (it varies, but up to $41,000) every year into a tax-free account. Keoghs are fairly complicated to create and the assistance of a financial advisor is required. There are several benefits to starting a Keogh retirement plan:

- Contributions are deducted from gross income.
- Taxes are deferred until the money is withdrawn.
- Interest earned is also tax deferred until withdrawn.
- Contribution amounts are more liberal than with IRAs.

Solo 401(k). This plan is great because of its high contribution limits. Like a Keogh, a solo 401(k) currently allows you to contribute up to $41,000 a year into your retirement account, but here, the amount you can contribute rises as you get older.

SEP IRAs. A Simplified Employee Pension Individual Retirement Account (SEP IRA) is a plan that allows you to contribute and deduct up to 20 percent of your income into a tax-deferred retirement account. SEPs are indeed simple: They can be created in a few minutes at a bank or brokerage house with no professional help required, and no annual government reports are required. They beat regular IRAs because they allow for larger contributions.

> You may be tempted to also set up a traditional Roth IRA. While that may be good for retirement purposes, it does little for you businesswise, as contributions are not tax deductible.

Note: If you do set up a SEP, solo 401(k), or Keogh, you have to offer it to your employees as well. This means you will likely need to make contributions that don't just cover you. Because of this, consult with an employee benefits pro before setting up any sort of retirement plan for you and your employees.

One last bonus for creating a business retirement plan: You can get a tax credit of up to $500 for the first three years of the plan if you have less than 100 employees.

Lease Your Property to Your Business

If your business uses property that you personally own, you can save on business taxes by leasing the property to the business. The lease expense to the business is tax-deductible, and the income you generate personally from the lease income is not subject to Social Security tax. You can then take any applicable depreciation allowance for the leased property.

> The IRS has an excellent site devoted exclusively to small business, with industry specific information, audit guides, links and more. Go to www.irs.gov/businesses/small/.

Use the Tax Laws

The Jobs and Growth Tax Relief Reconciliation Act of 2003 offered plenty of help for the small business owner. The best part of the bill is the generous change in the rules for depreciating business expenditures. Previously, equipment and business assets had to be depreciated over a five to seven year time span. Under the new rules, however, you can now depreciate and deduct 100 percent of the cost of almost all new and used assets in the year that you buy them. Also previously, the deduction topped-out at $25,000, but you can now depreciate up to $100,000 for any asset acquired after May 5, 2003.

Reexamine Your Business Structure

If you have been in business for a while and are profitable, it may be smart to change your legal form of business. For instance, a growing S corporation may want to become a C corporation to take advantage of benefit programs limited to C corporations, such as group-term life insurance and various health-plan options. A newly-profitable sole proprietor may want to form an LLC to get personal liability protection, or to form an S corporation to reduce the self-employment tax.

Pay Your Quarterlies

Make sure that you are paying your quarterly estimated taxes on time and in sufficient amounts to avoid penalties and interest down the road.

Delaying Your Receivables and Accelerating Your Expenses

At the end of the tax year, if your business expects to have significant income from accounts receivables, consider delaying those receivables until after the first of the year. Doing so will reduce your business' net taxable income for that year. Similarly, if you anticipate a large tax bite at the end of the year, consider accelerating some expenses into the current tax year. Expenses that can be accelerated include corporate charitable contributions, 60 percent of health insurance premiums for you if you are a self-employed individual, year-end employee bonuses, or any other tax-deductible expenses you are planning on making.

Deducting Your Home Office

If you use part of your home for business, you may be eligible for the home-office deduction. Here's the rule: (1) Your home office must be used "exclusively and regularly" for your business, and (2) The area must be either your principal place of business or where you meet with customers in the normal course of business. If you pass that test, then you can deduct a portion of your mortgage, insurance, utilities, and so on.

SURVIVING AN AUDIT

Even if you know your tax law and do everything right, the chances of getting audited are greater for you than for the public at large. Why? Because small businesses are audited more than any other entity. So if you do get that dreaded letter and do have to attend a tax audit, here is what you should do.

Get Some Help

If you have a CPA, consider hiring her to help you prepare and to attend the meeting. Your accountant should be your financial business advisor, and this is when you need her most. If you can't afford an accountant, you must do on your own what she would do: Prepare. Look at the return(s) in question and be able to substantiate (with those good records you were advised to keep) what is in the return. You, or you and your accountant, need to prepare all documentation for the audit.

Be Organized

Make sure your receipts are organized, your cancelled checks and credit card receipts are in order, and that all logs and other records are ready. Having your ducks in a row builds credibility. The success of your audit depends upon your ability to document your income and expenses. You will want to have ready for the auditor bank statements, cancelled checks, receipts, invoices, sales slips, petty cash vouchers, printouts of electronic records, bills, checkbook registers, ledgers, journals, appointment books, and any other physical documentation of your records. Without adequate records the IRS auditor can legally make assumptions about your income and deductions.

Prepare Your Listed Property Records

Equipment that has both personal and business use is called "listed property": things like home computers, cell phones, and autos. Provide the auditor with business records of your listed property.

Prepare Your Travel and Entertainment Records

T and E expenses must be proven by written record (IRS Code § 267). One way to document T and E expenses is with an appointment book or log.

As you can see, winning an audit will be much more likely if you have a practice of maintaining records, keeping receipts, and chronicling electronically what you do.

CHAPTER 20

Legal Ease I

It is easier to stay out than to get out.

—MARK TWAIN

Like taxes and insurance, law is one of those areas that entrepreneurs would rather not think about, and when they do, it usually is unpleasant. Yet you need to know what you need to know. There is a litigation explosion in this country, businesses are prime targets (known in the trade as "deep pockets"), and you need to arm yourself with knowledge. Therefore, in this chapter and the next, you get a primer on business law, so that you know what to avoid, and what to talk to your lawyer about if something does go wrong. One caveat: Although I am a lawyer, no book can take the place of an attorney who knows you, your situation, and the facts. As such, while the general information I provide can educate you, if you do find yourself in legal hot water, meet with a lawyer in person.

CONTRACTS

Contracts are the easy stuff. They are like your personal set of laws. As long as you bargain in good faith, and the subject of the contract is legal (i.e., you can't legally contract to open a house of prostitution), just about anything you and the other side agree to will fly. However, not every promise is legally enforceable; to create a legally enforceable promise, or set of promises, three requirements must be met that raise the promises to the level of a legal contract.

1. *Offer.*   The first part of any contract is a clear and unambiguous offer. "I will buy 200 pounds of your flour at $8 a pound" is a clear and specific offer, inviting a clear and specific response. On the other hand, "I think I would like to buy some flour" is not an offer because it is neither specific nor an unambiguous offer to accept specific terms.

   Offers remain open unless accepted, but may be revoked at any time. So if you offer to buy the flour for $8 a pound, find it elsewhere for half that price, *and* your offer has not been accepted, then you can still revoke the offer. However, if the flour seller has accepted your offer, you cannot revoke it.

2. *Acceptance.*   Like an offer, an acceptance must be clear and unambiguous: "I accept" is an acceptance, but "That sounds good, let me call you back in an hour" is not. The point of a contract is to allow a willing seller and a willing buyer to enter into a commercial transaction with clearly defined terms. Hence, the acceptance must be equally obvious.

   What if the seller says, "I'll sell you the flour for $10 a pound"? In that case, the $8 offer is deemed rejected, and the seller just made a $10 counteroffer, which you now have the power to accept or reject. This offer/counteroffer dance can go on ad infinitum. The one exception to this is a commercial transaction between merchants where there is an acceptance with minor changes that do not *materially* alter the original offer. In that case, pursuant to the Uniform Commercial Code (UCC), the offer is deemed accepted and the changes become part of the contract. What does "material" mean? That's what you hire lawyers for!

   There are times when offers are not actually accepted but are enforceable. This occurs, for example, when the acceptance occurs as actual performance. My offer to purchase 200 pounds of flour can be accepted by delivery of 200 pounds of flour.

3. *Consideration.*   To create a valid, legally enforceable contract, aside from offer and acceptance, you also need a bargained-for exchange (legally "quid pro quo," or "this for that"), called "consideration." In essence, this means that you have to give up something to get something: My money for your flour.

If I said, "I'll wash your car this afternoon" and you say, "okay" no contract has been formed, even though there has been an offer and acceptance. Why? Because there has been no consideration. You give up nothing for me to wash your car; it is just a promise on my part with none on your part, and therefore is not legally enforceable. You need offer, acceptance of that offer, and a bargained-for exchange to create a valid, legally enforceable contract.

There is one legal tenet that helps you get around the need for consideration. If you make a promise, and I rely on that promise to my detriment, and it was reasonably foreseeable that I would rely on that promise, I can get that promise enforced, even if we did not have a formal contract. For instance, if you say, "I will give you $5,000 if you drive my car to Los Angeles" and I do, I relied to my detriment on your promise, and I can enforce it in a court of law.

There are a few other things about contracts that you need to know:

- *It is good business to get every contract in writing.*   Although only certain contracts *have* to be in writing (most notably, those for the sale of land, for purchases over $500, and employment contracts that last more than a year), memories fade over time, and people choose to remember things wrong. If it's not in writing, there is no record of whose recollection is actually correct. Get it in writing. Avoid oral contracts.
- *Remember, too, that standard or form contracts can be modified.*   A contract is also known as an "agreement" for a reason—you need to

agree to it. If there is a clause in a standard contract you do not like, negotiate to change or delete it.

- *Be as specific as possible in your contracts so that nothing is left to chance.*   Ambiguity breeds litigation.
- *The first one to breach a contract usually loses.*   Yes, there are legitimate reasons that may excuse performance (the contract was entered into by mistake, fraud, or is impossible to perform), but usually the first breacher loses.

If you would like to draft your own contracts, or otherwise be your own lawyer, then go to www.Nolo.com. Nolo Press is the leader in do-it-yourself law and offers a wide array of excellent books and software to help you.

NEGLIGENCE AND LIABILITY

When ice on your walkway (ice that you already asked your employee to remove, but that he did not) causes a customer to slip, fall, and break her arm, that is legally called "negligence." Being found negligent can be one of the worst things that can happen to your business, since the damages can be astronomical. Whereas a breach of contract merely means that the loser has to pay the winner the value of the contract, a negligence suit can cost you hundreds of thousands, if not millions, of dollars, as you are obligated to pay the defendant for his pain and suffering.

Here is the standard of care you and your employees are obliged to maintain: *You must act as a reasonably prudent person would under the same or similar circumstances.* If you do not, and if that *breach of duty* causes someone damage, you will have to pay. In the case of the ice, a reasonably prudent employee would have removed the ice when his boss asked him to. If he did not, and that caused the customer to slip and fall and get hurt, then the business would be found liable because of its negligence.

This is why many small businesses enact standards, policies, and procedures for employees to do certain duties in a certain way. If the standards you adopt are adhered to, it is less likely that someone will get hurt, and even if they do get hurt, it will be more difficult for them to prove you fell below the standard of care, if you have policies and procedures in place intended to avoid just this sort of accident. Your policies and procedures prove that you are a reasonably prudent business owner, see?

But accidents do happen and people do get hurt. That is why you are also strongly advised to buy liability insurance. Yes, your premiums will go up if claims are made against your policy, but it sure beats paying the damages out-of-pocket.

> The most famous case in the history of negligence law is called *Palsgraf v. Long Island Railroad*. In that case, Mrs. Palsgraf was standing at one end of the platform of the Long Island Railroad after buying a ticket. A train stopped at the other end of the station, and a gentleman carrying a package raced for the car. A Long Island Railroad employee on the car held the door open, reached to help the gentleman in, and another guard on the platform pushed the man up from behind. The man's package dislodged, fell to the ground, the fireworks inside the package exploded, and shock of the explosion knocked over some scales at the far end of the platform near Mrs. Palsgraf, injuring her. Quiz: Did she win? Nope, the court ruled that the actions of the employees, while negligent toward the man, were not so in relation to Mrs. Palsgraf.

The key to avoiding negligence claims is to maintain a safe place of employment. Set standards and enforce those standards.

PRODUCT LIABILITY

If you manufacture, wholesale, distribute, or sell retail products, you need to be concerned with a special subset of negligence law called "product liability law." If a product you manufactured, wholesaled, or sold injures a consumer, everyone in the supply chain between you and the buyer may be legally affected.

In the case of a defective product, there are three legal theories to be concerned about.

1. *Negligence.* Here again, the injured party would need to show that the seller or manufacturer breached the standard of care. For instance, if a car's wheel fell off because it was not bolted on properly at the plant, the manufacturer of the car would be found liable for any injuries that resulted.
2. *Breach of implied warranty.* If you, the small business owner, make either an express or implied warranty or representation about what a product will do, and the product fails to live up to that, causing harm, you may be found liable for the injury under this theory. Many states have limited the use of this theory to business matters where the buyer has suffered economic loss only.

> Whatever representations you make, the product must perform up to that standard. So one way to limit your risk is to avoid making any representations in your advertising or marketing materials, as they may later be used against you.

3. *Strict liability.* This is the scary one. If an injured party can show that (1) the product was defective at the time the seller sold it and (2) the defect caused the injury, then you are on the hook. Unlike negligence, the injured party does not need to prove that you breached some standard. Rather, he needs to prove only that the product was defective, for whatever reason. Your prudence and care is no defense. That is why they call this *strict* liability. When Firestone tires began to explode, you can bet strict liability was a theory the plaintiffs' attorneys used.

There are several things you can do to minimize your risk of being sued for product liability. First, try to not ship or sell defective products—inspect what you can. Second, warn where possible. Warning of dangers is a valid defense (and now you know why you see those crazy warning labels on products). Next, be careful about what you say and promise in your promotions. Also, consider using disclaimers. A conspicuous tag disclaiming any liability for damage caused by the product may protect you in some circumstances. Finally, specify the useful life of the product. Harm caused after the expiration of the useful life cannot be attributed to you.

INTELLECTUAL PROPERTY

An altogether different area of the law, but one no less important to your business, is intellectual property law. It has to do with intangible assets, like words, phrases, and pictures. These may in fact be your most important assets. Let's use Nike as an example. How important is that swoosh logo? That is intellectual property (a trademark). What about the name Nike? That is also intellectual property (trademark). Its shoes? Patented. And its tag line, Just Do It—yep, that is intellectual property, too.

Intellectual property is no less important in a small business. You need to know how to protect your business name, logo, inventions, and so on. There are five areas of intellectual property that may help you: trademarks, copyrights, patents, trade secrets, and goodwill. Let's look at each.

Trademark

A trademark is a word, phrase, design, or symbol that identifies your business and distinguishes it from the competition. (A "service mark" is essentially the same thing; it identifies a service you provide.) Examples of trademarks are Dr. Pepper or The Portland Trailblazers.

Trademarking your business name or logo is quite easy. To get full trademark protection, register your mark with the federal trademark office. Log on to www.USPTO.gov (the web site of the United States Patent and Trademark Office) and follow the directions.

Copyright

A copyright protects the original, physical expression of a creative idea. This sentence is a copyrighted sentence. To be copyrightable, the ideas must be unique, tangible (written or taped, for instance), and a "work of authorship." Musical scores, magazine articles, choreographed dances, photographs, movies, and sculptures would be examples of copyrightable expressions.

Copyrights last the life of the author plus 75 years, and the creator owns the copyright, although if the creator created the thing working for someone else, the employer would own the copyright. You own the copyright to any works your employees create in the fulfillment of their duties. This is called work-for-hire.

One of the best aspects of copyright law is that there is nothing to register. As soon as you create the thing, it is copyrighted as a matter of law. This sentence is being copyrighted as I write it. Certainly you can register it with the U.S. Copyright Office, but it is not necessary. Instead, when you want to put the world on notice that you have copyrighted material, have "© All rights reserved" prominently affixed to the work.

Patents

If you invent or discover a new and useful "process, machine, manufacture, or composition thereof" you can apply for a federal patent to protect your invention from being used by others without your permission. Utility patents protect machines and industrial processes and last for 20 years. Design patents protect designs of manufactured items and last for 14 years. Plant designs protect new plant varieties and last for 17 years.

Patents are not inexpensive to obtain, and the assistance of a lawyer is almost always required. However, if you have invented something unique, definitely spend the money and patent it.

Trade Secrets

Most states have adopted the Uniform Trade Secrets Act. This law defines a trade secret as "information that has independent economic

At one time, R. Buckminster Fuller had the most entries in *Who's Who*. An inventor, mathematician, author, and cartographer (among other occupations), Bucky is most well known for having invented the multitriangular geodesic dome. He once remarked that he owed his fame and success to . . . his patent lawyer! Had it not been for the airtight patent his lawyer obtained for the dome, Bucky believed that his beloved invention would have surely been stolen, and, he says, "no one would have ever heard of me."

value by virtue of remaining secret." A customer or vendor list might be considered a trade secret. KFC's "17 herbs and spices" surely is a trade secret.

To be legally protected, make efforts to keep your secrets secret. This is not to say that you can never tell anyone the secret, but rather, that you attempt to retain the secret and act appropriately.

If you want to share something secret with another party, make sure they sign a nondisclosure agreement, or NDA. An NDA says that you will be sharing confidential information and that it cannot be used by the other side for commercial reasons and cannot be disclosed to a third party without your prior, written approval. You can find one at my site, www.MrAllBiz.com.

Goodwill

After some time in operation, your small business develops a positive reputation in the community and a valuable list of customers. This is called your goodwill. Goodwill is a business asset that usually relates to your exit strategy, when you are looking to sell your business. A significant asset to be sold at that time will be your business reputation, your goodwill. Protect it.

CHAPTER 21

Legal Ease II

> I can try a lawsuit as well as other men, but the most important thing is to prevent lawsuits.
>
> —CONFUCIUS

If you have ever been party to a lawsuit, you know only too well how true Confucius' words are. Lawsuits are a civilized form of war, pitting one side in a pitched battle against the other, both willing to do and spend almost anything to win, and both usually losing plenty in the process. Lawsuits are an expensive, time-consuming, exhausting, frustrating, and often ineffective way to resolve disputes. The point of this and the previous chapter, therefore, is to help you avoid the dreaded lawsuit. So learn what the rules are and do your best to follow those rules.

EMPLOYMENT DISCRIMINATION AND LAWSUITS

Employment discrimination lawsuits usually arise when employees were either fired or not hired, and they contend the reason was discrimination.

At-Will Employment

When can you fire someone without repercussion? While seemingly a simple question, the answer is not so simple. The basic rule is this:

Almost all employees are considered "at-will." An at-will employee can be fired at any time, for almost any reason. "Just cause" employees cannot—you need, well, a just cause to let them go. What makes an employee "just cause"? Usually, it is some sort of employment contract or promise of continued employment. If, for example, you have an employee handbook that promises job security, that could, by a court of law, be inferred as a promise of continued employment, and then your employees cannot be let go absent a valid reason like stealing or some such thing. Tough times and the need to cut back would not count as just cause.

It is harsh, but also smart, therefore, to have all employees sign a document acknowledging their at-will status. That way, it will be very difficult for them to come back and say you had no right to fire them because they were a just cause employee. A letter stating that they know they are at-will protects you.

Protected Classes

There are three times when even an at-will employee cannot be fired.

1. You cannot fire someone in retaliation for the exercise of a statutory right, such as filing a worker's compensation claim.
2. You cannot fire someone in retaliation for their exercising a legal duty, such as jury service.
3. Most importantly for this topic, you cannot fire someone on the basis of their color, gender, religion, age, ethnic background, or disability. Membership in the armed forces also cannot be a reason to fire someone, and neither can past debts or bankruptcy. In the law, these are called "protected classes."

For workers, most employment discrimination cases made against businesses fall under the category of "disparate treatment": They claim that the employer treated them unfavorably compared to other employees because of their membership in a protected class. As such,

> You are *strongly urged* to avoid questions into protected class status when interviewing prospective employees. Why? Because if you do, and then do not hire the person, they may sue for employment discrimination, claiming that is the reason you decided not to hire him or her, that your nonchalant question about his age, is evidence that you discriminate on the basis of age, for example. The only questions you should ask are those that relate to his or her competence and qualifications for the job.

plaintiffs in employment discrimination cases sue under Title VII of the 1964 Civil Rights Act.

If you are found guilty, either of not hiring someone for discriminatory reasons, or of firing someone for discriminatory reasons, the penalties are harsh indeed. If an ex-employee wins, she might be awarded back pay, reinstatement, attorney's fees, money for emotional distress, and even double damages as a way to punish you.

Preventing Claims

There are a few things you can do to protect your business from employment discrimination claims.

- Have an employee handbook that explains what is expected of employees, that they are at-will, how the discipline system works, and that explains that nondiscrimination is your policy and discrimination claims will be investigated promptly and thoroughly.
- Document, document, and document some more. Have regular written performance reviews. When you do have problem employees, *warn them in writing. Have them sign the warning. Have them sign any second warnings.* The more you can document that the reason you fired them was legitimate and not discriminatory (poor performance or whatever), the less any discrimination claim can stick.

SEXUAL HARASSMENT

Needless to say, the most prominent sexual harassment case in history was *Jones v. Clinton*. In that case, Paula Jones alleged that then-Governor Bill Clinton invited her to a hotel room and groped her. She sued, claiming sexual harassment. The judge in the case ruled that even if the event did happen as alleged, Jones suffered no damages. She never went to a psychologist, was never treated unfairly at work afterward, was never denied a promotion, nothing. One of Paula Jones' main arguments—that she didn't receive flowers on Secretary's Day as others in the Arkansas government had (although she was not Clinton's secretary)—was almost laughable to the judge: "Although it is not clear why the plaintiff failed to receive flowers on Secretary's Day in 1992, such an omission does not give rise to a federal [case] in the absence of some more tangible change in duties or working conditions that constitute a material employment disadvantage."

There are two types of sexual harassment cases to be concerned with at your small business. The first is a quid pro quo case, literally, "this for that." In this type of case, the victim is forced to have sex in exchange for a job benefit. If you promise your secretary a raise in exchange for a sexual favor, you have committed quid pro quo sexual harassment.

The second sort of case is called "hostile work environment." In this kind of case, the employee must prove that a supervisor or co-worker made unwelcome sexual advances or physical conduct, and that such conduct was pervasive enough to poison the employee's work environment and create an abusive workplace. Note that a same-sex sexual harassment claim under this theory is equally applicable in many jurisdictions.

Just as you should adopt an antidiscrimination policy in your workplace and employee handbook, so, too, should you adopt and make known to employees your antisexual harassment policy. A written policy that everyone knows about is both the right thing to do, and good business. Investigate claims promptly and discipline any offenders.

UNFAIR TRADE PRACTICES

Here, there are two issues to be concerned with: treating consumers fairly and legally, and protecting your business from ex-employee competition.

Consumer Protection Laws

The first consumer protection law to be concerned about is deceptive or fraudulent advertising. Your advertising must be truthful. You can boast, but like George Washington, you cannot tell a lie. If you do, not only can you be sued by consumers who claim they were damaged, but you can also get into trouble with the Federal Trade Commission, which investigates false advertising claims. The FTC can issue a "cease and desist" letter, or sue.

> Consider the case of the car dealer who promised in his ad a car for "1,000 bananas." Of course he meant $1,000, but when a customer came in with 1,000 bananas, the dealer would not sell the car. The consumer sued the dealer, and was awarded $1,000 in compensatory damages (the value of the car) . . . and $100,000 in punitive damages to punish the dealer for misrepresentation.

Aside from false advertising, you need to also avoid phony price comparisons. For example, there is nothing wrong with proclaiming that at your sale this weekend, the price for a particular $250 item will be "$100 off—$150!" However, if your normal price is not actually $250, but is really $200, then the sale price is only $50 off and you have broken the law.

Similarly, be careful when you use the word "free." In your ads, "free" better really mean free. "Free Printer!"* (with the asterisk explaining that the printer is free with a purchase of $1,000 or more) won't fly in most places. For instance, New York law states that "any limitations or conditions imposed on a 'free' offer must be disclosed in advertising . . . a description of the condition must be near the word 'free' (an asterisk plus footnote are not good enough), and in type at least half as large."

Therefore, avoid deceptive advertising and pricing, and treat consumers with honesty.

Ex-Employees

The issue arises when an employee leaves as to whether, and how, she can compete against you. Employees often learn confidential information in the course of their employment, information that would be useful should they decide to go into business for themselves, or jump to a competitor. Of course you will want to prevent them from using that information, but can you? It may be an illegal restraint on trade. Yes, usually you can stop former employees from competing against you, at least for a while. Here is how: Have employees sign some or all of these three documents when they come to work for you:

1. *A confidentiality agreement.* You need a document that specifically spells out what you consider to be your confidential trade secrets—customer lists, wholesale costs, that sort of thing. Have it say that the employee agrees to keep confidential this material, and then have them sign it. Both of you should keep a signed copy.

2. *An assignment of inventions.* Any invention an employee creates while at work is the property of the employer; that is the general rule. To be safe, however, it is wise to have all appropriate employees sign an agreement that states that they understand that the business will own anything they invent as part of their employment. If they invent something on their own time, that is different.

3. *A noncompete agreement.* This is the trickiest of the three, legally speaking. Our free enterprise system means that courts are loath to infringe on people's right to work. Yet courts also understand that there are times when competing would be unfair, and so a balance between these two competing interests is what is required. Noncompete agreements that are limited in length and geography usually fly. A noncompete agreement says that the employee agrees not to join a direct competitor, or start a directly

competing business, for a set time (usually two years is the maximum a court would allow) and in a specific geographic region ("The Greater Albuquerque Area" for example).

Laws in different states treat these agreements differently. In California for example, noncompete agreements are frowned upon and only enforceable in limited circumstances. Again, in most places, as long as the length is "reasonable," and the contract is limited to a specific geographic area, such agreements are usually acceptable.

When staffers do leave, make sure during the exit interview that they remember that they signed these sorts of agreements. It is far better to head off a lawsuit than to litigate one.

FINDING A GOOD ATTORNEY

Any lawyer can help you out of a jam, but a good lawyer can help you avoid the jam. Attorneys can help with incorporating, contracts, leases, hiring and firing, and a host of other issues. But this begs the question: Where do you find a lawyer who knows his stuff whom you can trust? The best way is through a referral. A satisfied client will tell you far more than any commercial. So if you know someone who has a business and a business lawyer, find out how he likes his lawyer. You need to find out:

- *Did the lawyer get good results?*   (Did the case settle successfully, was the contract beneficial, were taxes reduced?) Results are what count.
- *Was the attorney accessible?*   Too many lawyers are hard to reach and fail to return phone calls quickly. A call should be returned within 24 hours.
- *Were the fees reasonable?*   Of course you need to be concerned about fees when hiring a lawyer, but fees are not the most important thing to be concerned about. As in life, with attorneys, you usually get what you pay for. In this case, cheaper is probably not better.

- *Who does the work?*   Many lawyers (especially at big firms) use un-
derpaid, overworked associates to do a lot of the work. That is usually fine as associates are typically quite bright, and this does help
keep fees down. But know, too, that many associates are young, with
little experience, in both life and law. You need to know that when it
counts, the person you hired will be doing the heavy lifting.

If you can get a referral for an attorney who meets these criteria,
call him or her up and schedule a meeting. As you are looking to start
an important long-term relationship, expect to spend a few hours with
the lawyer. Get a feel for his personality. Make sure he knows what you
would be expecting. Ask about his background. Get referrals and call
them up. Certainly, you should not be billed for this meet-and-greet
with the lawyer. If you are, that is a bad sign.

Barring a referral from a friend or business associate, there are a
few other ways to find a good attorney. Look in the Yellow Pages; most
lawyers advertise today. In the back of the Attorneys section of the Yellow Pages is a listing for lawyers by specialty. Look under Business Law.
Find a few that look good and set up a few meetings. You need someone who is smart, experienced, and with whom you feel comfortable.

Finally, call your local bar association. The lawyers are listed by
their areas of specialty and the bar can usually refer you to a few of
its members with good reputations. As bar associations are nonparti-
san, you can rest assured that the recommendation will be pretty
trustworthy.

PART

Growing Your Business

CHAPTER 22

Successful
Advertising Strategies

Early to bed, early to rise, work like hell, and advertise.

—TED TURNER

Not advertising is like being alone in a dark room with the door closed. You know you are there, but no one else does. You absolutely have to advertise if you are going to succeed in business, because it is the basic way new customers learn you are out there. Yet it is surprising how many small business owners assume that their great idea, or ideal location, or big sign, or good looks, *or whatever* will bring people in the door. Here is what brings new people in the door: advertising. Sure, marketing is very important, as is networking, and customer service, and word of mouth, but advertising is the route with potentially the biggest payoff. Advertising turns the light on.

THE PROCESS

The problem for many a small business is that there are a lot of advertising choices, most are not inexpensive, and a costly mistake can be crippling to the budget. Absolutely understandable. And, as discussed earlier, one trait of the great entrepreneurs is that they reduce their risk to the extent possible. That is what we want to do here. Few small businesses have the cushion to absorb a costly mistake, so what is presented next is a process that allows you to greatly reduce the possibility that you will bet on the wrong horse, advertise in the wrong place, and lose a bunch of money. What should happen, instead, is that you will create a winning ad with little risk.

The good news is that creating a successful advertising campaign really is a joy. An ad that works will become a tried-and-true friend that your small business will rely on. Once you have one, you can breathe a little easier, knowing that when you roll it out, you will get predictable results. That ad the travel company runs in the Travel section of the Sunday paper is probably its bread and butter. They know that ad will bring in *x* number of dollars every time it runs. Whether it's a monthly ad in a magazine, a regular radio buy, or a cable TV campaign, a smart, well-thought-out ad campaign can be your ticket to success.

The key is to bet on the right horse, to pick the right ad and the right vehicle. How can you be sure of that? Creating an (almost) risk-free, winning ad campaign* is a five-step process:

1. Think ahead: What is the purpose, size, and budget for your campaign?
2. Decide what media work best for your business, brand, and budget.
3. Create an ad, one that builds on that brand.
4. Test the ad.
5. Finally, once you are convinced that you have an ad and/or campaign that works, roll it out.

BRAINSTORMING

The first thing you must do is decide the purpose of your ad campaign. There are basically two types of ads and corresponding campaigns.

---

*(When I say "campaign," I am referring to an ongoing advertising presence. Your campaign may be a multimedia plan organized six months in advance utilizing both electronic and print media or it may be an overnight radio buy that lasts a week. Either way, the process is the same.)

The first is a branding campaign intended to publicize your name and corporate identity so that people remember it when they need what you offer. In the extreme, we all remember those numerous Super Bowl Internet ads during the dotcom boom. Although sites like Web-Van and Pets.com mistook branding for a business plan, by sinking a ton of money into their ad campaign, at least they got the branding part right. Look! We continue to remember their names and I am writing about them still. Via advertising, they created memorable brands, if nothing else.

Therefore, the purpose of a branding campaign is to get your name out there so people start to remember it. Take the ad in the paper that says "Divorce for Fathers." This is a branding ad. Of course the purpose of the ad is to get customers, but unlike the second type of ad (next), which has an immediate hook and call to action ("SALE!") this type of ad is a bit subtler, as intended to build awareness of the business as it is to get a customer today. The plan is to have people see the advertisement again and again, so that when the time comes and some dad needs a divorce lawyer, he remembers whom to call.

A branding campaign takes time, but if you have the time and money, it can be very rewarding. By branding your business (recall from Chapter 10, Branding 101, your brand is your promise to your customers), you create long-term viability. Not done in a week or a month, branding is an ongoing process that pays more and more dividends as time goes by, but you must remember this: Fundamental things apply. Branding, when done right, will make a long-term difference but will not yield immediate rewards.

This brings us to the second sort of ad campaign, the one intended to generate sales NOW. This is a campaign that is usually shorter and more intense. Several media sources may be used to reinforce the same message. Whether you want to let people know about your sidewalk sale this weekend, a shipment of the new Harry Potter book your shop just got in, or a free drawing for a digital camera, this type of campaign is intended to create immediate dividends with a noticeable result. If a branding campaign is a marathon, this ad campaign is a sprint. It will be more periodic, maybe once a month or so.

Budget

The question arises: How much do you need to spend? The SBA suggests that you earmark two percent of your gross sales toward yearly advertising. Others believe the amount should be closer to five percent. If you gross $500,000 a year, assigning five percent of that—$25,000—as an annual advertising and marketing budget is probably not far off ($25,000 yearly is roughly $2,000 a month). If you want to continue to generate half a million dollars in sales a year, $2,000 a month for advertising is a little price to pay. This process, then, requires that you look at your gross sales and earmark an appropriate percentage of that toward your monthly ad budget. Your income determines the budget. This is called the "cost method."

If the cost method sounds too formulaic to you, there is another method to determine the right budget called the "task method." Here, you look at how many customers you need or how much product you need to sell to hit your sales for the year, and then, based upon past sales from advertising, calculate what you need to spend this year. If you spent $15,000 last year generating $300,000 in sales, and you want to grow 10 percent this year, you will need to spend more, maybe $17,500 or so. Your goal creates the budget.

So that is your first assignment, deciding what sort of campaign best suits your objectives and needs and what sort of corresponding budget you can afford.

CHOOSING THE RIGHT MEDIUM

Different media outlets have different strengths and weaknesses. Your campaign may utilize only one, or it may take several to accomplish your goals. The most important thing when advertising generally, and choosing your medium specifically, is zeroing-in on your target audience. Earlier in this book, it is suggested that you know exactly who your customers are. What is your target demographic? What do they watch, read, and listen to? Your earlier research and business plan should be consulted. Knowing whom your potential customers are takes a lot of the guesswork out of choosing the right medium. If your customers are men in their 20s, then a magazine like *Maxim* or an alternative rock radio station would probably be excellent choices. If they are business travelers, then *SkyMall* would be great. Without knowing *exactly* whom you are trying to reach, figuring out where to advertise is a shot in the dark. Do your research and reduce your risk.

Here are your main options.

Newspapers

Almost every home receives a newspaper, and in it you can target your audience quite specifically. By advertising in the right section of the paper (sports, comics, news, business, home and garden, etc.), you can reach different types of people.

The advantages to advertising in the newspaper are numerous. Newspaper ads can contain details, prices, and telephone numbers that are difficult to get across in the electronic media. You can pick your ad size, your section, your day. Even a small ad with a BIG HEADLINE can reap rewards.

> Your web site is a sitting goldmine. Whatever media source you choose, be sure to reference your web site. There you can give a lot more information and reel them in, for little extra cost.

Yet there are downsides. Unlike magazines, newspapers are read but once and discarded. Also, small ads have to compete with big ads and news articles for the reader's attention. Probably worst of all, you are not even assured that your target audience will see your ad. They may not read the section you are in, they may skip your page, or they may just gloss over your ad.

Your best bet against failure, therefore, is to have an excellent ad. While this is discussed in detail later, begin by calling your newspaper's sales representative for your area. Not only can your rep help you get the ad designed in-house, but she can also help you devise a budget and suggest the best sections and days to run your ad. The questions to an-swer are how big an ad to run, where, how often to run it, and how much to spend. Although bigger is usually better, it also costs substan-tially more. Ask your rep for help.

Newspaper advertising is sold by column and inch, and you can determine the size ad you want by looking at the paper. For example, an ad that measures two columns across and four inches down would be an eight-inch ad. If the inch rate is $50 per column inch, your ad would cost ($400 – $50 × 8 inches). Often a newspaper will charge you full price for the first day you run the ad and then give you substantial discounts the more days in a row you run it.

Keep in mind that:

- Although Sunday is the day newspapers are read most, it is also the most expensive day and the one with the most ads/competition.
- Because position in the paper is critical, if you can specify the page of the section you want (page three of your desired section is best because it is the first page with ads and what people see first when opening the paper), do so. Even if you have to pay to do so, it is usu-ally worth it. Finding your ad buried on page 21 is not a pleasant ex-perience.
- Request an outside position for ads that have coupons, as that makes them easier to cut out.

Depending upon your budget, newspaper advertising may make a lot of sense.

Television

Although television is the most powerful advertising medium ever in-vented (Budweiser does not spend all that money there for no reason), for most small businesses, television is both cost-prohibitive and unnec-essary. Here's the deal: You must be willing to make a substantial commitment of time and money, be willing to wait a few months for a payoff, and your small business must have regional appeal for a TV campaign to be worth the cost. A standalone bakery has no need to advertise on television, but a chain of bakeries might. If you do have a regional business or product, and you have the money and commitment to make a significant TV buy, the payoff can be huge.

> What makes a good television ad? First, it must be highly visual; TV is a visual medium. Because of remotes and competition, your ad must GRAB THEIR ATTENTION quickly. Be sure to repeat your phone number and the name of the business several times. Finally, do not make the mistake of making your ad more interesting than your business or product, or so amusing that people fail to remember what you are selling. Finally, do not be afraid to copy a good commercial that works.

Television, to be effective, must be used repeatedly. How often? A lot. Here is how to figure out how much: A GRP is a "gross ratings point." It calculates one percent of the TV households in the area. If there are two million TV homes in your city, one GRP is 20,000 households. To make a television buy worth your time, you probably need to buy at least 150 GRPs a month. The price you will pay for each GRP relates to which stations you want, the size of your city, and the competition. In a city like

> You can save money by trying these tips:
>
> - *Advertise at off-peak hours.*   Prime time (8:00 P.M. to 11:00 P.M.) has the most viewers and costs the most.
> - *Go with cable.*   Cable should allow you to advertise on a station that meets your desired demographic and is much less expensive than the networks.
> - *Consider a media-buying service.*   TV salespeople will quote you their standard rate card, maybe negotiate down a bit, but that's it. A media buyer charges 7.5 percent but can easily save you more than that, because they buy millions of dollars' worth of advertising a month and have a lot more pull than you do.

New York, you might expect to pay $2,500 per GRP. In a smaller place, say, Raleigh, it might be $100.

The bottom line is that TV makes sense only for a few small businesses. But if yours is one of those, and you have both the time and war chest to do it right, TV can reap tremendous rewards.

Radio

Radio is another medium that can allow you to target specifically your audience, and as such, can be a very effective advertising tool. It might be a Christian rock station, or a news talk station, or an oldies station; all cater to different demographics. Again, however, targeting that desired audience will probably not be cheap. The following chart shows what you might expect to pay, per minute, in the top 16 markets, on top-rated stations (top 3 or so), secondary stations, and tertiary stations.

Market	Top Tier	Secondary	Tertiary
New York	$1,500	$1,000	$350
Los Angeles	$1,500	$1,000	$350
Chicago	$1,200	$ 800	$250
San Francisco	$1,000	$ 750	$250
Dallas	$1,000	$ 750	$250
Washington, D.C.	$1,000	$ 750	$250
Seattle	$1,000	$ 750	$250
Atlanta	$1,000	$ 750	$250
Boston	$ 850	$ 600	$175
Denver	$ 850	$ 600	$175
Philadelphia	$ 850	$ 600	$175
Houston	$ 750	$ 500	$150
Minneapolis	$ 750	$ 250	$150
Phoenix	$ 750	$ 250	$150
Baltimore	$ 500	$ 350	$100
Portland	$ 500	$ 350	$100

It is estimated that people have to hear an ad six times before it sinks in, so the key is repetition. The key is repetition. The key is repetition. What is the key? See? And, of course, repetition costs money.

The important thing with radio, as with any other media source, is that the station you pick delivers your desired demographic audience. Speak with your sales rep and get verifiable information regarding the station and particular shows' audience size, rating points, listener, age, and income.

> Be sure to also check out Chapter 35, *Marketing on a Shoestring* , which gives many different ways to advertise and market your business on a shoestring budget.

Internet

Although Internet advertising has rebounded from its 2000 crash, remember that it crashed for a reason. You might be able to get some cheap banner ads or popups, but if no one reads them, it's just a waste of money. It is far smarter these days to put your Internet dollars into buying placement on various search engines. Those tiny boxed ads next to Google results, for instance, can be a great investment.

Magazines

Maybe more than any other medium, magazines can target your audience best. There are simply so many magazines today that it should be easy to find one that your customers read. Magazine ads are not inexpensive, but magazines do tend to stick around a house for months and are often read by many people. As such, you might get more bang for your advertising buck by advertising there.

Yellow Pages

When do you use the phone book? When you need to buy something and are not sure where to get it, right? That is why the Yellow Pages work. Many times a day, every day, people open the book ready to give someone their business. If you are not in there, then it is not going to be you. And even better than magazines, Yellow Pages are in homes and businesses for a year.

The bad news is twofold. First, because the Yellow Pages are so successful in creating customers, advertising in them is not inexpensive. A quarter-page ad may run you $500 a month or more. Also, more and more, people are bypassing the book altogether and simply searching online for what they need. Again, it might be smarter to put your money in search engine placement, or in the online version of the phone book.

But, even at that, many small businesses believe that they would be unable to keep their doors open without advertising in the Yellow Pages. So you should advertise in there, too, right? Maybe. Service businesses like plumbers and locksmiths would be silly not to advertise in the phone book. You can bet that a majority of their customers are people who see an ad there. But not every business benefits from placement, especially for the cost. Beware also that people who open the phone book are often shopping around for the best price and will call on many ads. If your business model does not compete on price, the phone book may not be your best choice.

Here are some Yellow Page tips:

- *Ask for a discount.*   First time advertisers should get as much as a 40 percent discount their first year.
- *Create a memorable ad.*   Look through your phone book. Which ads catch your eye? Often, they are the ones with color, or a picture, or a lot of white space. The problem with the Yellow Pages is that you are competing against a lot of ads for the same eyeballs, so you have to make your ad stick out.
- *Consider your category.*   There might be several different sections in which you could place an ad. Figure out a few different categories for your business, and then see which one has the most ads. The odds are, the largest section is the one that is read the most.
- *Read.*   A good book that you might want to get is *Yellow Pages Advertising: How to Get the Greatest Return on Your Investment* by Jeffrey Price.

CREATE A WINNING AD

Knowing your objectives and media options helps you create an ad or ads that reinforce your brand and allow you to fulfill your mission. There are many different theories as to what makes a good ad; whole books are written on the subject. But the truth is, if you are like most other small businesspeople, you probably do not have the time to read yet another book. Here then is an easy ad creation method that works. It is the tried-and-true AIDA method, which stands for Attention, Interest, Desire, and Action. The AIDA formula serves as a blueprint for creating a winning ad—any type of winning ad, be it in the newspaper, magazine, or on radio or television.

Attention

THE FIRST THING YOU HAVE TO DO IS GRAB THEIR ATTENTION! Once you have done that, then you can get potential customers interested in what you are selling, but if you do not get their attention up front, they will never hear a thing above the din of headline news, sports stories, or full-page ads. So you must first hit your prospect with a powerful, benefit-laden headline.

An attention-getting headline (again, either in print or electronic) must quickly capture a customer's attention, get them to want to know more, and do so in a few seconds. For example:

- "Amazing New Technique Relieves Arthritis!"
- "Free Pamphlet Makes Your Computer as Easy to Use as a Telephone!"
- "Save 50% on Office Supplies—Today Only!"
- "The Lazy Man's Guide to Riches!"

The idea is to intrigue them enough to want to know, read, watch, or listen more.

Interest and Desire

So, you grabbed their attention. Great. Then what? If a potential customer is reading your ad, it better sell them or your great headline will go to waste. Make a compelling offer in the body of the ad by describing the benefits of what you are selling in simple and interesting terms. To work, the Interest and Desire section of your ad must be well written, must clearly explain the benefits to the consumer, and must keep their attention. Easily explain in your ad how your product fills the need of the customer. If you solve some problem they have, and your ad easily explains that, bingo!

Action

Having grabbed their attention and shown them the benefits of buying from you, ask for the order. Give incentives for the customer to buy now, and make it easy to do so. It might involve a coupon, an 800 number, an e-mail address, an online order form, a fax order line, or some other means to make it easy and simple to buy or call.

Here's an example of an AIDA Ad:

Bankruptcy?
Free Seminar! Free Advice!

[This headline captures the
Attention of someone in debt.
Remember that "Free" is the
most powerful word in advertising]

This Thursday at 8:oo P.M. at the downtown Holiday Inn, local bankruptcy attorney Jay Rosenberg will be conducting a *free* bankruptcy seminar. All of your questions will be answered, and there is no cost and no obligation. [Interest and Desire]

Seating Is Limited. Call (212) 555-9000 for reservations.
www.freebankruptcyseminar.com
["Limited seating" is a call to Action.
Web site can give more details]

If you follow the AIDA formula, you should find that your ad will work, no matter what medium you place it in.

TEST THE AD

To avoid making an expensive advertising mistake, after coming up with your game plan and designing your ad, test it and make sure it pulls. Testing the ad could mean many things: running a smaller version of the ad in print, and then enlarging it or buying better placement once you are convinced that it pulls. It might also mean running it in a local paper before branching out regionally or running your radio spot on a less expensive station, or on a less expensive show, until you know it works.

Consider running the ad in different media sources at the same time, each with a different code that people need to refer to when responding ("Mention code 1122 when calling and get 10% off!"). That way, you will be able to track which ad in which source works best.

In the history of bad business decisions, maybe the worst of all was the decision by Coca-Cola to scrap Coke and introduce New Coke. How could this have happened? If you are going to toss out old Coke, you might as well ban mom and outlaw apple pie while you are at it. At the time, Coca-Cola was being challenged by Pepsi. Nervous executives at Coke began to secretly experiment with new formulations, until they finally found one that beat Pepsi in taste tests. Convinced they had a winner, Coca-Cola triumphantly rolled out New Coke—to huzzahs and ridicule. The problem, it was later discovered, was that Coca-Cola never test-marketed New Coke. The marketing wizards at Coca-Cola never took batches of New Coke, and tested them in stores in, say, Des Moines. Testing is key to avoiding expensive, painful belly flops.

Avoid sinking a lot of money into the ad campaign until you know for sure that your ad and strategy will work. After that, go for it!

ROLL IT OUT

If you have created an ad that works, it is time to roll it out, for it is your meal ticket. Run it as often as you can afford, avoiding oversaturation of the market. Maybe you recall an infomercial a few years back wherein an entrepreneur named Don LePre talked about how placing a "tiny little classified ad" could make you millions, as it had for him. LePre's strategy was to find a product or service to sell, create and test a small, inexpensive classified ad for it, test it, and when the ad pulled, to roll that exact ad out to hundreds of newspapers across the country. It worked and is essentially what you should do. Once you have found an ad that works, use it in as many places, and as often, as you can.

If you plan on advertising a lot, consider hiring an ad agency. They can help with the creation of your ad and buy you time or space at rates you probably could not get for yourself.

FEES

As you start this process, you will begin to meet and discuss pricing with a variety of media outlets. The first rule of media is *Never Pay the Rate Card*. The rate card is the price you will be quoted from their book. Yes, sometimes inventory is tight and you will have to pay the rate card, but just know that that is not always the case. If you will be buying a lot of time or space, or they need advertisers at that time, you can negotiate down their rate card rates. If you cannot negotiate down the rate card, see what else they might offer you. It might be free response cards, better position at no extra cost, free color, or ads in a special edition.

Advertising is one of the most important things you do in business. If you do it right, your small business should reap the rewards.

CHAPTER 23

Marketing Muscle

Image creates desire.

—J.G. GALLIMORE

Small businesses do not have unlimited funds; indeed quite the opposite is usually true. So just as you need to be thoughtful about how best to use your advertising dollars, so, too, do you need to be equally intelligent about your marketing efforts. Both must clearly reinforce your business identity. Marketing, advertising, and branding are the interwoven threads that make up the tapestry that is your business image. Together, they constitute your most powerful weapons for getting people to notice and buy from you. If these threads are disparate, if your advertising does one thing while your marketing does another and neither reinforces your brand, your tapestry will be, well, ugly. But if these threads do reinforce one another, if they communicate a unified message, then your business image will be a tightly woven whole with a clear identity that people can recall. That is the plan. There are so many small businesses out there competing against you for the same customers that the ones with the rich, memorable tapestry will get people to remember them above the din.

MARKETING OVERVIEW

Marketing, boiled down, is the combination of all your efforts to get people to remember your business. It includes everything—from how your phone is answered or how you deal with complaints to your signs, logos, letterhead, and promotions. Whereas advertising essentially brings in new clients, marketing not only does that, but it helps keep them around. Marketing, more than anything else, is what builds your brand, and an identifiable brand is the hook that gets people to remember your business. And if they remember you, they will likely buy from you. That is why marketing and branding are so important.

Think of it this way: Your business identity, your brand, is your business personality. It is what people remember. Just as we sometimes meet easily forgettable people with blah personalities, so, too, do we all run across far too many small businesses with little, if any, personality. Forgettable businesses—what a waste. But by the same token, when you meet someone with a large, identifiable personality, you remember them, just as you do when you run across a business with a distinctive personality.

Does Starbucks have a personality? You bet—hip, a bit laid back, friendly. How did Starbucks create that brand? By consistently reinforcing it with everything they do. From the décor of their stores to the personality of their baristas to the choice of music they play and sell (oh yes, and their coffee), Starbucks consistently tells you that theirs is a cool place to hang out, even if it does cost a bit more. That is what you want. You create that distinctive personality, that memorable brand, by marketing a consistent theme.

Peter Drucker, the guru of modern business, says that marketing is what your business is as seen through the eyes of your customers. So what do your customers see when they look at your business? A law office must be stately because the issues people need lawyers for are serious. Legal clients want to see excellence, so the law office needs an embossed letterhead, a prestigious address, and a proficient receptionist, for starters. Their marketing materials must be professional and elegant. All are different aspects of the interwoven marketing campaign intended to get clients to believe in the firm enough to hire it.

So marketing is the process of getting customers and potential customers to perceive value in what you offer. There are so many different marketing methods available that it is impossible to cover them all in a single chapter. This chapter, therefore, is devoted to relaying some of the more powerful, easily implementable ones. Chapter 35, *Marketing on a Shoestring*, covers scores of other ways to promote and grow your business with little money.

Marketing Plans

A marketing plan should not be new to you, but it probably is. If you drafted a business plan, your marketing plan is a major section, and it should be reviewed. However, the fact is, if yours is like most other small businesses, you have neither a business nor a marketing plan. That is fine. It is not required. The five-step process discussed in the previous chapter can easily be adopted here as well.

> According to the *Wall Street Journal*, only 14 percent of small businesses have a written business plan.

1. Think ahead: What is the purpose, size, and budget for your marketing campaign?
2. Decide what media might work best for your business, brand, and budget.
3. Come up with some marketing materials that build on that brand.
4. Test the materials, if applicable.
5. Once you are convinced that you have a marketing method that works, roll it out.

Just as you were advised to come up with an ad campaign and test it out before expanding on it, so, too, should you do the same thing here. Review the myriad of marketing tools presented next, pick the ones that make the most sense, test them out, and then go for it.

TOOLS YOU CAN USE

If you are like most other small businesspeople, you have already figured out a few marketing methods that work for you. It might be a stall at the Saturday Market, a monthly seminar, a regular sale, or an incentive program for referrals—something. That is good. But if you are also like most other small businesspeople, you likely have one or two or three methods at most. What I want you to do is Think Big. There are so many ways to market your business and to get new customers that it would be a shame if you did not consider and implement some new options. While your methods may work well now, the danger is that marketing materials do get stale and stop working. And even if they don't, the smart entrepreneur has multiple ways to bring in business so that if one income stream slows down, others are around to keep the money pumping.

> Another trait common to the most successful entrepreneurs is that they have "multiple profit centers," a term coined by Barbara Winter in her great book, *Making a Living Without a Job*. Amazon.com started selling books; now they sell everything. When book sales are down, CD sales may be up. Multiple profit centers allow you to withstand the dreaded business cycle. Adopting multiple marketing methods helps create multiple profit centers. See Chapter 36, *Small Business Success Secrets, I: Money*, for more information.

The Elevator Pitch

I do a lot of public speaking on business issues, and I was talking to another speaker a few years ago lamenting how slow business was when he asked what I talk about. "Well, small business success, basically," I replied. He was silent. After a pregnant pause, I finally asked, "Well, what do *you* talk about?" He said something like, "I speak to organizations that want to energize and excite their employees, get them working together, help them understand their core values, and allow them to realize what it means to be a team. My speeches are dynamic and funny, and I leave audiences invigorated, committed, wanting more, and I usually get a standing ovation." Given our respective answers, whom would you hire if you were planning an event and needed a speaker? I knew the answer, and it was not me. So ever since that illuminating encounter, I have been working on my elevator pitch.

We are all always asked what it is we do. Having a quick, interesting, powerful answer is the simplest of marketing tools, yet one of the most powerful; it may lead to opportunities that we did not even know existed. As they say, you only have one chance to make a good first impression. You want a pitch that will spark someone's interest and have him or her saying, "Tell me more."

Here are a few questions you must answer if you are to create a great elevator pitch.

What Is the Problem You Are Trying to Solve? Every great business solves a problem for someone. Why do you go to the local store to buy some bread? Because you have a need for bread and the store solves it. What problem does your business solve?

Can You Keep It Simple? Use plain English, be intriguing, and have conviction.

> There once was a Silicon Valley entrepreneur whose product protected digital signals. His original elevator pitch was something like, "We utilize the latest 20–50 key exchange using Duffle transponders, blah blah blah." After getting some help, he ended up with, "We protect communications."

Why Would People Want to Know More? Instead of saying, for instance, "I am a graphic artist," you might start with, "I help people get more business by illustrating their dreams."

Does It Accelerate Your Heart Rate? A great pitch is a passionate pitch.

Here's your basic pitch: "Hi. I'm Mara Sydney, president of Jillian Publishing. We publish architecture books." Here is an elevator pitch: "Hi, I'm Mara Sydney, president of Jillian Publishing. We publish books, newsletters, and video programs designed to help architects, drafters, and urban planners become more successful. Our best-selling title, *How to Become the Recognized Expert in Your Field*, was named Specialty Book of the Year by *Architecture* magazine."

Networking

Of course you should network, you know that, and most of us probably believe it. But it is sometimes easier said than done. First of all, networking takes time, and secondly, it is not always easy. Yet even so, some of your best prospects will come from networking, whether it is at a chamber social, by joining a group like LeTip International, or in some other social situation.

Because much of business is about relationships, it is indeed not what you know, but whom you know, and networking ensures that you will know more people. Is it occasionally uncomfortable to make chitchat with people you do not know? Sure. But here is some motivation. According to the book *The Millionaire Next Door*, most self-made millionaires network all the time, wherever they are: at the car wash, on the golf course, or at a business conference. They know that they never know which contact may be a big deal and lead to a big deal.

Here are two tips for making networking easier.

1. *Use your elevator pitch.* Having a prepackaged snappy opener is a great segue into a more meaningful conversation.
2. *Pretend you are the host.* Rather than sitting back, waiting for something to happen at the event, flip the situation around and pretend you are the host. How would you act? That's right—gregarious, self-assured, and positive.

Form a Strategic Partnership

We are not called *small* businesspeople for nothing. According to the SBA, of the roughly 23 million small businesses in this country, 17 million have no employees. Of the remaining six million with employees, the vast majority have 10 or less. The point is that we often need help. A large corporation has plenty of resources—marketing departments, accounting—you know the drill. But we don't.

One of the best ways around this dilemma and to grow your business (that, after all, is the purpose of marketing) is to team up with other businesses who are after the same customers as you and with whom you have some synergy. With the right strategic partner, you can combine and leverage, *for very little extra money*, your respective distribution, infrastructure, and knowledge for greater joint success. The teamwork could, for example, entail cross-promoting each other's product or jointly creating new products. For instance, a veterinarian and a local pet store might agree to cross-promote each other in their respective establishments. On a larger level HP, the giant computer maker, has long teamed up with Microsoft, the maker of software for those computers, to jointly grow their businesses.

Here is an example: All Systems Go! (www.a-v-designs.com) is one of the top home theater and multizone music design and installation businesses in the country, and its owner, Radames Pera, is a master of creating successful business partnerships.

You may also know of Pera from his earlier career. If a friend has ever held a rock in his palm and asked you to "snatch the pebble from my hand, grasshopper," then you are imitating Radames Pera. Yes, he was the child actor who played the young "grasshopper" in the classic television show *Kung Fu*.

Pera began All Systems Go! in 1988 because, he says, he always loved stereos and wanted to have a business that he would enjoy going to every day. Back then, surround-sound stereo systems were new, so Radames went around to various stereo and electronics stores in Los Angeles, forming relationships with salespeople and letting them know that he was available to install the pricy systems they were starting to sell.

This clever strategy meant that his business grew almost exclusively by favorable word of mouth. That he did great work for a fair price only enhanced his reputation. Expanding into the full range of audio and video home theater systems, All Systems Go! grew rapidly. How good is Pera at what he does? Word-of-mouth referral clients include Johnny Depp, Nicholas Cage, Sharon Stone, Phil Knight, Charlize Theron, and Ben Stiller.

When he decided to leave L.A., Pera had to start his business over. How did he do it? Via business-to-business partnerships. Armed with a list of satisfied celebrity clients, a stellar reputation in the entertainment capital of the world, plenty of experience, and a thorough understanding of the market, enticing and teaming up with the local stereo and electronics retailers was much easier. And again, his plan worked. "The business took off, right away," he says.

In fact, business was so good, and his reputation was such, that while he was living and working in Portland old clients in L.A. continued to fly him down for new jobs there as well. After a decade in Portland, Pera and his wife were forced to relocate, but his old strategy of linking up with retailers for once did not work because, he says, "the market had become saturated." Ever resourceful, Pera tried a new tack—marketing his services to builders and architects. And once again, creating strategic partnerships allowed him to successfully re-create his business in a new location.

To make a strategic partnership work for you, consider the following.

- *Make sure the other business is congruent with yours.*   Do you have the same goals? Discuss and agree upon the purpose of the partnership and what each side expects.
- *What are the downsides to the deal?*   Brainstorm both the positive and the negative.
- *Is the deal a win-win?*   Negotiate viable commitments that both sides can live with. How will disagreements be resolved?
- *What is the exit strategy?*   Having a set of definable objectives allows you to know when the partnership is, and is not, working. What will trigger an end to the deal?

Direct Marketing

Direct mail is one of the oldest, most tried-and-true marketing methods around. Using direct mail letters, flyers, coupons, and reply envelopes, you can sell your products or services to qualified prospects, increase awareness of your business, and create new customers. For instance, if you own an Italian restaurant, you could send out a flyer to all homes within a three mile radius offering a free glass of wine with dinner. There is no doubt that you would create some new customers in the process.

Via direct mail, you can announce a big sale, offer a new product, or provide a 10 percent off coupon (insert your idea here). The point is, direct marketing allows you to get your business noticed.

A Gallup survey of 251 businesses found that their top choice for educating consumers, creating sales, and introducing products was . . . direct marketing.

Creating a successful direct marketing campaign is a threefold process. First, you must find a letter/offer/flyer/coupon that works. This is a matter of testing, testing, testing. Again, start small, tinker, and analyze results. Our restaurant might try sending the free wine offer to $1/3$ of the homes in the area, a 10 percent off coupon to another third, and a free child's dinner to the last third. After tabulating the results, the owner would then know which coupon pulled best, and could then send it out every four months or so.

Step two requires that you acquire a usable list. One of the nice things about direct marketing is that not only is it a chance to attract new customers, but it is equally valuable helping you stay in contact with present customers, too. As such, your list could be self-generated, if the goal of the campaign is to get old customers back into the store. If the goal, however, is to find new business, then you need a broader list. Buy lists from list brokers (look in the Yellow Pages under Direct Marketing), and be very specific about the type of audience you are trying to attract when you buy your list: "I want a list of homeowners in the surrounding five counties," or "I want a list of men aged 25–34," or whoever is your target market.

> The new wave in direct marketing is direct e-mail marketing (no, not spam.) It is covered in the next chapter, *Your Web Presence.*

The final step in a successful direct marketing campaign is to get people to read your offer and respond. Here is how:

- *Hand address the envelopes.* Depending upon the size of the mailing, consider hiring some high school kids to address the envelopes. (Aren't you more likely to open an envelope addressed by hand than one computer generated? So are your potential customers.)
- *Remember that an effective offer answers the question for the reader, What is in it for me?* You must offer something they want; saving time or money often works.
- *YOU MUST GRAB THEIR ATTENTION, QUICKLY.*
- *Use a conversational tone, deliver credibility.* Customer testimonials are great as are guarantees. Also, give them an incentive to act— an expiration on the offer works well.
- *Be patient.* Often several letters are needed to get a response, and even then, remember that a good direct mail campaign response rate is about five percent. But think about it. If you send mail to 1,000 potential customers, it will cost about $500, but how much will you make with 50 new customers?
- *P.S.* Always include a P.S. because they are almost always read. The postscript is a great place to reiterate the offer or call for action ("Act now and get an extra 10 percent off !").

Have a Sale

What will you be announcing in your direct mail piece? Often it is a sale, one of the most powerful tools in your marketing tool chest. It reinforces your good name with old customers, helps attract new customers, gets rid of unwanted inventory, and creates a buzz, all at once. Not bad!

As with a direct mail campaign, obtaining a good list is critical to a successful sale. The most important thing you can do to create a successful sale is to develop your customer mailing list. An up-to-date, good list of even 500 people is far more valuable than, say, an unqualified list of 5,000. Begin your list by asking your regular customers to fill out a preferred customer card. Add them to your list. When customers write you a check, even if they didn't fill out the preferred membership application, copy their name and address to your list. See if you can obtain membership lists from local organizations like clubs and churches. Finally, buy a list if you must. When buying a list, make sure that you do not overspend for unqualified names. Be selective.

> Try buying lists from The American List Counsel: 1-800-822-LIST, or Edith Roman Associates: 1-800-223-2194.

This might also be a good time to review Chapter 12, Successful Pricing Strategies. Sales are loss leaders. You need to mark down enough items for the sale to be worth your customers' while, but not so many that you lose money. Markdowns are critical to the profitability of your sale. Generally, product that is less than four months old should be marked down no more than 30 percent. Product that is less than eight months old should be marked down no more than 50 percent. Items older than eight months can be marked down 75 percent. If you have something eight months old, move it; it is taking up valuable space from product that can be turned over again and again. Because sales allow you to convert inventory to cash, be aggressive when pricing old merchandise.

Before the sale, get your store ready. Of course you need to spruce things up, but beyond that, be sure to:

- *Mark everything clearly* with the reduced price. (Make it easy for your customers to see.)
- *Put the merchandise out where it can be looked at and touched.*
- *Organize everything* and have it arranged by size and category.

- *Keep in mind that the first week of your sale will always be the busiest.* Make sure that you have plenty of inventory and that the shelves are stocked.

During the sale:

- *Continue to keep displays full.* Customers will not buy if they think the best deals have already been had.
- *Watch for slow moving merchandise and mark it down more if necessary.* Something is better than nothing, and space for better selling merchandise beats the clutter of old merchandise.
- *Create a buzz.* Talk about what a great deal this or that is. Have big signs or balloons. Your outdoor SALE! signs are vital. Use different signs to attract attention.

> At Carpet World in Los Angeles, the owner had a huge sign in the middle of the store that proclaimed "Our Word Of Mouth Advertising Starts With You!"

Brochures

When you leave a car showroom, what do you leave with? Right, a beautiful, glossy brochure. For the right business, a brochure can be its most important marketing method. It is a chance to put your best foot forward, proudly display who you are, what you offer, why it is unique, and why people should buy from you. If a customer asks for a brochure, it is a rare chance to proffer your best offer, so be sure that you create a topnotch one. Here's how:

Brainstorm. Meet with your team and get their input. Find out what they think is important to have in the brochure. What do your customers need to know? What sells them? What needs can you fulfill, and why can you fulfill them best?

Decide upon the purpose of the brochure. What is the role of the brochure in your overall marketing efforts? Is it to be a tool for your salespeople? Will it be used at a trade show? Will it be at the point of sale?

Consider the competition. If your competitors have a slick brochure, can you legally use some of their ideas? At the very least, know what your competitor's brochure looks like and strive to best it.

Get some software. It used to be that creating a brochure was an expensive proposition: Hiring graphic artists, layout, design, and printing were not inexpensive. But today, things are much different. If you have (or buy) a graphic arts software program, and either learn it yourself or assign that task to a staff member, creating a brochure in-house should not be that expensive at all.

Create a mockup. You do not have to, and should not try to, get every important fact crammed into the brochure. Less is more. People are busy and do not like reading a lot of copy. Get the essential ideas across. Get them to want to know more. Use color, bullet points, white space, and pictures to spark interest.

Print it. Even if you do not have access to a color printer, you can always go to Kinko's or the like. Of course, you can always use a commercial printer where you will be dealing with a professional and should get excellent results. Just know that you do not have to anymore.

Publicity

A newspaper or magazine article about your business or a radio or television segment about it can do more than almost anything else to market and build your business. If you want to know how small businesses become big businesses, here is a trait they all have in common: At a critical moment in the growth of the company, the business invests in public relations and gets a lot of publicity. That publicity is then parlayed into additional business, and more publicity, and buzz is born.

But even if growing large is not your goal, you should not bypass the opportunities that await by getting some timely publicity. That article or story is independent verification of what a great business you created. For starters, the people who see the story will be tempted to patronize your business and check it out for themselves. Even better, however, is that you can link it to your web site, or tape or copy the show or article and use it forever in your later marketing materials. Say that you own a chain of florists and you get your local paper to do a story about your business. Maybe the hook is Mother's Day, or Valentine's Day; it does not matter. What matters is that this story can be reprinted and displayed in all your shops. A quote can be pulled and used in subsequent advertising: "Beautiful stores with a great selection," booms the headline.

To top it off, getting publicity is quite cost effective. What would it cost you to get on the front page of the Business section, if even you could? What would it cost to get a three minute segment during the local news? Now compare that to the cost of either hiring a public relations firm or even just doing it yourself, and you begin to see the bargain that is publicity.

If anyone knows something about marketing, it is the folks at Krispy Kreme. How do they create that tremendous buzz? First, they have an excellent product, based upon a recipe purchased in 1937 from a French chef (which today is locked in a fireproof vault at the company's headquarters). Second, they have a clever, memorable name, invented to represent the crispy outside of the doughnuts and the soft, creamy middle. Third, they offer something unique. If you have ever been in a Krispy Kreme store, you know that half the fun is watching the doughnuts being made and going down that conveyor belt. Finally, they manipulate supply and demand. When Krispy Kreme enters a new market, they give the local press plenty of warning, they give out plenty of free samples, they build the anticipation, and then, months later, a single store finally opens up.

Most of us won't create the next Krispy Kreme, but the lesson for us is clear: Create a unique business or product, have a memorable name, market it creatively, generate some publicity, and thereby create buzz. The results can be awfully tasty.

Newspaper editors and television producers have to come up with new stories every day. There is no reason why you or your business should not help them feed the hungry monster that is their daily story requirement. The way to do so is to give the editor/producer a news hook. They are not in the promotions business; they do not care if your business gets publicity or not. They are in the news business, and what they do care about is finding a newsworthy story. So if you are going to succeed in getting on the air, you need to couch your desires as news. You must give them a news hook.

How do you do that? There are two ways. First, you could hire a public relations firm. PR firms have both the expertise and contacts to get the story about your business out there. If you do not have the time or inclination to do it yourself, but see the value in having your business name publicized, then hiring a PR firm makes a lot of sense. They can be expensive, and you want your money well spent, so the way to find a good one is the same way you found the other professionals on your team. Word of mouth is best, but cold calling some firms out of the phone book can work just as well. Compare fees, sure, but more importantly, compare results.

The other way to get the word out there about your business is to do it yourself by drafting and sending out a press release. A press release is a one page article that explains the who, what, where, when, and how of your newsworthy story. It is intended to capture an editor's attention, to get her to want to know more, and then to assign a reporter to interview you. To get that to happen, be sure to:

- Send the press release to the editor—by name—who is in charge of your industry. Send it also to the reporter—by name—who covers your industry.
- Use a catchy headline.
- Make it newsworthy. Dog Bites Man is not newsworthy. Man Bites Dog is. Be unique. Be creative.
- Do not sell.
- Keep it short and sweet—no more than 500 words.

Here is an example of a press release.

For Immediate Release   [Today's date]
Attorney Wins Prestigious Award

Jay Rosenberg, a local attorney specializing in criminal law, was awarded the state bar's Young Lawyer of the Year award at the state bar convention this month. The award is given to attorneys under the age of 40 who have shown leadership in their area of the law. Says state bar president Sam Davis, "Jay Rosenberg has given selflessly to needy, indigent clients. He is to be commended for his hard work in his community. He is an up-and-comer." Rosenberg is the owner of the Rosenberg Law Firm, with two offices in town.

For more information, contact Raphael Arons at:

555-555-5555 or

Raphael@AgencyPR.com

CHAPTER **24**

Your Web Presence

The Internet is a marketing medium.

—JAY CONRAD LEVINSON

If you have been in business a while, I am assuming that you have a web site, and if you are new to the world of small business, I am assuming you are getting a site. If you do not have one, get with the program. This is the twenty-first century. A web site is one of the most powerful, inexpensive, and useful marketing and sales tools ever invented. Whether you buy a program and design it yourself or hire someone to build a web site for you, you must get online. That is not the question. The real question is: What do you do and how do you make money once you have a Web presence? In this chapter, we discuss how to get people to come to your site, what they should find when they get there, how to fulfill the orders you receive, and how to use the power of the Internet to create even more business.

GETTING TRAFFIC

Commercially speaking, many small businesses find the Internet frustrating, although some do find it exhilarating. If you are like a lot of other small businesses, though, you probably spent a sizable sum to get your site up and running, only to find that, while it is sort of a cool

225

e-billboard, it does little to actually drive sales. The problem usually is that people do not know you are out there. The issue therefore is: How can you get people to find your site?

Getting Listed on Search Engines and Directories

More and more, people are leaving the Yellow Pages and searching for what they want online via Internet search engines and directories. And because many of those looking are other businesses, the possibility of your creating some very lucrative commercial customers is also quite possible online, again though, *only if* they can find you. Therefore, you must get listed on the various search engines like Google, Yahoo!, and Ask Jeeves. There are two ways to do this.

> A search *engine* is a tool that compiles and lists computerized results from an inquiry. A search *directory* is an inquiry result created by humans listed by category. The listings on the Yahoo! homepage are a directory. The Yahoo! search tool on its homepage is a search engine.

1. *Do it yourself.* Here, you physically submit your web site address (or URL) to the different search engines and follow up to see that you get listed. Because submitting your site is a very preliminary step, it does not mean that you will be ranked high, merely that the engine or search directory knows your site is out there.
2. *Use an automated service.* Since there are hundreds of search engines, finding and physically submitting your site to every one is time consuming. Note, though, that the ever-present 80–20 rule is said to apply here as well—80 percent of the searches are done on 20 percent of the sites, and even then there are only about a half dozen major ones.

A good plan then is to use a service that simultaneously submits your site to literally hundreds of search engines. One such service, for example, is www.submitit.com. This site, for a small fee, will get your site listed on up to 400 search engines, and it also resubmits your site periodically to make sure you stay listed. Another excellent submission service is www.submissionpro.com.

Submission Tips

Getting the engines and directories to know about you is all well and good, but it will do little to build your business. What really drives traffic, and therefore sales, is your ranking and being listed in the directory. Being stuck on the third page of a query result will not help your cause much, but getting a top 10 ranking will.

Begin with the submission process. Whether you will be submitting your URL yourself or hiring a web service to do it for you, you need to create a list of 25 words or so describing your site, including three key words that you think people will use to get to your site. For instance, if you have an athletic shoe store in Boston, your three words might be "athletic shoes Boston."

Paid Submissions. The wisest course is to submit your site first to Yahoo! Why? Although Yahoo! charges a fee for commercial listings, it is a human-based engine and directory. If you pay the flat $300 fee (for a year) you *will* get listed and linked. When that happens, you drastically increase your chances that your site will be found by Google, and that's the ticket. Google sends out a "web crawler" that automatically searches and analyzes the Web for good links. The more sites that link to yours and the better the Google software thinks your site is, the greater the chances you will get accepted by Google (for free), and the higher the likelihood that you will get a higher ranking. A listing and link on Yahoo! starts this process.

If money is tight and you cannot afford to pay $300 to Yahoo!, work on getting reciprocal links with other sites. Google may then find you anyway.

> The $300 annual fee to be listed on the Yahoo! directory is for commercial sites only. If your site is not only about selling merchandise, you should also try submitting via Yahoo! Express, the free submission tool for noncommercial sites.

Aside from Yahoo!, the other directory/engine that you should pay money for is LookSmart, because LookSmart's listings are distributed to, among others, the popular MSN Search service. If you want to try the free submission at LookSmart, you need to go to Zeal.com (owned by LookSmart), where volunteer editors will review your submission.

Crawlers

As mentioned, and as you likely know, the most important search engine is Google, which uses a web crawler to find and rank sites (Google presently also powers AOL Search). Crawlers look for links, so getting sites to link to your site is vital; the more, the better. Although Google accepts submissions as Yahoo! does, and while it is wise to submit to Google, just know that submissions are not their primary way of finding and ranking sites.

Another crawler service to submit to is Inktomi, as it provides results to MSN Search. Like Google, Inktomi looks for links to your site. For less than $50, you can submit your site to Inktomi.

> Crawler-based search engines have three elements. The "spider" visits web sites on the Internet every month or two and reads the web pages. This information then goes into the master "index," or catalogue. The "search engine software" then sifts through the index to match the search query with the already-indexed pages, and then ranks those pages it thinks are most relevant.

There are three last crawler sites that you want to be sure you submit to. The first is AllTheWeb because it provides results for the popular Lycos search engine. The other is Teoma, because it powers Ask Jeeves. Finally, be sure to submit to Alta Vista, which, though less popular than in its late-1990s heyday, is still used by many people.

HIGHER RANKINGS

So you have submitted your site to the appropriate engines and directories, built some reciprocal links, and now want results, right? You may get them, and you may not. Different sites use different methods for ranking search results. To some degree or another, each uses a different set of complex algorithms analyzing the words most used on your homepage and the number of links associated with your site to analyze what you offer. What can you do? Two things: first, optimize your site for search engines, and second, spend some more money.

Get Your Site Ready

Search engines rank sites for a query based in large measure on three things: first, by the keywords that appear at or near the top of your homepage; second, by the frequency keywords appear in relation to other words; and third, by the links to and from the site. Maybe you are thinking that you can surreptitiously have "athletic shoes Boston" written one hundred times at the top of your homepage and you will be assured a high ranking. Wrong. That is a type of spamming that will assure you a low ranking. And in any case, the link analysis plays a large measure in how high you will be ranked.

So how do you get higher rankings?

Pick Your Keywords Carefully. The words that you think people will use to find your site are your keywords. For me it might be "small business success" or "small business expert." What about you? Each page on your site will be spidered and indexed, so you need keywords to reflect each page's content.

If you would like to sign up for my free online newsletter *Small Business Success Secrets*, go to my site, www.MrAllBiz.com.

Pick Your Keyword Placement Carefully. I do not want to get overly-technical here, but the code that is used to create your web page is called HTML. At the top of each page, as part of the HTML code, are things called "meta tags" and "title tags." These help create and explain your page. The title tag, for instance, is what people will see and get if they go to bookmark your page to their Favorites or Bookmarks. Because some crawlers look at these meta and title tags, speak with your webmaster and make sure that your keywords are made part of your meta and title tags. Similarly, the titles to each page need to use the keywords you want associated with those pages.

Have Specific Pages. Create pages with HTML content and keyword placement that are specific enough to catch a spider's eye.

Get Linked Up. It is important to reiterate that getting other sites to link to you is one of the best ways to get better rankings.

Expect this process, from submission to listing, to take several weeks.

How do you get good links to your site? Here is one way: Go to your favorite search engine, type in your keywords, view the results, and then visit the sites that are ranked the highest. Send e-mails to the sites and see if they would be interested in a link exchange.

Buying Good Rankings

No, you cannot buy a high ranking, but you can do something that is pretty darn close. Think about Google for a second. When you get your query results, what do you also see? To the far right are several small boxed ads. At Lycos, the paid results appear *above* the actual search results. If you are willing to pay, you can buy such exceptional placement. With some sites, you pay per click; that is, you might pay 25 cents for every person who sees your ad and clicks it. With other engines, you pay a flat monthly fee. Either way, the great thing is that by agreeing to pay, you can be assured that, while you may not be ranked the highest, you can still end up on the first page people see when they type in your keywords. The different engines and directories have many different advertising methods that you can choose from to get your site noticed and linked with appropriate search results. Given the ever-increasing use of the Internet by shoppers, this can be a very good use of your money, and a powerful way to increase sales.

GETTING PEOPLE TO BUY

Getting people to your site is good, but for you to make money online, they have to buy something. For insight on what it takes to sell online, we turn to the man who probably knows it best, Jeff Bezos, founder of Amazon.com. So what does Bezos think? He says that the key to business success in the virtual world is offering the customer something that cannot be replicated in the physical world.

Amazon started out as The World's Biggest Bookstore, and it worked because whereas a typical book superstore may carry thousands of books, Amazon was able to list, literally, more than a million books. Because that sort of inventory cannot be duplicated in the real world, Bezos created and offered something unique, thus driving people to his site. So you must do this if you are going to be an online success—and not necessarily on the scale that Amazon did to still be successful, either.

Here is a small business example: Bryan Caplovitz is the founder and president of Speakermatch.com. Speakermatch began as a speaker's bureau, an agency that matches public speakers with meeting planners. As part of that business, Caplovitz created a web site. While his bureau began as most other businesses do—with a modicum of success—it was when he had his Big Idea and began to follow Bezos' dictum—*you have to offer something unique to succeed online*—that things began to change, rapidly, and for the better. Caplovitz realized that there was a great need not being met by traditional speaker's bureaus, a need that could best be met online. Although Bryan Caplovitz never met Jeff Bezos, he instinctively knew Bezos' lesson. Caplovitz realized that one of the great frustrations for many a speaker is that finding speaking gigs takes a lot of time. Similarly, for meeting planners, finding the right speaker is also time-consuming. Instead of having a physical speaker's bureau, Caplovitz realized that he could match these two groups online. "It became the Monster.com for the speaking industry," says Caplovitz.

On the site (www.speakermatch.com) meeting planners list—for free—their events and speaker needs. Speakers pay a monthly fee to the site for the right to peruse and pursue the leads that match their abilities. According to Caplovitz, since he started using his revised business model, "the site and customer base have grown every month." He has two pearls of wisdom, learned the hard way, for those who want to start their own successful online business:

- *The smartest thing he did was to create an opt-in subscription list for his speaker marketing newsletter.* By opting-in to that newsletter, visitors to Speakermatch are instantly prequalifying themselves for Caplovitz's services. They want what he is selling, and they have agreed to give him their e-mail address. It's a powerful marketing tool for any would-be e-merchant.
- *The dumbest thing he did was to purchase an opt-in list from a broker.* "It's a waste of money," he advises.

Creating an opt-in, e-mail newsletter is an excellent way to create a viable customer list, stay in touch with customers, and generate increased revenue. To be successful, your newsletter must provide information, discounts, or services that customers want badly enough to agree to give you their e-mail address, a.k.a., "opt-in." By opting-in, these customers are telling you that they are *very* interested in what you have to offer. So use that. Sure your newsletter must be full of valuable content, but do not miss the opportunity to pitch new products or services.

So the Amazon and Speakermatch lesson is clear: If you want to create a successful online business, then offer something unique, something not easily duplicated in the physical world, serve a market need, and watch the money click in.

DROP SHIPPING

Fulfilling orders online through your shopping cart is fairly basic. After a visitor goes to your site and clicks to purchase, you will get notification of the purchase and if you have a merchant account, the money will be deposited directly into your bank account. You then ship the product as you would any other order.

If you are new to this, you need to get a merchant account. If you cannot get one, you should strongly consider signing up with PayPal, which will notify you when you do get an order, tell you what was ordered, collect the fee (and a small percentage for itself), and either hold or deposit the money into your specified account. It is a very good service for your basic small business web site.

What if you don't want to go through the hassle of actually physically fulfilling orders? One of the best things about having a viable e-commerce site is that you do not have to actually physically have stock on hand to sell merchandise. "Drop shipping" is an arrangement between you and a wholesaler or distributor whereby you virtually stock your online store with their products and take orders. You then inform the wholesaler or distributor of any sale, and they ship off the merchandise. In essence, you are just a middle man (though no one knows that; it looks to the entire world as if the merchandise is stocked and sold by you). Via drop shipment, you can sell first-rate merchandise on your site and make a healthy profit, but without actually having to stock and ship product.

Here is an example: Say that your athletic shoe site carries a product called The Best Tube Sock Ever, and a package of 10 sells for $44, plus $6 for shipping and handling. When a visitor clicks and purchases this item, you get an e-mail notification. You then send the tube sock manufacturer an e-mail (in many systems, this, too, is automatically generated by the sale), the manufacturer ships the package off—using your label—and sends you a bill for its cost, say $35. PayPal takes your money and deposits it into your account. You make $15 on every purchase, and all you had to do was take the order.

You are right if you are thinking this is a great business model, because it is. You do not have the labor expense for shipping and handling, you can stock name brand items, you can easily add and delete items on your e-store, and you do not have to buy inventory. Start this process by deciding what products you want to carry and then speaking with the manufacturer of those products to see if they have a drop shipping system. If they do not, then work on finding a distributor (a business that has an inventory of products and distributes them).

> The Thomas Register lists thousands of companies, their brands and products. The company web site says that it is "the most comprehensive online resource for finding companies and products manufactured in North America, where you can . . . view thousands of online company catalogs and web sites." Go to www.thomasregister.com.

As with any other business deal you do, negotiate the best deal you can. When you find a wholesaler or distributor you want to use, find out

- How their wholesale prices compare to retail, so you can calculate your profit
- How and what they charge for shipping
- How they will bill you
- How they deal with returns and refund requests

Drop shipping is an easy, affordable way to sell online. Avoid those companies that want to charge you a fee for selling their products (they are out there, so beware), and be sure to choose quality products that reinforce your image and brand, and that afford you a healthy profit margin.

eBAY

If you already have products to sell and do not need a drop shipper, one of the best, easiest, least expensive ways to create another profit center is to begin an eBay business. Moreover, if you have old merchandise that you have not been able to sell, you might be surprised to find a ready market for it on eBay. Going online at eBay costs very little; if it works, great, and if not, all you have lost is some time.

> People sell an estimated 12 million items on eBay every day, generating about $40 million in sales.

As you know, on eBay, you sell items via an auction system, although a recent change allows customers to "Buy It Now," supplementing the auction. You can sell almost anything on eBay, with the most popular items being collectibles, books, movies and music, furniture, cars, and sports memorabilia. Note, though, that almost anything might sell on eBay—everything from a pig farm to a rubber ball can be found there.

One secret to selling on eBay is the old dictum to buy low and sell high. Remember the motto of our antique dealer, It's All in the Buying. He knew that if he could buy items at a cheap price, reselling them for a healthy profit would not be that difficult. That is especially true on eBay.

eBay Strategies

Several things you can do to increase the likelihood of eBay success are first, be sure to set a proper, hidden "reserve price" for your auctions. The reserve price is the lowest fee your auction will accept for your product, thereby assuring that you will make a profit on the sale (if you sell it). Second, focus on customer service. Potential customers will e-mail you questions, and those questions need to be answered promptly. Similarly, once you make a sale, stand behind your product, and be sure to ship it promptly. Other things you can do to make sure your foray into eBay is successful are:

- *Use photos.* People want to see what they are buying.
- *Write a great headline.* Redundant but true: Headlines grab people's attention.
- *Be thorough.* Giving a full description of the product can make a big difference.
- *Accurately estimate your shipping costs.* Even though eBay buyers usually pay for shipping, you still will eat into your margin if your actual shipping fees are more than what you are charging your buyers.

Learning how to sell on eBay is not difficult. Visit ebay.com/education to get a full tour of how the process works, or check your local bookstore—there are several good books on the process. All in all, eBay is a great, low-risk way to grow your business, or start a potentially lucrative, small business with very little money.

> Want to make a high-tech impression? Consider getting a micro, or mini, CD business card. Specialized businesses can burn small CDs for you (roughly the size of a regular business card) with several minute's worth of information. The CD cards come in many shapes, can handle all sorts of multimedia, and some even have e-commerce functionality.

E-MAIL MARKETING

One of the easiest ways to grow your business using the Net is to tap the power of e-mail. No, not spam, but rather, targeted e-mails to qualified customers and prospects. Personally, I have used this method with great success to syndicate my *USA TODAY* column to business sites all over the world.

The idea is to offer goods or services to specific customers via e-mail. In that sense, it is not unlike the more traditional direct marketing method discussed in the previous chapter, the difference being that you can find your list of potential recipients via a web search, and your communication is electronic. For instance, say that you are an architectural drafter. You could e-mail architects across the country, explaining who you are, telling them how inexpensive your services are, showing that you are Web-savvy, and offering to create a virtual partnership. The trick is to make your initial e-mail intriguing enough that the recipient would want to know more. That e-mail should be fairly short, no more than five paragraphs, and should explain the many benefits of working with you. If the architect is interested, he or she will e-mail you back, and presto! You have another new client.

CHAPTER 25

Exodus

Be prepared.

—BOY SCOUT MOTTO

There may come a time in the life of your business when you want to move on, or at least start preparing to move on. People leave businesses all the time—to start another business, to cash out, to let a child finally take the reins, to retire—the reasons are many. But any exit strategy requires preparation, something that many entrepreneurs are loath to do. In this chapter, we tackle getting out, made easy.

SUCCESSION PLANNING

No, no one likes to think about their death, but should you die without a plan, what would happen to your business, to your family? Succession planning is your way to ensure the continued viability of your vision and, therefore, should be part of any small business plan. If something does happen to you, or to other key team members (should someone die or leave unexpectedly), would the dream live on? Succession planning ensures that it will. You need not only to create a succession plan for your own sake, but it is something you owe your employees, vendors, shareholders, and/or investors. They all depend on your business to some extent for their livelihoods. Succession planning is the process whereby replacements are identified and groomed, not only for the CEO/president, but possibly for key managers as well.

Consider the cautionary tale of Marty, the owner of a flooring chain. As he got older, Marty decided that he needed a succession plan and so created what he thought was a foolproof one. Then the unexpected actually did happen: At the age of 50, Marty died suddenly and his plan had to be implemented. When Marty's will was read, everyone discovered that Marty's right-hand man was given 25 percent of the business and was to run it. The other 75 percent was equally divided among Marty's three children, two of whom were still minors. What Marty had never imagined was that his plan would create more problems than solutions. His oldest son wanted to run the business, but Marty's will had specifically given that responsibility to Marty's employee. Then, after a year or two, the employee came to resent working full time, but having to give 75 percent of the profit to Marty's kids. In the end, the children sold their shares of the business to the employee, and Marty's master plan and dream had, like Marty, prematurely died.

As you start to create a succession plan, you need to answer three questions. First, what is your vision for the future of the business in your absence? Second, who can best implement that vision? Finally, what plan can you create to see that the vision is carried out?

Start by deciding what you want for the business if something happens to you, your partner, or other key people. Do you want the business to continue? Would that signal instead that it is time to wrap things up? Legally speaking, the death of a partner ends the partnership, unless otherwise agreed to. In an LLC or corporation, death does not ipso facto end the business. If the business does continue, who will own the deceased's share of the business and how much say would she have in running it? These are questions you need to answer.

> Whatever plan you create needs to be memorialized in two places. First, it should become part of the operating agreement for the business. Second, if ownership shares are being transferred, that must be handled in your will or living trust.

Next, if continuing is appropriate, you need to decide who is capable of replacing the person in question, be it you or someone else. You and your team have duties. Who around can best handle those duties? Look around your business and think about who might best replace key individuals. You do not necessarily want a clone of yourself, but rather someone who can step in and lead. Examine skills, personality, leadership ability, and intelligence. You may even want to give potential candidates a self-assessment test to see how they view their strengths, weaknesses, skills, and vision. They do not need to know the reason for this test if you do not want them to.

Finally, once you have identified the person you think would be the best candidate to fill the position—say, for instance, your position—speak with him or her about this and get their perspective. If it is your son who is going to take over, you need to not only broach the subject of succession, but discover whether he would like to become the boss. If the answer is affirmative, thereafter actively begin to groom him for the position. Teach him what he needs to know. Answer questions. Expose him to all aspects of the business, your vision, and the plan. But be careful as you do this. Choosing a successor can also create hard feelings. Qualified candidates who are not selected may leave, and the process itself may cause companywide anxiety. Your best political skills will be required.

> In 1991, GE Chairman Jack Welch said that the thing that preoccupied his mind, the thing he spent the most time on, was succession planning. This was *nine years* before he stepped down.

Finally, put your succession plan in writing, so that there is no mistake regarding what you want.

SELLING YOUR BUSINESS

Maybe you want to sell your business because you were unable to locate a successor, or simply that it is time to move on. A business sale re-

quires forethought because it is a complicated, time-consuming transaction. Finding qualified buyers, going through your books and inspec-
tions, transferring real estate, and closing the deal can be protracted.
Certainly it could take a year or more, all told. So, to make sure that you
actually are able to find a viable buyer and close in a reasonable amount
of time, a few tips are in order.

Line Up Your Ducks

Like the sale of a home, the sale of a business requires that you increase
the business' curb appeal, among other things. You will want to paint
what needs to be painted, fix what is fixable, clean up the back room,
and otherwise get the place ready to show.

Get a Business Valuation. A lot of small business owners overesti-
mate the value of their business, especially their goodwill, thinking it is
worth more than it is. It is wise, then, to pay for a professional business
valuation early in this process so that you know what to expect and will
be able to honestly evaluate the offers you receive. The value of your
business is based upon its profitability, goodwill, assets, and liabilities. If
you hire a business broker, as discussed later, he will be able to accurately assess the value of your business as part of his services.

Get Your House in Order. One reason buyers buy businesses is because they want to reduce their risk, and the only way they can see
whether your business is risky or safe is by looking at your books. All
records—P&L statements, tax returns, contracts, permits, leases,
everything—need to be in order.

Boost Your Profits. People buy businesses because they are profitable. It follows, then, that one of the best things you can do to ensure
a lucrative sale is to increase sales and profits, to the extent possible.

Speak with Your Advisors. Your attorney and accountant may have
some good ideas about the sale of your business; they may even know
of potential buyers. You need to talk to them beforehand, tell them

your plan, and then have them ready to review the deal as it nears completion.

Hire a Business Broker

Having decided to sell your business, and having spruced up the office in preparation, the inevitable question is: Where do you find buyers? You have two options. You could either advertise the sale yourself or hire a business broker. If you decide to sell it yourself (akin to selling a home without a real estate agent), advertise in the following places:

- *The classifieds.* The classified ad section of your local paper has a section called Business Opportunities. That section lists various small businesses for sale, their prices, and locations. Many buyers start there.
- *Magazines.* The backs of trade magazines also usually have a section for businesses owners who are selling their business.
- *Online.* If you type "business for sale" into your favorite search engine, you will get a list of sites that broker business sales.

While you might do just fine selling your business without a broker, consider what it would be like to sell your home without an agent. You would not have access to the agent's expertise and experience, nor her access to the multiple listing service, nor her contacts and colleagues. So, too, in the world of business sales. Brokers have a listing service and associates, both of which are excellent ways to find buyers. So the first advantage of hiring a business broker is that you will have access to many more qualified buyers than you could find on your own.

While not cheap (usually they are paid a percentage of the sales price), business brokers can be an invaluable resource when selling a business. A good broker will help you decide upon the right price, be an important sounding board, negotiate a good deal, and handle the closing. Maybe best of all, a good business broker will separate the real buyers from the looky-loos, bring in more qualified prospects, and thereby usually garner a better price for the business.

If you are considering hiring a business broker, be sure to find out the following.

- *The broker's experience.*   Good brokers need to know business valua-
  tion, sales, business financing, negotiations, and more. You want someone
  with experience who really understands the world of business.
- *Whether the broker is certified.*   The accreditation you want is from the
  International Business Brokers Association (IBBA) and is called a Certified
  Business Intermediary (CBI).
- *The services provided.*   Will the broker help you value the business?
  Does he do more than negotiate the deal? A good broker should be an
  overall financial advisor for your end of the transaction.

The upshot is that the purchase of a business is a major event, and a good business broker can help make sure it is a successful one.

The Price

How much should you expect to get for your business? It is a fair question, though not an easy one to answer as every business is so different. When it comes to price, there are basically four questions to answer:

1. *What does the business own?*   A business with assets is obviously more valuable than a business without. Of course assets include things like trucks and equipment, but they also include contracts, intellectual property rights, goodwill (i.e., the reputation that the business has in the community), and so on.
2. *What does the business owe?*   The value of your business is offset by its liabilities. Less is more, of course.
3. *What is the business' profitability?*   Again, the same principle applies; bigger profit equals a bigger price.
4. *What about the intangibles?*   What makes the business unique? Do you have a great location, a favorable lease, or valuable employees? These can make a difference.

These four items are then taken into account and used to determine the value of your business. There are three ways to go about doing so. The first is called *price building*. The second method is called *return on investment*. The third is the *multiplier*.

> To learn more about how to sell your business, pick up a copy of *How to Sell Your Business* by C.D. Peterson.

Price Building. Price building is a valuation method that simply looks at the hard numbers—assets, profits, accounts receivable, goodwill, leases, and so on. For example, yours might look like this:

Real estate	$400,000
Equipment	$100,000
Inventory	$ 50,000
Goodwill	$ 50,000
Subtotal	$600,000
Less liabilities	$100,000
Total	$500,000

Return on Investment (ROI). ROI looks at the profit, per year, to help determine what a buyer's return on her investment will likely be. For example, say that you decide that $500,000 is the asking price. Is that fair? Using the ROI method, and assuming some numbers, we would see that:

- Net profit is $200,000.
- Business sale price is $500,000.
- Return on investment ($200,000/$500,000) is 40 percent.

Using ROI, and these numbers, the buyer would be getting a 40 percent return on her investment. Given that a good passive investment may return a yield of 10 percent or so, a 40 percent return for an active investment may be high. Thus, a higher price for the business may be in order.

Multiplier. The last method, and a common one, is the multiplier. Again, look at the earnings, but multiply it by some factor—it varies depending upon the industry—to get a final price. A factor of 3 would result in a $600,000 asking price. Of course, the battle is what that factor should be.

If all of this is too complicated, and it can be, then consider simply getting an appraisal and/or hiring a business broker (look in the Yellow Pages under Business Brokers). It will probably be worth it to ensure that you get a fair price.

BANKRUPTCY

Sometimes, the decision to get out of the business is a necessity, not a choice. Many things can precipitate a bankruptcy: illness to you or a partner, divorce, losing a big customer or contract, anything. Although bankruptcy is a frightening word, it need not be.

I spent many years as a bankruptcy lawyer and came to really appreciate the bankruptcy process. Here is what I know: Most of the law is about retribution, except bankruptcy. Indeed, lawsuits and criminal courts are dedicated to helping people and society get revenge. But rather than revenge, bankruptcy is about forgiveness. It forgives your debts, forgives your mistakes, and gives you a chance for a "fresh start" (that phrase comes straight out of the bankruptcy code). Forgiveness is a rare thing in life, let alone the law. So the first piece of good news is that there is good news. A fresh start—does that not sound nice?

Does bankruptcy harm your creditors? Yes, of course it does. And no, it is not easy for the debtor, either. It is never easy walking away from debts, especially those owed to people you have been doing business with for some time. Walking away from such debts is no simple thing, but if you are contemplating bankruptcy, it should be a relief to know that you can walk away if circumstances so dictate.

So bankruptcy puts you back in control of your business finances. If you are at a place where bankruptcy is a viable option, then it is safe to assume that things are pretty bad right about now. Creditors are probably calling, threatening to sue, or already suing you and your business.

The second piece of good news is that as soon as you file your paperwork, the bankruptcy court issues a federal court order called an "automatic stay." The stay is sent to all of your creditors and it instructs them to leave you alone. Once you file bankruptcy, you should receive no more calls, threatening letters, or lawsuits; all lawsuits are halted by the stay, no matter how far along they are in the proceedings.

There are four types of bankruptcies available to your business. The type you file depends upon your situation and goals. Here are the four types (Note: Each "Chapter" is a chapter in the bankruptcy code).

1. *Chapter 7.* The vast majority, 95 percent, of all bankruptcies are Chapter 7s. For an individual it is quick (four months), fairly inexpensive, and almost all debts are completely wiped out (called "discharged" in the lingo). The problem for a business is that Chapter 7 (also known as a "straight bankruptcy" or "liquidation") shuts down the business. If this is your goal, good, because this is what will happen. If your small business files a Chapter 7 bankruptcy, all operations must cease, your doors will close, and a bankruptcy trustee will be assigned to sell the assets of your business for the benefit of your creditors. Most, if not all, business debts will be discharged, as will all personal debts if the business is a sole proprietorship or a partnership.

   However, if you want to stay in business, then you need to file one of the other chapters.

2. *Chapter 11.* When you hear about a company emerging from bankruptcy, that is a Chapter 11. Chapter 11 is used to restructure business debts. Under this chapter, existing management of the business continues to run it, although the bankruptcy court must approve significant business decisions. Creditors are appointed to a committee who work with the business to develop a plan of reorganization. The plan may allow the company to pay 10 cents on the dollar to its creditors, or it might be 100 cents. It varies. Once the

plan is fulfilled and the debts are paid (it usually takes several years), the company emerges from bankruptcy.

3. *Chapter 12.*   Chapter 12 is for farmers.

4. *Chapter 13.*   Chapter 13 is like a mini Chapter 11. Whereas Chapter 11 is usually used by larger corporations, Chapter 13 is a reorganization plan for smaller companies that want to keep their doors open, such as sole proprietorships.

While not the optimum path you wanted your business to take, bankruptcy is not as bad as most people fear. Sometimes, you just need a little forgiveness to get back on track.

PART

V

Dealing with People

CHAPTER **26**

Hiring and Firing

You're fired!

—DONALD TRUMP

It is often said that your employees are your most valuable asset, but that may not necessarily be true. It would be nice if they were, and sometimes they are, but employees are also a lot of work. Hiring them, dealing with the myriad of issues and troubles that arise, letting go of the problem ones—employees take plenty of time and effort. So as you deal with them, especially the hiring and firing part, there are a few things you should know to make things easier and to keep you out of hot water.

EMPLOYEE OR
INDEPENDENT CONTRACTOR?

It is not surprising that you might want to hire people and call them independent contractors. Although an employee and an independent contractor often perform similar duties, your obligations toward independent contractors are minimal compared to obligations to an employee.

- You rarely need to provide an independent contractor with worker's compensation insurance. (Check with your state.)
- You need not match an independent contractor's unemployment insurance payment.
- Most importantly, you need not pay any portion of an independent contractor's Social Security or Medicare taxes.

So yes, it would be nice to hire independent contractors to do the job of employees (many employers do), *but only* if they really are independent contractors. There are two main distinctions between an employee and an independent contractor. First, employees have to follow directions, whereas independent contractors must truly be independent; they get to decide how, when, and where they work. Sure, you can oversee what they do and approve or disapprove of the project, but you cannot control the actual process of when and how they do it. Second, employees are exclusive, that is, they usually work for only one company, and certainly never work for competitors at the same time. Independent contractors on the other hand must be able to offer their services, not just to one business, but to the public at large. Indeed, they often work for several similar businesses at the same time.

That is why they are called "independent contractors"—they must be independent. You may be tempted to save money and hassles by saying that the position calls for an independent contractor, but if the person is really an employee (because they are not truly independent), the results can be severe. If you get caught (and you will probably get caught—employees resent this tactic), not only will you owe back taxes, and interest and penalties to the federal government, but you very well may owe money to the employee for lost benefits. On top of that, you will also likely get into trouble with your state's labor department. All in all, taking this shortcut is a mistake to avoid.

HIRING EMPLOYEES

Hiring employees should be a fairly enjoyable process. Finding and hiring the right people is a chance to implement your vision for your business. It is when you get to locate the type of people you would like to work with and with whom you think your customers would like dealing. As much as you look at background, education, skills, and intelligence when hiring, you should equally consider personality and compatibility. You spend plenty of time with your employees and you want to make sure that yours will be an enjoyable place to work.

Finding and hiring good employees, therefore, is one of the most important things you as a small business owner can do. Employees help set the tone, do the work, deal with customers, and are the ones on the front line. If they blow it, they give you and your business a bad name, and conversely if they do things properly, you all win.

So how do you hire the right ones? Essentially, this is a three-step process.

The Three Steps

Step 1: Preparation. Before hiring anyone, have a very clear idea about what the position will entail. Write up a job description that includes duties, hours, responsibilities, and so on. Based upon the job description, consider how much schooling and experience the person should have, what sort of people skills they need, what you want from them, and so on. Some of this can be gleaned from an employment application.

Sample Employment Application

Personal Information

Name:
Address:
Phone number:
Social Security number:
Position applying for:
When would you be available to start:

Employment Information

Please list your employment for the past three years.

Date　*Employer/Supervisor*　　*Address/Phone #*　　*Duties*

Special skills and qualifications:

Other:

Education

School　　　*Years of Attendance*　　*Did You Graduate?*

References

Please list three references.

Name　　*Relationship*　　*Years Acquainted*　　*Address/Phone #*

Date:　　　　Signature:

After receiving the application and weeding out the undesirables, have ready an interview questionnaire that you can use as a guide. Explore the candidate's background, experience, qualifications, ideas, intelligence, and references. Be sure to include open-ended questions that require the applicant to explain things. Have several questions ready regarding each important attribute for the position.

Step 2. Finding Qualified Applicants. Once you know what you want from an employee, you need to find a stable of potential candidates to interview for the position(s). Of course, a "Help Wanted" ad in the classifieds, in your window, or on a site like Monster.com can draw a pool of applicants, but don't overlook such options as:

- *Temp agencies.* The best thing about hiring a temp is that you can "test-drive" an employee before making a long-term commitment.
- *Seniors.* Older workers usually have an excellent work ethic, and are responsible and eager to please.
- *State employment agencies.* Every state has job placement programs. If you tap this resource, you will find that the state will not only post your job listing on state job boards, but just may prescreen applicants for you.
- *Colleges.* Universities are a good place to find inexpensive, part-time, smart employees.

Step 3. Interview. Discover whether the interviewees are responsible, why they left their last job, whether they can take directions, if they have ever been fired, why they want this job, and their qualifications for the position. Also as much as you want someone who meets your qualifications, do not overlook their personality and how well you may or may not get along. Be sure to get references and resumes.

Remember, since you cannot discriminate in hiring because of race, gender, color, national origin, religion, finances, or disabilities, any questions along these lines should be avoided. Concentrate on job-related questions.

Coachability

It is hard to underestimate just how important the employee-hiring process is. A good employee may be a new profit center or simply another pair of valuable hands—selling, helping, assisting clients, and boosting morale. On the other hand, the wrong person can steal, create havoc, anger customers, and hurt sales. Worse, if you fire him, the unscrupulous employee might even sue for "wrongful termination" (that is, illegal termination), even though you were legally and morally correct in letting him go.

You cannot be too careful therefore when interviewing potential employees. Of course honesty, intelligence, skill, and affability are important. You can garner much of that information from resumes, references, and interviews. Knowing what people did in the past is a pretty good indication of what they will do in the future. Really, that is rather standard stuff. Most small business owners have a pretty good sense of what they want and are looking for in an employee. You know about checking references.

However, one area that is often overlooked is something I call "coachability," and it is vital to making a smart hire. Coachability is the ability of an employee to take directions and make changes, to listen and adjust, to think and respond. Just as not everyone is cut out to be an entrepreneur, so, too, not everyone is cut out to be an employee.

Running a small business and hiring the right employees is like running a sports franchise. There are good teammates and bad teammates. There are employees who make everyone around them better and those who hog the ball. And just as in sports, having uncoachable employees can ruin your team. You have to stock your business with employees who are willing to do things your way, who listen, who can take constructive criticism, who are willing to try new things, and who are adaptable and positive—who are coachable.

So when interviewing those prospective employees, be sure to find out what kind of teammate they have been and will probably be. As much as skill and smarts, their coachability can make or break your season.

THE NEW EMPLOYEE

Whenever you hire new employees, there are several agreements that you may want to consider having them sign. The first three are discussed in Chapter 21, Legal Ease II, but as a reminder, they are:

- A reasonable noncompete agreement if the employee might learn things that can be used against you later
- A nondisclosure agreement (NDA) to prevent employees from disclosing confidential trade secrets
- An assignment of inventions or "work for hire" agreement if the employee will be involved in creative endeavors

You should also consider having an employment contract as it can be a good way to memorialize your agreement with the employee. *It is critical that the contract state clearly and boldly words to the effect that "nothing in this agreement is intended to guarantee employment or alter the fact that [name of the employee] is an at-will employee."* This document can help clarify your relationship with the employee, but may also be an important defense in any future litigation. The agreement might cover:

Compensation. This section details the employee's base salary, and benchmarks for bonuses or commissions.

Job description. Here, explain *in detail* what is expected of the employee, her hours, duties, sales quotas, everything. Be expansive and explain that other responsibilities may be added later on.

Benefits. Your benefits package should be explained. You should reserve the right to change the benefits plan.

Stock options. If you offer stock options as part of your benefits or incentive program, the process by which they are attained and exercised needs to be explained.

Arbitration. Litigation is expensive, and many employers have mandatory arbitration clauses in their employment agreements.

Immigration status.   The employee needs to verify that she is a citizen of the United States, or has the proper work visa.

If you do decide to have some sort of employment contract, go over it with your lawyer. Then both you and your employee need to sign the contract, and you should keep a signed copy in a safe and secure place.

Consider also having an employee handbook that explains important policies and procedures, such as workplace safety, antidiscrimination policies, how complaints are handled, discipline, sick leave, and vacation policies. This handbook should also reiterate that employees are considered at-will.

If you have 50 or more employees, you are required to abide by the Family and Medical Leave Act. The FMLA mandates that eligible employees be given up to 12 weeks of unpaid leave during any 12-month period for the birth of a new child, the adoption of a new child, to care for the health of an immediate family member with a serious health problem, or to take care of their own serious health issue.

LEARNING FROM NEW EMPLOYEES

If you are a good employer, you do a lot of listening. Employees are one of your very best resources for learning how to improve your business; they will see things that you missed. However, on the totem pole of valued employees, the newer employee usually is near the bottom. That may be a mistake as new employees especially can give you a perspective other, more entrenched, employees lack or lost.

So after an employee has been with you for a few months, consider giving her a survey to fill out. The results will probably be illuminating. For example, your survey might look like this:

1. Name:
2. Position:
3. Please describe your job:

4. What are the most important things you do in your job?

5. What is the best part of your job?

6. What is the worst part?

7. What would you change about your job?

8. Does the job reflect what you were told during the hiring process?

9. What improvements could be made to our hiring process?

"IT JUST ISN'T WORKING OUT"

You may be tempted to have a probationary period of, say, six months when you hire new employees. You should avoid this. Why? Because by creating a probationary period, you are implying that different rules apply before and after the probation. You do not want that. You should have one set of rules for everyone, whether it is their first day or tenth year.

You may also be tempted to fire someone immediately when things go wrong. It is far better, and helps you avoid litigation, if you document problems first. Yes, it is true that an at-will employee can be fired at any time, but creating a paper trail can only help you. Document every transgression in writing giving the employee a letter explaining what they are doing wrong, what they can do to reverse course, and have them sign it.

> Remember, you cannot fire, without repercussion, any employee because of discrimination, retaliation, or if they have a long-term contract.

To avoid an ugly and expensive wrongful termination suit, here is a checklist of things to consider before terminating an employee. Of course, not all items will apply to all employees, but this does give you an idea of issues to consider prior to firing.

1. Analyze whether the problem is the fault of the employee, or your business procedures. If it is how your business is run, firing someone will not solve the problem.

2. Make sure that you have documented the employee's transgressions in writing.

3. If you have a grievance or complaint procedure, be sure that it has been followed.

4. Determine whether similar employees have been treated similarly to the employee in question. Disparate treatment equals litigation. •

5. If the employee is a member of a protected class (handicapped, a minority, older), be sure that the reason for the termination is valid and double-check to make sure the problems with the employee have been documented.

6. Make sure the employee is not being fired in retaliation for exercising a legal right.

7. Make sure the employee does not have a contract for continued employment, either written or implied.

If you determine that firing the person is required, it has been found that it is best to do so in the morning, usually midweek, although late on Friday afternoon may work well, too. Break the news in the employee's office or a conference room, and endeavor to do so gently. Make it brief and dignified. If you are concerned that the employee might become violent, have a security guard ready nearby (hire one for the day if needed).

> The opposite of an at-will employee is a just cause employee. Employees with long-term employment contracts (such as a tenured teacher) are just cause employees. Just cause employees may be legally terminated only if you have, well, a just cause. Just cause reasons may include illegal behavior, excessive absenteeism, insubordination, sexual harassment, or serious incompetence. Firing a just cause employee requires investigation, notice, and hearings.

After the employee has left the premises, you may need to change the locks or the access code if he had a security clearance. Finally, write a disengagement letter to the ex-employee after he has gone, handling any necessary housecleaning matters and reiterating what happened in the termination meeting.

A necessary part of small business, letting employees go can and should be done in a way that minimizes your risk.

CHAPTER **27**

Employee Benefits Demystified

A man to carry on a successful business must have imagi-
nation. He must see things as in a vision, a dream of the
whole thing.

—CHARLES SCHWAB

People work for many reasons, compensation being but one. If you are
to create and sustain a successful small business, take into account the
many things people want out of work. From the noble (the desire to
make a difference) to the mundane (to get health insurance), work
means different things to different people. While pay will be the main
way you compensate them for a job well done, it is by no means the
only way. In this chapter a smorgasbord of benefit options is offered for
your consideration.

WHAT IS REQUIRED?

By law, you are required to give employees only certain benefits, although they are probably not what you think. You must

- Pay them at least the prevailing minimum wage.
- Provide worker's compensation insurance.
- Withhold and match FICA taxes.

- Pay unemployment taxes.
- Have employees work no more than 40 hours a week, or pay overtime, unless they are exempt employees.
- Give employees time off to serve in the military, on a jury, or to vote. •

You are not required to give employees benefits such as

- Bonuses
- Health insurance
- Paid vacations
- Sick leave
- Retirement plans
- Stock options
- Life insurance
- Christmas, New Year's, or other legal holidays off

Of course, while you are not required to offer such benefits, if you want to create a place where people want to work, a place that is special, a place that engenders loyalty, you must provide some or all of the benefits just listed.

The quality of your benefits package is definitely something employees will look at when deciding whether yours is a place where they would want to work. And since the quality of the employees you attract has a direct impact on the quality of your business (and the quality of your bottom line), offering a full benefits package is an important criterion to consider, albeit an expensive one.

BONUSES

Money is a mighty motivator. Offering bonuses, therefore, can be a valuable incentive. Bonuses can be structured in two ways. First, individual employees can be given benchmarks to hit, and a sliding-scale bonus can be offered as the employee hits each goal. But because this sort of system usually works best mainly with sales staff, the other sort of bonus plan may work better companywide. Under the second system, goals for the entire business are communicated to all employees, and as the company hits these goals, a pool of bonus money is created. Each goal reached fills the pool more, and at the end of the year the pool is divided equally. Goals could be sales, or reduced overhead, or less shrinkage.

> *Shrinkage* is a reduction in inventory caused by accounting error, employee theft, customer shoplifting, administrative error, and/or vendor fraud or mistake.

There are several advantages to this system. First, it helps teach your employees about business, and the more they know, the less likely they are to waste. Second, it gives everyone a stake in the outcome, not just your salespeople. Third, it creates a sense of teamwork and helps employees feel invested in the business.

STOCK OPTIONS AND OWNERSHIP

Another trait shared by the great, most successful small businesses is that they often give employees a stake in the business, an ownership share. Rather than it being just another place to work and draw a salary, a small business that an employee partially owns makes that employee a committed entrepreneur. As a result, they usually are more motivated, more dedicated, and more conscientious. Moreover, the possibility that the business could hit it big and thereby make the employee rich is another powerful motivator.

> At one time, during its late 1990s Internet heyday, Amazon.com was trading on the Nasdaq for almost $600 a share. It turned ordinary employees into instant millionaires (if they sold at the right time.) These days the stock is back down to earth, trading at less than $100.

There are three types of stock ownership plans:

1. *With a stock option plan* your business would award the option to buy company stock at a specified price, and the employee then has a certain amount of time to exercise the option and become a part owner of the company. Approximately 10 million employees in business both public and private hold stock options at any one time.

2. *An employee stock ownership plan (ESOP)* is a sort of retirement plan akin to a 401(k), but instead of creating a diversified portfolio, with an ESOP the retirement funds are invested in the stock of the employer. Under this scenario, the company contributes cash to buy its own stock (usually from the owner), which is then shared among the employees. There are significant tax benefits available under this plan. It is estimated that about 8 million employees invest in ESOPs.

3. *An employee stock purchase plan (ESPP)* allows employees to buy stock at a discount (usually around 15 percent). The employee can then either sell the stock for a profit, or hold onto it.

> For more information on creating some sort of employee stock ownership plan, contact the National Center for Employee Ownership at 510-208-1300—NCEO.org.

OTHER RETIREMENT PLANS

For employers and employees alike, the most popular employer-sponsored retirement plan is the 401(k), as contributions are tax deductible for employers and tax deferred for employees. Participation is optional, although employees today know they need to fund their own retirement and usually appreciate the opportunity to do so. You, the small business owner, must decide whether you can afford to match funds contributed by employees. It is expensive to match employee contributions dollar for dollar, even if they are tax deductible.

Investments made by the 401(k) contributions can be made by employees or by the plan administrator; know, however, that with a 401(k), the more options you give your employees, the more expensive administration will be. Expect administration costs to be at least $1,000 a year, as reports must be filed with the IRS, the Department of Labor, plan participants, and so forth.

To set up a 401(k) plan, or some other tax-deferred retirement plan as outlined in Chapter 20, Legal Ease I, you need to speak with a financial planner or your accountant.

HEALTH INSURANCE

Employees consistently rank health insurance as among the most important benefits supplied by an employer. The problem for the small businessperson is that the cost of insuring your employees continues to rise at frightening rates. Moreover, unlike larger businesses that have the ability to at least partially pass on or absorb increases, small businesses have neither luxury. So what to do? There are options, but no great answers. In all honesty, too many options for reducing your health care costs while still providing employees with coverage involve cutting benefits or shifting costs onto your employees. While that may help you keep costs down, it does not make for a happy workplace.

The first and easiest thing to do is shop around. There are all sorts of plans to choose from, with varying degrees of costs and coverage. Online, ehealthinsurance.com is a good site for comparing health plans. You should also speak with your insurance agent or broker. The plan you bought a few years ago may have cheaper alternatives today. Remember, too, that an insurance broker can shop your needs to many different providers, whereas an agent works exclusively with one company. By shopping, you can compare quotes for scores of different plans.

Options

Your basic options are these:

Traditional Health Insurance. This type of insurance allows employees to pick any doctor or specialist they want. They need to first meet the deductible, and there is usually a cap on out-of-pocket expenses. This is the most flexible, and most expensive, sort of plan.

Health Maintenance Organizations. HMOs direct employees to providers within the system. Their primary care physician is the gateway to all other medical care. Co-pays are small, and meeting deductibles is usually not a requirement.

Preferred Provider Organization. A PPO allows employees to see any health provider they want, but if they choose a doctor outside the system, their co-pays are higher.

Point of Service. With a POS plan, as with an HMO, your staff has a small co-pay and are encouraged to see doctors in the network. If they go outside the network, they must meet a deductible and also pay a percentage of the fee.

There are two relatively new healthcare options on the block that you should also consider:

Health Savings Accounts. HSAs are like IRAs for medical care, with two parts. The first is a health insurance policy that covers expensive hospital bills. The second is that employees can contribute money tax-free into an interest bearing investment account in which the money deposited can be withdrawn tax-free for medical care. If employees do not need to use the money they save, the money accumulates with tax-free interest until retirement, when they can withdraw it for any purpose.

To learn more, go to www.hsainsider.com.

Health Purchasing Alliance. Here, instead of joining one health plan, employees join an alliance of many health plans, all of which are being jointly administered. Because all are competing for your healthcare dollars, you get the best possible prices and are able to shop for various coverage options in one place.

Finally, you should find out whether your business may be eligible for discounted healthcare plans from an association. Chambers of Commerce often offer this, as do trade associations.

Alternatives

A few other things you can do to reduce your small business' health care costs are first, consider cutting back on the extent of your plan. If, for example, your plan offers dental and vision, you may have to cut those. Unpleasant, yes, but at least your employees will still be covered in the areas where it really counts. No, I certainly do not enjoy advising you to cut employee benefits, but I also understand that health care costs are a major concern for many small businesses, and cutting benefits is better than cutting jobs.

Also, if you have a plan that requires co-pays, as most do these days, you can reduce your premiums by increasing employee co-pays: The higher their co-pay, the lower your premium. Similarly, you can increase prescription co-pays: By increasing the amount your employees pay for their prescriptions, you can again reduce your premiums.

Whatever you choose to do, it has to be thoughtful and maybe even something you decide with your employees. Because health care is so important, you must weigh carefully your need to reign in costs against your employees' needs for adequate health care.

HOLIDAYS, SICK LEAVE, AND VACATION

Time off work for holidays, sick leave, and vacation days are not rights that employees have but benefits you offer. According to the Fair Labor Standards Act, you are not required to give paid time off for holidays, sick days, or vacation days. But just because you do not have to be a good employer, it does not mean that you should not. If you want to recruit great people, you have to create a great place to work, and this is one place to start.

The Traditional Method

Small businesses usually set up a leave policy whereby employees get x number of days for sick days, and y number of days for holidays, and so forth. You simply decide on how many each employee will get a year, whether they will be paid days or not, put the leave policy in writing, and let everyone know. Typically, new employees usually get about 16 days off per year, allocated evenly between vacation days and sick days. Most employees expect a paid week or two off per year.

Most employers provide paid holidays for New Year's Day, Memorial Day, the Fourth of July, Labor Day, Thanksgiving Day, and Christmas Eve and night. When it comes to other religious holidays, the norm is to allow employees to take them off without pay, or to allow employees to use vacation days. Most small businesses also allow about four days off, paid, to attend to a death in the family.

Innovative Options

Consider this new idea: Pool these various types of days off into a bank of hours that employees can use as they see fit. For example, instead of giving employees 11 holidays and 5 vacation days a year, you might decide instead to give everyone 100 hours a year off to use how and when they want.

This sort of plan has many benefits. First, it promotes honesty. Employees could schedule days off without having to call in sick. Also, it respects employees as adults, in effect telling them that you trust them and you assume they know best how to balance their lives and work. Employees are responsible for their choices for using their time off. They may use a half day here, a full day there, a week for vacation, save it for sick days, or just save it to be used later.

Some employers allow employees who bank more than, say, 75 hours, to cash in the extra hours for money at their current rate of pay.

Another innovative option is the flex-holiday plan. At the beginning of the year, you create a list of major holidays (there could be 25 or more): Everything from Christmas Day to St. Patrick's Day, Kwanzaa, or President's Day should be on the list. Employees then can select any 11. This plan also respects employees as adults and allows them to decide what is important.

INTANGIBLE BENEFITS

Benefits can take many forms. Aside from offering options like health and retirement plans, you can create policies that will be appreciated by your staff, policies that are every bit a benefit as money.

For instance, your small business could be family friendly, allowing employees to leave when family commitments arise, during soccer season, maybe. You could welcome their children when they come to the store. You could offer job-sharing so that a new mom can have her job, and her baby, too.

What else could you do to make your workplace better? The great thing about innovative policies is that employees appreciate them almost as much as anything else you offer, yet the policies may not cost nearly as much as those other, expensive benefits packages.

CHAPTER **28**

Training and Motivating Your Staff

Help me help you!

—JERRY MAGUIRE

Some employees are hired, trained a bit, and expected to do their jobs competently. Others are hired, trained properly, expected to do their jobs competently, and the training continues. Whom do you think will be more effective? Right. Yet even so, it is understandable when a small business owner fails to properly train her employees. After all, training takes time, and time is probably our most precious commodity.

All small business owners are guilty of making the mistake of spending too much time working *in* our business, rather than *on* our business. It is so easy to get so lost in the day-to-day minutiae of our business that we miss big picture. Training and motivating employees is one way to counteract that, ensuring that your plans and vision are being carried out, even when you are busy doing other things.

TRAINING

Good training creates better employees. It may be as simple as explaining a new policy and showing employees how to implement it, or it might be a several-weeks-long process in which employees learn something new. Either way, adequately training your staff is vital to the continued success of your small business.

Nancy Clark owns two retail dance apparel stores, so it is physically impossible for her to be at both places at once. Accordingly, she is a big believer in proper training: She spends up to a month training new employees before allowing them to work on their own. During the training period, which she conducts during regular store hours, Clark makes sure new employees learn everything, from opening and closing procedures to knowing the merchandise to operating the cash register. Clark trains her staff "from the ground up," so that when something arises, the employee is able to handle it. "Thorough training creates knowledgeable staff, and that in turn creates a well-run business," says Clark.

To be most effective, begin training employees the day they start work and cover everything they need to know. By creating a training process that covers all the bases, you create better employees, which in turn allows you to concentrate less on problems and more on the areas of your business you enjoy. Your initial training can cover many things, such as:

- Philosophy: Employees should understand your way of doing business.
- Brand: Teach your employees what your business is all about and what you want the company "personality" to be.
- Policies: Explain overtime, vacation, sexual harassment, workplace safety, and other policies.
- Operations: Show them how to operate the alarm, the lights, the point-of-sale system, their computer, and so on. Explain how to restock the shelves, how to handle a complaint, and other similar issues.

- Expectations: Employees need to be taught what you expect of them.

> At Long & Levit, a law firm on the West Coast, new lawyers were not only trained in the essentials, but every day for an hour, they were given a workshop in basic civil litigation. The crash course was unique in that it rapidly accelerated the new attorneys' ability to contribute to the firm. By training their lawyers properly from the start, by teaching them not only how to be good employees, but how to be better lawyers, too, the firm helped the bottom line.

Many small businesses spend the bulk of their training on the one issue that is both the most important and often the hardest for employees: Sales. (Because sales are so important, issues beyond training are covered in the next chapter, Extraordinary Sales and Exemplary Customer Service.) Sales training not only gives employees a valuable skill, but is equally a chance to teach your troops your way of doing business. Among the things to cover in your sales training:

- Attitude: Is your staff to be friendly, chatty, professional, reserved, or what? Some small businesses want their employees to be aggressive; others want them to be almost invisible. What say you?
- Products: Employees need to learn about your product line, why you sell what you do, how it ties in with what you are trying to accomplish, and how that fits the needs of customers.
- Money: How should they handle cash sales, credit cards, and checks?
- Operations: How to handle returns, refunds, and so on?

> One of the best ways to train new employees in the art of sales is to have them shadow your best salesperson for a few days.

Ongoing Training

If employees want more out of work than just a paycheck, what are those things? One of them to be sure is additional skills. Today's workforce is so mobile and forward-looking that one of the best things you can do to create a semblance of loyalty is to train employees well and add to their skill set. By so doing, you will increase your employee retention rate and also create a better business. *Inc.* magazine puts it this way: "Make 'train to retain' your company mantra."

Beyond retention, there is much more to be gained by adopting an ongoing training program:

- You create a stronger, more business savvy workforce.
- You build loyalty.
- You create a stronger "bench," that is, a better pool of people to promote from within.
- You reduce layoffs; rather than letting someone go, some additional training may solve the problem and avoid the hassle of having to train someone new from scratch.

As I have said, small businesses can learn plenty from, and emulate, larger businesses. KPMG, one of the world's largest accounting firms, is dedicated to ongoing training. According to its literature, "Our training doesn't stop between the major events of an individual's career. We offer an ongoing program to help keep KPMG people sharp and up-to-speed. These additional training programs include: technical updates, industry conferences and enabling skills training. For you, this thorough, comprehensive and continual training process helps ensure that your skills and abilities always fit perfectly with the teams you join."

Ongoing training can take many forms. The most popular are additional computer skills, financial management, technical training for individual occupations, and career path training. None of these need cost a fortune.

The California Chamber of Commerce conducted a survey of 100 of the most successful small businesses in that state. One of the questions it asked was this: The real key to business success is:

- Hard work and perseverance
- Fine products and service
- Advertising
- Knowing the fundamentals of business
- Employees

What was the most popular answer? The last one.

Training Managers

Not only do regular employees need adequate training, managers do too, maybe more. Managing people is not something that always comes naturally, so the more you can help them help your staff, the more successful everyone will be. Because managers are already motivated to succeed they are in the position they are in, but managers do need to be taught how to coach, as essentially, that is their job. They need to prod, push, and praise just so, in order to bring out the best in their people.

How do they do that? Four traits you can teach can help any manager be more successful:

1. *Listen.* Is it true that Ernest Hemingway was referring to managers when he said, "Most people never listen"? Probably not, but he could have been. Managers are wont to talk, too much usually. If you can get a manager to listen to what your employees say, they will probably begin to listen to what the manager has to say. Respect breeds respect.
2. *Ask.* No one likes being told what to do, and this is even truer as employees get older. Managers will get far more from your staff if they avoid the barking orders and ask for help, instead.

3. *Be reasonable.* Of course a manager has to be assertive and get the job done, but you usually get better results with honey than with vinegar.

4. *Prioritize.* Great leaders set priorities and enlist people around them to get those priorities accomplished.

Maybe the best management book ever written was *The One Minute Manager*. In it, authors Ken Blanchard and Stuart Johnson explain the value of one minute goals, one minute praising, and one minute reprimands. It works this way: Managers create a one-page set of goals for each employee summarizing the top 20 percent of tasks for that employee. The employee then gets to work and the manager follows up consistently, giving either one minute behavior-based (not personal) praise, or one minute behavior-based reprimands. Both praise and reprimands keep employees going in the right direction.

Training Techniques

Properly training your staff and managers need not be boring, as people learn best when they are engaged. Accordingly, any small business looking to improve its training should consider doing something more than lectures alone. For example, you might try:

Shadowing. As mentioned, sending people into action with already trained employees is a fast way to get someone up to speed.

Videos. Because people recall what they see, videotapes can be a very effective training method for employees and managers alike. Videos can teach people how to sell, how to open and close, how to spot and deal with potential theft, how to motivate, and so on.

Role-playing. Staff members can take turns pretending to be the thief, or the reluctant customer, or the irritated patron. You can then show them the proper way to handle these situations.

The Internet. Online training is a booming business, and convenience and low cost are two reasons. Do a search, and discover how many options there are.

Review. Have staff contribute botched sales calls or success stories to the class to use as examples.

The bottom line is that your commitment to training and education can retain employees, help them provide better service, boost morale, and increase sales. All in all, it is a pretty good idea.

MOTIVATION

There are two ways to motivate employees: with money and without money.

Money Motivators

It is no secret that money motivates employees. Sales contests, offering bonuses, and dangling raises are tried-and-true ways to motivate people. The benefits package you offer is a similar motivator, which begs the question: Why does it take money to motivate an employee? Because the possibility of making more money transforms the employee into an entrepreneur, which is based on the premise that hard work and ingenuity will be rewarded. Isn't that how you think? "If I implement that plan, we could increase sales by 10 percent!" Well, that is precisely what an employee thinks when offered a money motivator. "If I sell more than anyone else this month, I win that trip to Hawaii!" So the secret to motivating with money is to tap into, and use, this mind-set for mutual benefit.

First, you can always link an employee's pay to performance. That is exactly how commissioned salespeople work. Similarly, you could link bonuses with desired outcomes. For example, you might offer your director of operations a nice bonus if he can reduce overhead by 10 percent for the year. A manager might get 10 percent of any increased revenues for his store for the month. There are many ways to structure such a compensation program.

The most important thing when creating a money-motivated system is that the reward is linked to an outcome that the employee can control. The director of operations can directly affect overhead but cannot increase sales, so a reward based on increased sales would not work with him. If the reward is based upon overall company performance, the employee will only be motivated to try harder if he can affect overall company performance. As long as the reward and the desired action are linked, the motivation will be there.

> Contests are a wonderful way to build excitement and create desired behaviors and outcomes. Successful contests use realistic, achievable goals, are limited to a short period of time, have desirable prizes, link rewards to performance, and have uncomplicated rules.

Motivation on a Shoestring

Employees who are disengaged usually have a reason. The Gallup Organization's annual survey of employment has found that employees are unmotivated when they do not know what is expected of them, when they feel stagnant in their work, and when they do not feel appreciated. People also lose enthusiasm for a job when it becomes boring and routine, when bosses are clueless, and when their employer seems to care more about money than people.

So if you want to motivate employees without money, the first thing is to engage them. Learn what excites a problem employee workwise and begin to foster that. This individualized approach is the opposite of what many managers do—notice the problem and try to fix it. That motivates no one. What motivates people is feeling appreciated as individuals and contributing what they have to offer.

There are many simple ways to motivate people, to have them feel appreciated, without spending a lot of money:

- *Show appreciation.*   Thanking employees for a job well done is so simple, yet so effective. Thanks can take many forms: a pat on the back from a manager, a call from the president, a special parking spot for a week, a night out with your team, increased territory, a massage and facial, or a round of golf. FedEx inscribes the names of special employees' children on the nose of new planes to thank the employee for a job well done. How often do you see a plaque naming the Employee of the Month?
- *Recognize them.*   Letting everyone else know that someone did a great job works wonders. A survey by the Minnesota Department of Natural Resources found that 68 percent of employees said that being appreciated was important to their job satisfaction. At Blanchard Training in Escondido, California, praise from customers or managers is reprinted in the company newsletter. What about sending a press release regarding an accomplishment to your trade journal?
- *Ask for input.*   Listening to employee ideas, and taking them, makes people feel like they are part of a team and that what they say makes a difference. At Grumman Corporation in New York, employees whose suggestions are implemented get gift certificates. Fel-Pro of Skokie, Illinois, has a yearly drawing for $1,000 for all employees who participated in the employee suggestion program.
- *Offer freebies.*   Employees who do something above and beyond the call of duty can be given an afternoon off, or a gift certificate to Nordstrom's, or tickets to a game. At H.B. Fuller Company in St. Paul, employees get a paid day off on their birthday. Mary Kay Cosmetics gives the birthday girl a lunch voucher for two.
- *Make yours a special place to work.*   What about having a massage therapist come by every other week for a complimentary 15-minute back massage at employees' desks? What about an in-house yoga class? Have a yearly picnic with spouses and children. Organize a rafting trip down the river. None of these cost a lot, but all would be appreciated, and appreciation *is* motivation.

Be creative. Take suggestions. Employees are much more motivated when they enjoy their workplace. A few changes can reap
tremendous rewards.

According to Michael LeBoeuf, author of *The Greatest Management Principle in the World* , the Top Ten rewards for good work are: (1) money, (2) recognition, (3) time off, (4) ownership shares, (5) favorite work, (6) promotion, (7) freedom, (8) personal growth, (9) fun, (10) prizes.

CREATING AN EXCEPTIONAL CULTURE

Training and motivating your staff can take you only so far. At the
end of the day, what will make a difference is the culture of your
small business. All businesses have a culture, some by design, most
by default. A negative culture is created by employees who feel un-
appreciated, by workplaces that are unharmonious, by managers and
bosses who are incompetent.

On the other hand, if you communicate a sense of direction, of mission, if you foster teamwork and cooperation and fun, you begin to create a positive culture, a place where people want to work. Your
corporate culture should be a reflection of your goals and ideals. Creating this sort of culture allows employees to act appropriately, to understand what you are trying to accomplish, and to implement that vision
in their own unique way. It gives work meaning, gives employees direction, and in the end, it boosts profits.

So how do you do create a superior culture? Start by having a
mission.

The Mission Statement

We have all seen them: Mission statements seemingly created by force
at some corporate retreat, prominently displayed, cockeyed, on some
wall somewhere, meaning nothing to no one. But a real mission statement, if done correctly, can actually be a very effective business tool be-

cause it tells you, your employees, and your customers just what your business is really all about and where it is supposed to be headed. Knowing your mission also helps everyone know whether their daily activities and policies are helping or hurting the cause, not only keeping you focused, but also helping employees understand what is expected of them.

You can create a mission statement by answering the following questions:*

- What personal values do you want to be embodied in your business?
- What qualities and characteristics should be best exemplified by your business?
- What resources are at your disposal?
- What is your niche?
- What is your grand vision for your business (think BIG!)
- Based upon your values, vision, characteristics, and resources, what is the purpose of your business?
- Which of your personal qualities do you want to be infused into the business?
- How can your business best serve your clients, family, employees, and investors?
- How much money do you want to make? What are your markets? Who are your customers? What is your responsibility and commitment to them?
- Are you willing to commit to your mission, your vision, your dream? Are you willing to pay the price, whatever that is?

Based upon your answers, based upon your values, dreams, plans, niche, resources, and market, draft a mission statement (between 50 and 400 words) that incorporates any or all of these. Make it large, bold, and fantastic, something you believe in with all of your heart. Surrender to your purpose.

---

*Excerpted with permission from the Speaking Success System by Burt Dubin, the No. 1 Speaking Success Resource in the World. www.speakingsuccess.com.

Missions and Culture

A mission statement that you actually believe in is the first step toward creating a superior corporate culture. Here are six more things you can do to create a valuable business culture:

1. *Have clear goals and values and live by them.*   Businesses usually set goals but just as often lose track of them. Successful small businesses, however, have a plan of action that they get the entire team to buy into. Think about what your business values and goals are, and then enlist your people into living them on a daily basis. Your mission statement is a good place to start.

2. *Communicate.*   If you communicate what you want and expect, if you listen to what they want and expect, and if you involve employees in decision-making process, people begin to own the results. Communication could be a quarterly state-of-the-business report, or it could be a one-on-one meeting devoted to career goals. The important thing is that employees hear what is going on, know where things are headed, and feel free to offer feedback and suggestions.

3. *Make employees feel that they are part of a team.*   A sense of teamwork creates a superior business culture. Go to a game together. Help a charity together. At McKormick & Company in Baltimore, employees are encouraged to work one extra Saturday a year for the charity of their choice. They donate their pay for the day to that charity and the company matches their pay dollar for dollar. Ninety percent of employees participate.

4. *Reward your staff.*   This chapter is about rewards. Whether they are big (profit sharing) or small (a gift certificate), rewarding employees makes a big difference.

> *1001 Ways to Reward Employees*, by Bob Nelson is a great book chock full of easy ways to reward your staff.

5. *Demand excellence.*   Demand the best of yourself and look for the best in others. Reward excellence. Have fun. Do your best, help

employees do their best, and work together to create results of which to be proud.

6. *Have fun.* The whole point of leaving the corporate world and striking out on your own is to create a business that you love. Sure it can be serious and stressful and difficult and demanding. But do not lose the forest for the trees. Workplaces where employees are encouraged to do their work *and* have fun have been shown to be more productive than places where work is everything. See the book *Fish! A Remarkable Way to Boost Morale and Improve Results* by Stephen C. Lundin to learn more.

Finally, beware of negative influences. Employees who are bored, or berated, or who are not challenged, or who are unhappy are people who can sabotage your business. They need to get on board or get off the bus.

Implementing even a few of these ideas can go a long way toward building a small business that will not only be a great place to work, but will prosper in the process.

CHAPTER **29**

Extraordinary Sales and Exemplary Customer Service

> Every sale has five basic obstacles: No need, no money,
> no hurry, no desire, no trust.
>
> —ZIG ZIGLER

People can make or break your small business. The preceding chapter was about caring for the internal people you work with, your employees. This chapter is about caring for the external people who make your business possible, your customers. If you take care of both constituencies, then small business success is yours.

SALES

You probably know a thing or two about sales by now or you would not still be in business. But even so, sales are one of those areas where even the smallest little trick or new idea, once implemented, can reap surprising rewards. Brian Tracy, maybe the world's best salesperson, tells the story of how his first sales job was selling soap door-to-door to earn his way to YMCA Camp. He heard rejection after rejection until he oh-so-slightly rephrased his sales pitch. Instead of asking, "Would you like to buy a box of soap?" he said instead that he was selling soap, but that "it was only for beautiful women." Thereafter he says, getting to camp was a breeze. So yes, the smallest sales secret can often make the biggest difference. Let's look at some sales secrets and strategies that may make a difference for you.

Rapport

Rapport, once established, will make your sales almost effortless, because one of the obstacles mentioned by Zig Zigler in the opening quote will have disappeared: lack of trust. Once you create rapport with someone, he begins to trust you, and with trust, walls and reasons melt away.

One sales strategy suggests that if you quietly mimic your customer's intonation and physical movements you will subconsciously create rapport. This sure does seem sneaky. Consider instead building rapport the old-fashioned way: Be your best self, find things in common, and be friendly and helpful. People rarely buy from someone they do not like and, conversely, will go out of their way to buy from someone they do.

> One successful saleswoman says, "Your job is to create rapport, inform them about the product, avoid pressuring them, let them make an intelligent decision, and if they leave before buying, make sure they have everything they need (your phone number, e-mail address, brochures, and so forth) so they can easily make the purchase later on."

One of the best ways to build rapport is to focus on the needs of the customers. They are there, wanting to buy, for a reason. Customers have needs or wants they think you may be able to fill. If you can focus on those, and if they get that what you are really interested in is fulfilling those needs or desires, then the sale becomes exponentially that much easier.

Ask questions, and then actually listen to the answer. Salespeople often make the mistake of falling in love with their own voice, convinced that if they spin just one more angle, the sale will be theirs. Actually, the opposite is usually true. If you listen at least as often as you talk, sales usually increase. In fact, master salesman Tom Hopkins says, "The human body has two ears and one mouth. To be good at persuading or selling, you must learn to use those natural devices in proportion. Listen twice as much as you talk and you'll succeed in persuading others nearly every time." When asking questions, keep in mind that

- Questions that require a yes or no answer do not add much either to your knowledge or to your rapport.
- Questions that relate to price or technical aspects of the product similarly do little to help.
- Open-ended questions that invite customers to explain their needs and motivation for buying do help.
- Asking follow-up questions, requiring more explanation, helps even more.

Go the Extra Mile

Because it costs so much more to create a new customer than to keep an old one, foster your relationships with your current clientele. Do your homework and keep up-to-date on where your customers are and what they need. A little extra effort into learning about a customer, for instance, by studying trends in their industry or knowing a bit about a competitor, can go a long way toward impressing that customer and keeping her around.

> Visualize a pickle or olive jar for a second. Think about that first pickle or olive. Getting the first one out of the jar takes some work, right? But once you get that first one out, all the other pickles or olives come out quite easily. So, too, in sales. Getting that first sale with a customer takes extra work, but once you get it, all subsequent sales with that customer come much easier.

Similarly, going the extra mile for potential customers can reel them in. There is the story of the sports agent who flew cross-country just for the chance to have a brief meet-and-greet with a potential client.

The sports star was so impressed that he signed up with the agent, concluding that kind of personal service was what he wanted from an agent.

Remember, it can take up to *six interactions* to close a sale. Going the extra mile means being willing to see a potential customer again and again, continuing to build rapport, until the sale is made.

Finally, going the extra mile also means following up. Thank-you notes and checking in to see if the product is working out build rapport for future sales.

The moral is that all sales are built on relationships.

Cold Calls

One of the hardest things to do in sales is to make an effective cold call, precisely because you have not yet established rapport. Here are a few tips to make cold calls easier:

- Begin with the right attitude. Know that cold calls are not easy but are valuable. Cold calling requires a competitive spirit.
- Before calling, smile, to put you in the right frame of mind.
- Remember that cold calling is a numbers game. Smile and dial, smile and dial.
- If they balk at setting up a meeting say something like, "All I need is 10 minutes of your time. I wouldn't waste my time coming all the way out to see you for 10 minutes if I didn't think it would really benefit us both."
- When asking for an appointment, do not say, "Can we meet next week?" Instead, be specific. Say something like, "How is next Thursday at 11:00 for you?"

Golf Lessons

If you have ever played even a little golf, you know that the harder you try, the less successful you are. But when you ease off the throttle a bit and trust your natural abilities, when you stop trying so hard, that is when the great shots appear. To a certain extent the same is true in sales. It is a paradox: Just as you make the great golf shot by not caring about the great golf shot, so too can you get the sale by not worrying about the sale. A customer can sense when a sale is your priority, and will back off accordingly. But once he is convinced you are more concerned with helping him solve his problem than being more concerned with selling, you will birdie the sale. Stop trying so hard.

Solve Problems

If you want to succeed in sales, you will focus on the benefits to the customer, on how your product solves their problem. *Do not* focus on your product's features. Benefits, not features, is Sales 101. When customers come in to buy a drill, what do they really want? They want a hole. The drill is a means to that end, so if you focus on the features of the drill (for example, its aluminum casing), you will miss the sale. Your customer does not care about your drill's aluminum casing; instead he needs to drill a hole. So if you focus on the benefits to the customer, if you show how well this drill could solve his need for a hole, the sale is yours.

This is true in any sales situation. Sure, the cool functionality of your product is nice, but that alone will not create a sale. Those things come into play only once the customer sees the product benefits him.

Once the customer sees that a product like yours can solve his problem, the next question inevitably is, "Why your product and not someone else's?" Once they have settled on this sort of product, people will buy from you if it is in their self-interest. Usually your product has

---

The purpose of a sales meeting is to help your sales staff sell more. Yet too many sales meetings become boring lectures and time wasters. The key to a successful sales meeting is to make it interesting, useful, and positive. Have an agenda and stick to it. Do not ramble. Start by congratulating and thanking them for something. Avoid chastising them. Do not make threats. Keep it upbeat. At least one positive war story should be a part of every meeting. Ask them for their opinions and find out what they are hearing from customers. Attendee participation in some form is a must. Employees want to feel respected. Consider bringing in a customer occasionally to explain why he or she buys from you. Finally, keep the meeting short and sweet. Meet for more than an hour and watch them fade out.

to be less expensive, faster, more convenient, or of higher quality. The smart salesperson will have several reasons ready when the customer gets to the "What is in it for me?" stage.

Sales Secrets of the Car Salesperson

Who better to learn sales from than a car salesperson? Despite their unseemly reputations, car salespeople know how to sell, almost better than anyone else. So do they have some secrets to impart? You bet.

To the car salesperson, selling is a game, and it is a game they play for a very good reason—it works. The goal of the car sales game is to sell you a car at the highest possible price, today, and they do so by enlisting you in their game and by getting you to play by their rules. That is their first valuable lesson: The best salespeople consider selling a game, not a chore. The right attitude can take you far.

How is the game played? Using several pre-planned steps:

Step One. The car salesperson gets you to trust her: Car salespeople are nice and friendly because they know that creating rapport with you is essential. Once they create rapport, trust occurs. She then starts to ask some seemingly innocent questions, but innocent they are not. In only a few minutes, the salesperson can learn:

- Whether you are ready to buy, and if so, how much you have to spend
- How much you know about the product
- How much you know about the game

Step Two. She starts to get you excited. That small talk and those innocent questions allowed the salesperson to learn some valuable things about you, especially regarding what benefits you think are important. So, like some Tiger Woods of sales, she casually takes you to a car she thinks you might like and does the walk-around, discussing the things she has concluded are probably important to you: safety, color, roominess, and so on.

Next, she invites you to sit in the car. Why is that? There is a phenomenon in the car business called "taking mental ownership." The longer you sit in the driver's seat, smelling and touching the car, the more invested in the car you become.

> Some real estate professionals have their own name for this same concept, called "falling under the ether." Once a real estate agent has learned what a client is looking for, he immediately schedules tours of appropriate properties. Before long, during some walk-through somewhere, the client usually finds a house he or she loves, and becomes invested in owning it. They have "fallen under the ether."

Step Three. This is critical; the salesperson gets you emotionally invested in the car. How does she do that? You know. She asks you if you want to take a test drive. Test-driving a car is fun and exciting. The salesperson knows that when you get excited about a car you will be more apt to make an emotional, rather than a logical, decision. Sure, the car may be nice, and yes, it may be the one you want, but even so, making a $20,000 decision based upon a 10-minute test drive is illogical. Yet it happens every day because car salespeople get patrons excited about the purchase.

Step Four. Create a sense of urgency. Maybe you are told, "The boss wants this car off the lot" so a special deal is available, or "Someone is coming by this afternoon to look at it again." You would be foolish not to buy NOW.

Yes, some car salespeople are too pushy, but not all are, and most know what they are doing. By playing the game to some extent, they sell cars, lots of cars. So you might want to learn the game, too. It is as simple as creating rapport, finding out what the customer wants, getting him or her emotionally invested in the sale, and then giving an incentive to make the purchase today. Try playing the game and see if you don't sell a few "cars" in the process.

What about that step in the car buying process when the salesperson goes to talk to his manager? Usually, they are just discussing strategy; trying to figure out how to get you to raise your offer. The manager then comes out and explains why your offer is too low. This authority figure becomes the person who can make the deal happen, and usually does. The lesson for you is that it might help sales too if you add a closer to your sales process.

The Sales Presentation

Of course, sales the car salesperson way can work only in certain situations. Just as often, a more professional approach is required, and sales presentations are the standard method, which is a five-fold process:

1. Create rapport.
2. Introduce the topic or product.
3. Ask questions to see what they need.
4. Highlight benefits.
5. Ask for the sale.

While the process is simple, what makes it work is preparation. Organize your presentation, prepare your selling points, and consider possible objections. Creating rapport at the start may be the most important aspect of the presentation. Here is an easy way to create that rapport: Within the first few minutes of your presentation, ask the audience/group some questions they can easily answer. That dialogue builds rapport quickly. During the presentation, be sure to take plenty of notes, listen, and deal with negativity with positivity. "There is always a solution" should be your motto. Finally, ask for the sale. It might be as subtle as "well, how should we proceed?" or it might be more blunt; it depends on your style and how the presentation proceeded.

Here are two excellent ways to close a sale at the end of a sales presentation: First, offer a one-time incentive. "If you want to do this today, I will throw in an extra hour of my time for free." Second, offer a 100 percent money back guarantee.

CUSTOMER SERVICE

"Great customer service" is something we all hear about, something to which many small businesses give lip service, but is equally something few small businesses ever really incorporate into their daily way of doing business. Sure they try to treat their customers well, but that is not the same thing. For some, lack of real customer service is because the culture of the business is so hectic that employees are too rushed to take the extra effort with customers. For others, it just is not important. Yet offering excellent customer service is one of those things you can do that will distinguish you from the competition, and it need not be either expensive or cumbersome. By implementing a few changes, you may just see increased sales and a more loyal clientele.

Say that you own a little coffeehouse. A customer who buys coffee and a bagel from you once, or only every so often, is nice, but nothing special. His share of your total revenue for the year is about $5. But what about that customer who comes in three times a week? If he spends even $10 a week at your shop, that translates into $520 for the year. The repeat customer is your most valuable customer and it does not cost much to keep him.

But what it does take is customer service. For people to patronize your business three times a week for a year, or to become a regular customer of any sort, they have to feel welcome and appreciated. Customer service means that he is treated as an individual, treated well, is respected, and finds your shop easy, not difficult. The café customer is rewarded for his patronage: by getting good coffee and food, by being greeted by a friendly face, by someone knowing his name. According to Michael LeBoeuf, author of *How to Win Customers and Keep Them for Life*, "Fancy sales pitches, high-powered marketing strategies, and clever advertising can be very important attention getters. And they

---

Want to know how your employees treat your customers when you are not around? Hire a mystery shopper. She will come into your store, shop and buy, and then report back to you what she observed.

may persuade people to become your customer. But keeping customers for any period of time depends on how well you reward them."

If great customer service becomes part of your business culture, your business will be the better for it. You know one of those stores where "We love our customers!" is more than just an empty slogan. Those small businesses treat you well, exceptionally even, and you enjoy the experience. It is not hard to turn any small business into that prototype, but what it does take is commitment. Teaching employees how to treat customers right should become part of your initial and ongoing training, reinforced daily. Among the other things you might consider doing are these:

- *Reward customer service stars.*   Consider the restaurant that has a plaque in the lobby listing waiters and waitresses who had learned "100 customers' names." Lens Crafters gives employees bonuses for outstanding customer service.
- *Poll customers.*   Ask your customers for feedback regarding your business' customer service, and how it could be improved. Hand out surveys and find out what your customers like and dislike generally about your business. Customer service is not just about saying yes or handling complaints; it is also about making your store the best it can be to serve the needs of your clientele, and getting feedback from them is one easy way to do that.
- *Just say yes.*   When possible, do what the customer asks. Saying yes keeps them around.

Customer Disservice

Just as there is a way to treat customers right, so, too, is there a way to treat customers wrong. Yet far too often, what I call "customer disservice" creeps in. Here then are the Five Commandments of Customer Disservice.

1. *Thou shalt not put phone calls ahead of real customers.*   How often has this happened to you? You wait in line someplace, you get to the front, it is your turn, when suddenly the phone behind the counter rings and the person on the phone is suddenly more important than you. Actual people who visit your business in person are almost always more important than the phone callers. Make sure that your employees know that and are taught to treat your face-to-face customers with the respect they deserve.

2. *Thou shalt not become a nopey.* Do you remember Gumby? Gumby had a pal named Nopey. No matter what you said to him, no matter what you asked him, Nopey's answer was "No!" Sound familiar? Far too many employees flex their muscle by saying no. It gives them a sense of power. But the Nopey employee is a problem employee. They are the ones who anger already unhappy customers and they are the ones who turn customers into ex-customers.

3. *Thou shalt not be a strict constructionist.* In the law, a strict constructionist is one who says that laws and policies do not evolve, that the document as written must be strictly interpreted. While that might be a valid legal argument, it makes for poor customer service. Sometimes the smartest choice is to bend policy and make an exception. The customer will remember it, and your business will probably not be harmed by it.

> At Outback Steakhouse, if something is not to your liking, your waiter or waitress can fix it *without having to go to their manager*. He or she can give you a free drink, comp you a meal, or take other similar actions to make sure you are happy. Bending policy to make customers happy is the norm, not the exception, at Outback.

4. *Thou shalt not have bad manners.* Your customers should not be thanking you; you should be thanking them. Common courtesy and good manners can go far toward leaving your customers with a good impression of your business.

5. *Thou shalt welcome complaints.* Feedback from your customers, whether positive or negative, is one of the most valuable things your business can get. An SBA survey found that 95 percent of dissatisfied customers would do business with a business again if their problems were solved quickly and satisfactorily. So solving the customer's problem is your job, even if you disagree with his or her complaint.

When you get a complaint, the first thing to do is ask the customer how he or she would prefer the problem be resolved, and resolve it that way if possible. If he wants a refund, it is usually in your best interest to honor that request. If an employee is involved in a dispute, retrace the problem and provide the employee with retraining, if necessary. If you are convinced that your business is not at fault, apologize, offer something to placate him, and explain how he can avoid similar situations in the future.

Take care of your people and your people will take care of you.

Franchises

CHAPTER 30

Selecting the Right Franchise

In business for yourself, not by yourself.

—RAY KROC, FOUNDER OF THE
FIRST FRANCHISE, McDONALD'S

Starting a business from scratch is akin to baking bread from scratch. It takes trial and error, and several bad batches, before you figure out what works. On the other hand, starting out by buying a franchise is like getting a good recipe right from the start. Because the franchisor has already baked some bad loaves and has learned how to avoid repeating those mistakes, because the trial and error stage has already been handled by someone else, and because you will be buying, among other things, that expertise and wisdom, buying a franchise greatly reduces the risk inherent in entrepreneurship. There is less chance you will burn your bread and a greater chance to make some dough when you buy a franchise.

FRANCHISE BASICS

There are both pros and cons to buying a franchise. Let's consider each.

> Franchise terminology: The *franchisor* is the company offering its name and business system to the buyer, or *franchisee*. The business the franchisee buys is called the *franchise*.

Pros

Maybe the best part of buying a franchise is that you are buying into a (hopefully) proven system. Here is how it is supposed to work: Say that somewhere some business owners created a successful business they believed could be duplicated. The reasons and methods for their success were things that could be systematized and taught. So the business owners reduced their success to a step-by-step plan. That system, that business model, is the franchise. The idea is that if you do what they did, you will get the results they got. A good franchise, then, is a systematic way of doing business whereby you agree to do things the franchisor's way and are being allowed to use their business name, logo, system, and so on. So the first benefit of franchising is that you theoretically reduce your risk of failing as you are buying a proven system.

> To learn more, visit the International Franchise Association web site—www.Franchise.org.

However, reducing your risk is true only *if* you buy into the right system. Not all franchises are created equal, so do your homework before buying a franchise. This piece of advice is reiterated several times throughout this chapter, but it bears repeating: The very best thing you can do before buying any franchise is to talk to current franchisees. See how they like the system and the franchisor. Discover how much money they make (as opposed to what the franchisor might have represented). Find out if they would buy into the system again, knowing what they know now.

The second good thing about buying a franchise is that you should get plenty of help. Ray Kroc put it best: You might be in business for yourself, but with a franchise you are not in business by yourself. Whereas when you start a business from scratch you are on your own, when you start a franchise, the franchisor is there (or should be) to help you succeed. They offer expertise in a wide variety of areas. A good franchise system trains you to be a successful businessperson. Furthermore, there will be other franchisees in the system with whom you can learn from and work. That, too, should be a great resource.

The last benefit of franchising is that you will get assistance with your advertising and marketing, and with the bigger franchise systems, you will get the benefit of their national advertising campaign.

Cons

While the benefits of buying a franchise are significant, the downsides should not be minimized. The first is that it can be fairly expensive to buy a franchise because when you are buying one, you are buying the franchisor's name, logo, goodwill, expertise, system, and training. That can be worth a lot, especially to a well-known franchise. Although many are quite reasonable, just know that if you want to buy a name-brand franchise, you will pay for that right.

The second major drawback to franchising is that you will have less independence as a franchisee than you would as a regular entrepreneur. You will agree in your franchise contract to run your business according to the system, even if you don't agree with it. That ice cream franchisee who does not want to give free cones away one summer evening every year has to, if the franchisor says so. Because the franchisor trusts you with its brand and goodwill, you are supposed to do things their way.

This brings us to the last shortcoming with franchising. You will be in an unequal relationship with the franchisor. The very nature of the business arrangement, as well as the contracts you sign, put the franchisor in the power position. This is difficult for many franchisees, especially when something does not go right. There have been many lawsuits by franchisees against franchisors whom the franchisees feel are overreaching and domineering. Then again, there are plenty of franchisors with whom it is easy to work.

Remember there are good franchisors and bad ones, so it is in your best interest to do plenty of research so you can rest assured the company you decide to partner-up with is a good one.

RESEARCHING THE FRANCHISE

When starting your franchise analysis, start globally, then narrow it locally. Begin by looking at the universe of franchises available because there may be franchises that would be perfect for you, if only you start out thinking broadly. After that, you narrow down the choices to the ones you like best and think would work well in your area.

Begin by picking up a copy of the *Franchise Handbook*, or go online to www.FranchiseHandbook.com. The *Franchise Handbook* is a must-have quarterly publication that lists most franchises, what they are about, and what their fees are.

Attend a franchise expo in your area. These are held fairly regularly, and the *Franchise Handbook* site lists many of them. The problem with an expo, though, is that only a few franchisors of the thousands available will be there. But even so, it does give you a chance to get some face time with actual franchisors.

Here is what you want to discover when speaking with franchisors at a franchise trade show:

- What is the total investment required?
- Do they offer financing?
- What sort of training and support can you expect?
- What sort of advertising do they do?
- Are there some current franchisees with whom you could speak?

After looking at the franchise universe, narrow the choices down to a few industries that you like best and that seem to have the most potential. Which ones match you, your skills and interests, and your financial wherewithal best? Does there seem to be a market for that type of business in your area?

As you narrow your choices, start to contact those franchisors who seem like the best and request information. Visit their web sites. Just don't rely on those materials alone to make your decision. Find franchisees of the franchisors you like best and go speak with them. *The most important thing you can do in this process is to talk to current and former franchisees.* They can tell you what the franchisor is like to work with, what to be concerned about, and a whole lot more.

What to Look For

Of course you want a franchise that will be interesting and lucrative; that is a given. While you can never be guaranteed of that, there are traits the good franchisors have in common you should know about:

- *There is plenty of support.* The best franchise systems are the ones where the franchisor sees its relationship with the franchisees as a partnership. The former head of Pizza Hut, Steve Reinemund, puts it this way, "Franchisees are only as successful as the parent company and the parent company is only as successful as the franchisees." That is the attitude you want to see. Support can mean many things: extra assistance during difficult times; good communication at all times; and superior training and materials. The franchisor may help you select a site for your business, negotiate your lease, finance the fees, or provide other services. Support is an attitude that says the franchisor is only as successful as the franchisee.

Get all promises of support in writing.

What kind of support should you expect? This is typical:

- Local and national advertising.
- Support and feedback from a field representative.
- Updated operating manuals.
- Continuous training for you and your managers.
- Communication: newsletters, intranets, and e-mails are the most common.

- *Advertising is key.*   Not all franchises are dependent upon advertising, but enough are that this is an important distinction. New customers must come from somewhere, and a superior franchise system will help you get those new customers with its advertising campaign.
- *The franchisor is flexible.*   The nature of franchising is that there are processes and procedures to follow. That sort of uniformity is one of the things that make franchises attractive—customers know what to expect. And while that is good, franchise rigidity is not. You want a franchisor who understands that creativity and independence are part of being an entrepreneur, even a franchised entrepreneur. The good franchisors know that it is franchisees who often come up with the breakthrough idea. The Big Mac was invented by McDonald's franchisee Jim Delligatti in 1968. Avoid the rigid franchisor.
- *The franchisor keeps up.*   An offshoot of the preceding issue is that a flexible franchisor should also be a modern one. Tastes and values change, but not all franchises do. Look for a franchise system that puts money into research and development, constantly testing new products and ideas.
- *The franchisor has a solid reputation.*   Checking with past and current franchisees certainly helps, but do not stop there. Do an online search. Go to the library and find any articles discussing the franchisor. Contact the Federal Trade Commission to see if there have been any complaints about the franchisor.
- *The franchisor is fairly large.*   A large number of franchises is a good sign, indicating that the business model works and that the franchisor has a successful, established business. This is not to say that newer franchises with fewer units is a bad thing, only that they are less tried and true. A smaller, newer franchise is a bit more of a gamble, and one point of buying a franchise is to reduce the gamble factor.
- *The franchisor is franchisee-friendly.*   Buying a franchise is a long-term investment, so make sure the franchisor is someone you can work with.

NARROWING YOUR CHOICES

All of this research should enable you to narrow your choices down to a few select franchisors. Then it is time to set up some face to face meetings, where a few things should occur. First, you should get adequately answered every question you have. Get a feel for the franchisor, their system, and whether you are compatible. The last thing you want is to invest a lot of money and make a long-term legal commitment to a franchisor whose values and modus operandi are different from yours. Finally, at this initial meeting get a copy of the franchisor's Uniform Franchise Offering Circular (UFOC; see later).

What to Ask

By the time you have narrowed your choices to a select few franchises, you should have a slew of questions for each franchisor. Yes, you may be very excited and might be ready to get started, but slow down. Do not fall under the ether! Now is the time to be prudent and thoughtful, to be, well, a businessperson. You will want to discover:

- The total fees you will have to pay, for what, and when. Is financing available? If not, do they have a relationship with a lender with whom you can talk?
- Will you need to buy real estate? Do they help you find a location? Do they offer architectural blueprints for building the store? Do they have a deal with contractors with whom you can work?
- What sort of equipment is required? Do you buy or lease it? What are the initial and ongoing inventory requirements? Who is the supplier?
- How extensive is their training program? How long is the initial training, where does it take place, and when are follow-ups?
- What sort of advertising and marketing support do they offer? How much is the advertising fee?
- What sort of research and development program do they have?
- How long is the initial franchise agreement, how long is the renewal, and who has the option to renew? Can you sell or assign your franchise, if desired?

> Also ask how much money you reasonably can expect to make. But do not be
> surprised if they say they cannot tell you. That is probably true. If they say, for
> example, "You will make $80,000 a year," and you do not, then what? You
> might sue them for misrepresentation. Thus, most franchisors are tight-lipped
> about potential profit. You can gather this information, though, during your re-
> search phase, as you interview other franchisees.

The UFOC

By law, at the first in-person meeting where the subject of buying a
franchise is discussed, or at least 10 business days prior to signing any
franchise contract requiring a payment by the franchisee to the franchisor, the franchisor must present the potential franchisee with the
UFOC. The UFOC contains extensive information about the franchise
and is intended to give you a chance both to learn about the franchise
and to make a rational decision.

> Not only must you get the UFOC at least 10 days before signing any contracts,
> but you must receive a copy of all contracts at least 5 days before the signing
> as well.

The UFOC, though written in legal gobbledygook, has nevertheless
a wealth of information. There are 23 standard items in the document.
The important areas to concentrate on are these:

Number 2.   This section discusses the experience and background of the directors, officers, and managers of the franchisor.
Know thy franchisor!

Number 3.   Examines the litigation background of the franchisor, as well as the people listed in Number 2. Beware of excessive lawsuits, or regulatory actions by government entities. Be

on the lookout especially for lawsuits by franchisees against the franchisor.

Number 4.　This section will list any bankruptcies for either the business or the people mentioned in Number 2.

Numbers 5, 6, 7, and 10.　This is where you discover the money commitment. Franchise fees, ongoing royalties, and the estimate of the total investment can be found here. Item 10 discusses whether financing is available.

Number 11.　This section is critical. It discusses the franchisor's obligations to you, such as training and so forth.

Number 19.　This section is not required by law, but if it is present, it will discuss potential profits.

Number 20.　Also important, this section details the number of franchisees that have either entered or left the system recently. Importantly also, this section lists the names, addresses, and telephone numbers of current and past franchisees. That alone makes the UFOC very valuable.

Number 21.　This is the section to review with your CPA. Here you will find three years' worth of audited financial statements.

FEES

There are usually four costs associated with buying a franchise. The first is the franchise fee. This is what you pay to buy into the system, use their logos, get trained, and so forth. The franchise fee might be as little as $2,500 for a small, unknown franchise or it might be $50,000 for a well-known outfit. Second, you will pay an ongoing royalty of between three percent and six percent of gross sales per month to the franchisor. Third, expect to pay some monthly or quarterly fee for the advertising pool.

The last cost is usually the largest one, the amount it will cost you to build out the store (if it is a retail franchise) in accordance with the franchisor's mandates. Again, this could be minimal, or it could be $500,000 or more. Why so much? Here are some of the things you may have to pay for:

Real estate. You may have to buy land and a building and put down security and utility deposits.

Design fees. You may need an architect to draft plans for your store.

Construction fees. This can include everything from constructing the building to remodeling and landscaping.

Equipment and fixtures. You may need to buy tables, chairs, telephones, display counters, computer systems, and cash registers.

Décor. Signs, pictures, lights, and interior design may be required.

Other costs associated with opening your doors might include:

Inventory. You have to stock the shelves.

Insurance. You will need worker's compensation, property, liability, property, and other insurance.

Labor costs. Your staff may be required to get initial training from the franchisor.

Costs vary widely. McDonald's estimates that new restaurant costs range from $455,000 to $768,500. Subway estimates that new restaurant costs range from $97,000 to $222,800. ServiceMaster says that its capital requirements range from $10,200 to $52,000.

THE FINAL DECISION

Do not be intimidated by the costs previously listed. Constructing a standalone restaurant franchise is an expensive proposition, but the vast majority of franchises are not standalone restaurants. There are literally thousands of choices out there. If you do your homework, you can find one that has a solid reputation, offers a fair return on your investment, is interesting to you, and is affordable. Good luck!

CHAPTER **31**

Franchise Success Secrets

The secret of success is to know something nobody else knows.

—ARISTOTLE ONASSIS

Running a successful franchise, indeed running any successful business, requires several traits and abilities. Yes, working hard and working smart count a lot, but other equally important factors go into the business success equation. Some, like strong sales skills, are seemingly obvious. Others, such as exceptional employee relations, are not so clear-cut. In this chapter the secrets of the best franchisees are yours for the taking.

SURVEY SAYS

Fred Berni is the President of Dynamic Performance Systems Inc., a company that helps franchisors select successful franchisees. Franchisors have a vested interest in finding strong franchise candidates, Berni says, because unsuccessful franchisees lead to franchisor aggravation, employee morale problems, unflattering media exposure, and possible lawsuits. So franchisors want to find and recruit potential franchisees who have a high likelihood of success.

In an effort to help his clients, Berni and a staff of psychologists undertook a survey of hundreds of franchisees over a several year period in many different industries. Asking more than 600 questions covering a wide range of attitudes, personality traits, and skills, the study examined how and why successful franchisees differed from less successful ones. The purpose of the study, Berni says, was to, "find a way to identify which candidates had the greatest likelihood for success, identify whether personality characteristics could predict performance, and identify what the mystery 'other factors' are."

> "Some years ago, I became aware of the frustrations that franchise professionals had in predicting how well a particular candidate would eventually perform. My clients told me, and research backed their claims up, that personality seemed to have no great track record in predicting performance. Obviously, there must be other factors in place of or in addition to personality at work here. So I decided to find out what these other factors were."—Fred Berni. www.franchise-profiles.com.

The results were illuminating, to say the least. The first interesting thing that the survey discovered was that, as Berni says, "Attitudes, not personality, are the best predictors of franchisee performance. Beliefs drive results." Berni's survey found that successful franchisees shared many common core values and attitudes. Though a franchisee's personality and skill-set were important, they paled in comparison to having the right attitudes and values. "Initially, we were somewhat surprised to learn that preexisting skill-sets had no predictive value. Upon further reflection though, this makes perfect sense. After all, every franchisor trains candidates in those skill-sets necessary to actually run the business," he says.

So just what attitudes and values make a difference that separate the excellent from the mediocre franchisee? Hang on, because the results, listed in order of importance, are illuminating.

1. *Successful franchisors involve their employees in the business.*
Maybe the most fascinating fact is that the way a franchisor treats

his employees is *the single most important factor in determining franchise success*. The survey found that:

- Successful franchisees truly believe that their employees are a valuable business asset, not a burden or business expense.
- Successful franchisees manage in a participative, as opposed to domineering, style.
- Successful franchisees treat employees with decency and respect.

Because of such enlightened thinking, franchisees who do treat their employees right tend to have less staff turnover, fewer hiring expenses, more contented employees, a happier workplace, and, thus, more loyal customers. Happy employees offer better customer service, which in turn translates into increased profits. Conversely, if your employees think you are a jerk, will they go out of their way to make a customer happy? If you do not help your employees, they figure, why should they help you?

2. *Successful franchisees are optimistic.* Having a positive outlook on life generally and your franchise in particular have been found to be major factors in franchisee success. It is not difficult to figure out how this attitude translates into day-to-day activities. If valuing your employees creates happier employees, which in turn equals happier customers, the same will be true for optimistic, positive franchisors. That positivity filters down through all areas of the business, raining light on everything and everyone associated with the business.

3. *Successful franchisees are moderately independent.* Yes, the nature of the franchisor-franchisee relationship is one where independence is not a paramount virtue. But surprisingly it is those franchisees who, in fact, are somewhat independent, who have ideas and try them out, who think for themselves and are self-determining who are most successful. The best franchisees find a balance between following the system and being entrepreneurial. Balance is the key. The good news is that you do not have to be a corporate clone to be a successful franchisee.

4. *Successful franchisees are adept at sales and marketing.* This trait is linked to the independence factor. Franchisees who are most successful do not just wait for business to appear, or for their franchisor to roll out a new marketing campaign. The most successful franchisees work at becoming knowledgeable businesspeople. They learn new marketing tricks and try them out, schmooze and sell, network and pitch products. They know sales is a game and one they enjoy playing.

The best franchisees take off their manager hat and do not expect their staff to do all the selling. The excellent franchisees are out there, in the store, talking to customers, making suggestions, and making the sale, too, knowing that if they have a "selling attitude" their employees will, too.

All of these traits are not just amorphous attitudes but are beliefs that create actions promoting success and sales.

5. *Successful franchisees are sociable.*   Business is a social game, and the best franchisees know that. Although you cannot really help being an introvert or an extrovert, being extroverted and gregarious directly affects the bottom line. Employees like you better and relationships with customers are strengthened.

> Are you introverted by nature? Do you find selling difficult? Sorry, but too bad. If you are going to be successful in your franchise, you will need to lead by example. Fake it 'til you make it. Since your staff takes their cues from you, if they see you being quiet, this will become the corporate culture of the business.

Therefore, franchisees who are most successful know that people come first. If they treat their people right, other things fall into place. It is the franchisee who is dictatorial, resentful, restless, or negative who has the least chance of success.

OTHER FACTORS

Aside from the traits, attitudes, and actions previously listed, several other factors foster franchisee success.

Successful Franchisees Follow the System

No, this is not contradictory to the precept mentioned earlier, that independence is important. If you were not independent, you would never have gone into business for yourself. But you did buy into your franchise for a reason, and evidence shows that successful franchisees follow the system.

Becoming a franchisor and creating a successful operating system are no small feats. Not only must franchisors have created a successful business to start with, but they had to have been able to reduce that success to a repeatable, teachable system. By the time you bought your franchise, the hood on that system had been up many times, and the engine that is the system had been tinkered with, analyzed, fine-tuned, turbocharged, and perfected. Mistakes had been made long since, funny noises had been fixed, and the bugs had been worked out. The system is what it is for some very good reasons.

If you do what they did, you should get what they got; that is the plan. If you wanted to do things your way, then starting a business from scratch and being a prototypical entrepreneur would have been a better choice. But if you are at a place where you already went a different route and bought a franchise, then it would behoove you to get with the program.

Be a Jack-of-All-Trades

Clay Werts is a no-nonsense man with salt-and-pepper hair who has been a very successful franchisee for more than two decades. An owner of three Baskin Robbins franchises, all popular, Werts has some strong beliefs, learned in the trenches, about what it takes to make it in the franchise game. He is, first of all, a big believer in the axiom, "If you are a jack-of-all-trades and a master of none, you are most likely to be a success." Why is that? He says that running a franchise requires many different skills: promotion, management, financial, and so on. Being able to handle all the different facets of the business is critical, he says.

To illustrate his point, Werts talks about the couple he knew who owned (notice, past tense) an ice cream store not far from his. The husband was the king of promotions and the wife the queen of ice cream decorations. Yet they went out of business within a year. According to Werts, although the couple did two things well, that was all they did well. The couple were especially bad at cash management. The money they made in the summer was not saved for the inevitable downturn an ice cream shop has in the winter. Cash management is as important as marketing is as important as a beautiful product.

> Clay Werts is also a big believer in the power of having a good location. You can stay in business with a great location, he says, even if you are not the best businessperson. But if you have a bad location, no matter how good a businessperson you are, your possibilities are inherently limited.

What is his final piece of advice for franchise success? "Think big," he says. "If you are an optimist, are willing to take a risk, and work your tail off, anyone can make it."

Advertising and Marketing

Superior franchisees are proactive when it comes to creating business. They accept the challenge of finding new customers, relish it almost. Of course they like and benefit from the franchisor's efforts, but they know they cannot rely solely on what the franchisor does. "If it's to be, it's up to me" might be their motto.

Too often, franchisees either fail to advertise sufficiently or their advertising is wasted on an unfocused approach that fails to zero-in on the people who are ready, willing, and able to purchase their products or service. Instead of marketing to their specific audience, these franchisees target a broad audience in an attempt to reach everybody, but usually reach nobody.

> One famous advertising executive once remarked that the best ad he ever saw read, "Farm fresh eggs available today!" The tight ad conveyed a feeling ("farm fresh"), the product (eggs), and a call to action (fresh today only, supposedly).

To avoid this unenviable fate is easy. Know your target market. Know who your customers are, what they like to watch, read, and listen to, what they buy and why, and how you fill those needs. Then, picking the vehicle to deliver your message to that market becomes much easier. Knowing their audience up front, and actively and consistently marketing to that audience is a hallmark of successful franchisees.

Location, Location, Location

We have all seen them—McDonald's, Pizza Huts, Taco Bells, Olive Gardens, and Hardees lined up in a row down the street like so many dominos. Then you pull into the mall, visit the food court, and there they are again—Sbarro's Pizza, Dairy Queen, Orange Julius, and Edo, all awaiting your business. Why is that? Do they not cannibalize one another's business by being so close together? The surprising answer is usually no.

By building near one another, many successful franchisees have found that, rather than fostering competition, being close builds business. There can be a synergy when you locate your franchise near other franchises; you create a destination. But to succeed in this environment, your business has to be very good, because if it is not, the competition will eat you alive. Tough, yes, but having a busy location is worth it.

The moral of the story? Whether your franchise lends itself to a cluster model or not, for the retail franchisee, location makes a big difference.

PART

VII

Home-Based Businesses

CHAPTER 32

The Home-Based Business

There's no place like home.

—DOROTHY

Working from home is an attractive option to many. Avoiding the overhead of an office, working from a place they enjoy, and chucking the rat race can indeed be great, and do not forget that easy commute to the extra bedroom. But having a home-based business is not all milk and honey, not by a long shot. While your chances of having a successful business increase if you work from home due to the lower overhead, there are nevertheless challenges aplenty when you work from home. Here we explore the promise and problems of the home-based business.

MAKING THE DECISION

There are two types of home-based businesses. First, there is the one that started with the intention that it will remain a home-based business. Because working at home can be easy, pleasant, and inexpensive, many people start their business from home because that is where they intend to be for the long haul. The second sort of home-based business is the one where people start their business from home with the intent to move it out as soon as it is economically feasible. These entrepreneurs know that the startup phase of a business is critical, money is usually tight, and that starting their venture from home allows them to earmark their precious capital on things other than on rent and commuting. It, too, is a smart strategy.

If you work in a home office or otherwise spend a lot of time sitting down, you may suffer from back pain. Well, the Moller Orthopedic Back Support may be just what the doctor ordered. The business began in the home of its founder and president, Frederik Wendelboe, who planned to move to an outside office as soon as it was feasible (it took about a year). Wendelboe's business brainstorm began after he was introduced to a secret European design superior to anything else on the market. "I have always had an entrepreneurial bent and was committed to creating a great business. The Moller Back Support allowed me to do just that," says Wendelboe. His unique angle was to get empirical evidence that his product was truly superior, so he had it subjected to extensive laboratory testing. Moller can now say that theirs is the only *medically proven* back support system for the relief of back pain. Clinical tests confirmed that it significantly reduces strain and pain throughout the lumbar region, and people who sit all day typically say that it makes them feel more energized. Wendelboe created the best back support on the market, starting from home (www.mollersupport.com).

Whether you already have a business that you are considering moving into the home or are thinking about starting a home-based business from scratch, know that it takes a certain temperament and an iron will to be successful at it. Do you make the cut? Let's find out. Take the following quiz. For every yes answer give yourself five points. For every no answer, give yourself zero points.

1. Do you have space at home to create a private office?
2. Are you self-disciplined enough to work when your family is around?

3. Do you have, or can you get, the technology required to run a modern home-based business: a separate phone line, e-mail, cell phone, and fax machine?
4. Are you willing to work alone, cut off from old colleagues and associates?
5. Are you self-disciplined enough to avoid going to the refrigerator, television, or Internet throughout the day?
6. Does your business model lend itself to working by yourself at home?
7. Are there minimal distractions at home: no noisy neighbors, loud babies, or intrusive friends with nothing else to do but hang out with you?
8. Will your customers still take you seriously if you work from home?
9. Are you excited about the possibility of working from home?
10. Does your family support your plan to work from home?

Scoring

35 and up: You have both the temperament and support necessary to work from home.
20 to 35: You might be able to start a successful home-based business, but be sure to line up all your ducks.
Below 20: Working from home is not for you.

The Home Business Boom

It has never been easier or more popular to work from home. Technology has made it so that the home-based entrepreneur has all the tools he needs not only to succeed, but to look like a pro in the process. Computers, laser printers, web sites, digital voice mail, and the like allow any small, home-based entrepreneur to look and act like a sophisticated, major operation. Moreover, attitudes have shifted so that working from home is often viewed more with envy rather than curiosity, as in days past. Combined, these changes in technology and attitudes have created a seismic shift in how work is done, meaning that more and more people are moving their office into their house.

Number of Part-Time or Full-Time Home-Based Businesses in the United States	
Year	Number of Home-Based Businesses (in the millions)
2000	20.3
2001	21.8
2002	23.3
2003	25
2004	26.1
2005 (estimated)	27
Source: International Data Corporation	

If present trends continue, it is estimated that within 10 years one of every three households will have someone working from home. *Entrepreneur* magazine estimates that almost $500 billion is generated each year by home-based businesses. In a recent survey, the SBA discovered that almost 25 percent of all home-based businesses had a yearly gross income between $100,000 and $500,000.

So yes, these days, working from home has a bit of a cachet. It is hip. It is also smart. One of the main advantages of starting a business from home, either initially or for the long-term is that it dramatically reduces your overhead, which is significant. Another trait that successful small businesses have in common is that they keep a close eye on the bottom line. This is not to say they are cheap; rather, frugal might be a better word. These businesses know that if spending gets out of hand, profits are hard to maintain. So a home-based business makes a lot of business sense since major expenses such as rent, labor, and travel are almost nonexistent, so the potential for success is greater.

Pros and Cons

Just as there are pros and cons associated with buying a franchise, so, too, are there pros and cons regarding the home-based business option.

Pros. First, as indicated, because home-based businesses are less expensive to operate, starting a home-based business is practical, doable. Finding the funding to buy an expensive food franchise, for example, is a very difficult task. But starting a small business from home is very, very affordable. Moreover, not only is your rent less, but you put less mileage on your car, have less need to wear out expensive clothes, and enjoy significant tax deductions.

Secondly, people who work at home tend to like working at home. They are a happy lot. A *Prevention* Magazine survey found that home-based businesspeople say they eat healthier, have more free time, exercise more often, and have a better sex life than when they were employees. The survey also found that those who work from home spend more time than before with family members. Mothers or fathers with school age children are more available.

Finally, working from home is a very flexible option. Because your office is just down the hall, it is easy to make a work schedule that works for you. You can work when you want, and if that is at midnight when you cannot fall asleep, well, bully for you.

Many businesses you know started out as a home-based business:

- Microsoft
- Apple
- Disney
- Amazon.com
- Xerox
- L.L. Bean

Cons. I said earlier that working from home requires discipline, a fact I know from personal experience. Having worked both inside and outside the home extensively, I personally like working outside better, because the detriments of working from home are significant.

The first problem is that there are a lot of distractions when you work at home, distractions that are not present when you work at an office outside the house. If you have children, the good news is that when you work at home, you see your kids a lot. The bad news is that you see your kids a lot. Crunching to meet that deadline or taking that important phone call is more difficult at home because, frankly, those around you do not always realize that even though you are at home you are also at work. If you do not mind being interrupted, that is good, because you *will* be interrupted.

Second, home-based businesses require self-discipline in many areas. If you want to sleep in, you can. If you want to work in your bathrobe, you can. It is easy to find yourself watching too much TV, or playing too much golf, or surfing the Net too often. Goofing off: Who would have thunk that is a home-based business hazard? Conversely, instead of working too little, it is similarly easy to work too much when you work at home. Your office after all is right down the hall. Why not go put a couple of extra hours in and get that project out the door? Workaholics need self-discipline, too.

> Bette Nesmith was a single mom who worked as a secretary at a bank in the 1950s. Though she was a fine artist, she was a lousy typist, making far too many typos. Because of her artistic abilities though, the bank had her paint the Christmas scene every year on the bank's windows. One year while painting the holiday scene, she made a mistake. She painted over it, as artists do, and thought to herself, "I wish I could paint over my typos when I type." Then she realized she could. Nesmith thereafter secretly brought some Tempura paint into work and began to paint over her typos. After a while she decided that this revolutionary idea would make a great business, so she started one out of her house. At home at night after she had gotten off work, Nesmith began to experiment with different permutations of paint, and in the process invented Liquid Paper.

Finally, a nice thing about going to a regular office every day is there are people with whom to interact and socialize, and this simply does not happen when you work at home. Meeting new people, sharing ideas, hearing the latest joke—you give all of that up when you open your own home-based business. Yes, you may hire employees down the road, but when you start out at home, you're usually alone.

TAKING THE PLUNGE

If you decide that a home-based business is right for you, it is vital that you do it right. First, do not make the mistake of thinking that you can get by cordoning off some space in the living room. You can, but it will not work. You need a separate room, both because your work will require it and because you will need it psychologically to reinforce that you are at work. Also, if you want to claim the home office deduction on your income taxes, you need to have a room devoted solely to the business.

Start by picking the right room. Maybe there is no choice to make; you have but one room available. If, however, you do have a choice, try to pick a room that:

- Has plenty of space.
- Has enough electrical outlets.
- Has a view.
- Is off the beaten path of the house.
- Is private.

You need room for a desk, chair, computer, phone, file cabinet, storage, bookshelves, and workspace for assembling materials, stuffing envelopes, that sort of thing. If you will be meeting customers, you will need enough room for chairs or a couch, and a table. Depending upon your business, you may also need space for employees, a waiting area for clients, or production facilities.

Once the office is ready to go, so are you. After that, starting your home-based business is not much different from starting any other business (review Part I). Get a business license, decide on an image and brand, begin to market yourself, and so on. The one difference has to do with having the right insurance.

Here is what you will need when equipping your home office:

Electrical. If possible, install extra outlets at desk level. If your office will use a lot of equipment, consider installing a separate circuit breaker.

Telephone. You need at least two phone lines, one for the phone and one for the fax machine, in addition to your regular home phone line.

Internet. You will need DSL or cable Internet connections. You may also want to install a wireless connection, which costs only about $100 and can be purchased at your local office superstore. Handling e-mail next to the pool is pretty nice.

Insurance

The mistake many new home-based entrepreneurs make is thinking that their homeowner's insurance will cover them if they have a loss and need to make a claim. In fact, some homeowner's polices specifically exclude businesses from coverage. Review your policy and see whether your home-based business would be covered or not. If not, call your agent and see what it would take to get covered.

The other mistake to avoid is to not tell your carrier about your home-based business, figuring that if you ever do need to file a claim, they will never know the difference. The problem with that thinking is twofold. First, if you have a lot of computer equipment, business software, inventory, or other signs of a business, the insurer probably will figure it out. Second, if they conclude that you did in fact have a home-based business, and part of your claim is for business losses, they can legitimately deny the claim for the business losses. Pick up a home-based business endorsement that specifically covers your business.

CHAPTER 33

Successful Home-Based Business Strategies

We are built to conquer environment, solve problems, achieve goals, and we find no real satisfaction or happiness in life without obstacles to conquer and goals to achieve.

—MAXWELL MALTZ

For those who have done it, creating a successful home-based business is a true accomplishment: Carving out a niche in a competitive world, doing something you love, where, when, and how you want it is most certainly something of which to be proud. What does it take? What distinguishes excellent from mediocre home-based businesses? Like many other things in this book, it requires both attitude and strategy. Model both, and you are on your way.

BALANCING ACT

There is a direct correlation between creating a thriving home-based business and your ability to strike the proper work–home balance. Working from home requires that you not only find a balance, but that the people around you do, too. As discussed in the previous chapter, you need to learn, fairly quickly, when and how to take on and off your work hat. When you work at home, there is a nebulous line that is too easy to cross. By setting down some ground rules, you give your work the rigor it may lack but certainly deserves:

- *Create a schedule, and keep to it.*   Sure you can deviate; that is half the fun. But deviating from your schedule should be the exception, not the rule. By sticking to a schedule, you signal to yourself and to the world that though you are at home, you really are at work. If you take it seriously, they will, too.
- *Dress appropriately.*   When you work at home it is too easy to make every day casual Friday. While you certainly do not have to wear a suit to the office, you need not be a schlub either. By dressing professionally, you again are saying, with deeds not just words, that your home-based business is the real deal.
- *Keep your office separate.*   To the extent possible, your office should be your office. If it doubles as a children's playroom or the laundry room, not only is it hard to get work done, but the delicate work/home balance will be out of whack.

When you take your home-based business seriously, when you create boundaries and parameters, others will, too, although it may take a while and some training. People who do not work at home often quietly resent those who do, and certainly think that you have plenty of extra time on your hands if you work at home. Visions of lazy afternoons and midday naps dance in their heads.

Your ground rules are the antidote. Your rules may be that when your door is closed, no one can bother you, or that from 10:00 to 11:00 A.M. you return phone calls and should not be disturbed. Maybe your entrepreneurial friends who also make their own schedule know that you *can* be bothered on Wednesday and Friday afternoons, when you take time off. However it is, your business, and growth, will come easier when you and those around you know and follow your rules.

Who minds the store after you leave the house? If you are like most other home-based businesses, the answer is nobody. With a little techno-savvy on your part however, your computer can become your virtual assistant. The right software allows your PC to receive faxes and phone calls, take messages and e-mails, and then *tells you* who communicated, when, and how. It can page you whenever you receive a designated voice mail or fax, or you can phone in and get your messages (in whatever form) whenever and from wherever you want. Check out ACCPAC's Simply Messenger PRO for starters.

GROWTH STRATEGIES

There comes a time in the life of many home-based businesses when it seems like it is time to move up and out of the house. But if you have grown accustomed to the place, accustomed to the pace, how do you leave the creature comforts of home and still grow? The answer is, you don't have to. Here are some simple ways to continue to grow and still work in your slippers when the mood strikes.

Use an Executive Suite

Executive suites are offices that you can rent by the hour, day, week, or month and share with other small businesses. They are fully furnished, have secretaries and receptionists on hand, and offer all the amenities (conference rooms, Internet access, copy machines, and so on) of your own full time, out-of-the-house office but at a fraction of the cost. Most usually are in beautiful, modern downtown offices, so you are assured of impressing clients.

Fees vary depending upon your needs. For example, you may want to continue to work at home and simply use the address of the suite on your stationery. That works. Most suites offer an affordable virtual office option (a couple of hundred dollars a month, tops) that allows you to use their address, have them receive your mail, and have them answer your phone (transferring the calls to you at home) and get a few hours of conference room time, too, for meeting clients. The more office time you need, the more you pay. These are great places to meet clients and make an impression.

By utilizing an executive (or professional) suite, you can put a shiny external face on your home-based business if you desire, and at a very affordable price.

Regus Business Centers offer executive suites at more than 400 locations worldwide in incredible, state-of-the-art buildings. They offer fully furnished offices, the ability to pay only for the time they use, a professional staff, a prime business address, and high-tech, wired conference rooms. Maybe best of all, once you are part of the system, you can use any office in any of their other locations. If, say, you rent a virtual office in Manhattan and have to go to Los Angeles to meet a potentially big client, all you need to do is call your New York Regus office and have them book you a room in the southern California office of your choice (www.Regus.com).

Rent the Space You Need

Many successful home-based businesspeople continue to run their business out of their home while renting the space they need to grow. Barsahrin Travis is a fantastic yoga teacher. She used to hold sessions in the quiet living room of her house, but when her classes grew too popular, she decided to rent space at a nearby studio. She continues to manage her thriving business from home, but uses space outside the house to grow.

It may be that you need warehouse space, a place for inventory, a location for your workshops, space for employees—the reasons for wanting more room are varied. The important thing is not to think of it as an either-or situation. You can continue to work from home *and* rent space and continue to grow. You do not have to move out of the house to get bigger.

Remember, too, that it is fairly easy to remotely access your computer; working in one place and logging on to another computer (back at home, for example) is easy. The latest version of Windows offers this sort of interface, as do web sites like www.GoToMyPC.com. Having a small business server also allows you to remotely access your office, which makes having two workplaces much easier.

Get Help

When you face the happy dilemma of too much growth and not enough room, another option is to contract with another company or individual who can handle the overflow for you. Yes, hiring people as either an employee or independent contractor to do work you could do yourself costs money, but that is what businesses do—they segment duties and hire staff to handle jobs. It is a sign that your home-based business has reached a more mature stage of development.

Aside from taking those duties off your hands, the other benefit of hiring help is that it frees you to concentrate on matters more important. Far too many small businesspeople spend far too much time working *in* their business and not *on* their business. You only have so much time, and when you spend it stuffing envelopes, filling orders, or collecting past-due invoices, you take time away from doing something else, usually a better, smarter use of your time. Hiring staff enables you to have more free time to think bigger and plan better.

Go Virtual

If you do not want the expense and responsibility of hiring employees and finding space for them to work, consider instead hiring a virtual assistant: an independent contractor who works from her own home or office, handles duties for you, and communicates with you via telephone, fax, and messenger services. Virtual assistants, or VAs, have become quite the rage. According to the International Virtual Assistants Association, "A Virtual Assistant (VA) is an independent entrepreneur providing administrative, creative and/or technical services. Utilizing advanced technological modes of communication and data delivery, a professional VA assists clients in his/her area of expertise from his/her own office on a contractual basis."

VAs are especially good at handling unwanted administrative duties such as collections, marketing, travel planning, research, and accounting. They might even help with your web site, prepare your newsletter, or schedule appointments. VAs are affordable, typically less than $50 an hour. You pay only for the time you use. Maybe best of all, by hiring a VA, you get all the advantages of having a guy or gal Friday without the associated overhead—no related employment costs or taxes, no rent for office space, nada.

A VA can really help your business grow. A good one is committed to your success, knowing that if she does well, you will do well, and if you do well, she might do even better.

> For more information, contact AssistU: www.assistu.com, or the International Virtual Assistants Association, www.ivaa.org.

ADD AN ADDITIONAL PROFIT CENTER

If your home-based business has topped-out, if you find that you make x number of dollars every month, month after month, then you need a new strategy. Some of the more lucrative home-based businesses add profit centers. Most home-based businesses, indeed, most small businesses, make a fundamental error not long after startup. It goes something like this: "Hey, I'm doing it! I am on my own and making money. I successfully ditched that stupid job and started a business." The new entrepreneur has figured out a few ways to get money in the door. It might be a product that moves well, an ad that brings in business, or a niche that no one else has filled, but she figured out something that works.

Then she stopped. Therein lies the rub. Having figured out a successful strategy or two, the average small businessperson usually begins to rest on their laurels. Whereas in the beginning she was probably very creative and active, trying different plans and ideas to see what worked, once she discovered one or two, if she is typical, that creativity and activity ended.

One secret to longevity and continued growth, then, is to continue to plot, plan, and implement new strategies; add more products; advertise somewhere new; create another niche. The best small business have not just one or two profit centers; they have multiple profit centers. They have many different ways of attracting business and many different facets of their business. That way, when one slows down for whatever reason, the others continue the cash flow. Richard Branson started Virgin Records as a small business by bartering for space above a shoe shop in London. The record store soon begat another profit center, a recording studio. That in turn begat another profit center, a talent agency. More profit centers were invented: An airline, a cola, and a phone company to name a few. Combined, all of those various profit centers are now called The Virgin Group.

That is what you may have to do, too. By creating new profit centers, you, too, can ensure that your home-based business will continue to grow and prosper.

> There are all sorts of affordable profit centers to be had. One example: Carlson Travel offers SeaMaster Cruise franchises as a home-based business. The estimated initial investment to buy into the franchise, including the initial franchisee fee, ranges from $5,500 to $16,445 (www.CarlsonTravel.com).

GET PAID WHAT YOU ARE WORTH

A problem for many small, home-based businesses is that they set their prices when they first open their doors and fail to raise them, ever. Afraid they will drive away customers, these businesspeople get stuck in time, charging and getting paid amounts that are years out of date. So how do you raise prices, earn what you are worth, and not lose customers in the process? There are several steps to take.

Step one: Decide upon a reasonable amount. If it has been a while since you have raised your rates, you may be a bit out of touch with what the market will bear. What do your competitors charge? That is a good place to start. Like Goldilocks, you do not want to be too hot or too cold. You want to be just right (unless what you offer is qualitatively different). Decide upon an amount you think is fair and reasonable.

Do you hate hourly billing? Consider the beauty of the flat fee. With a flat fee, you can estimate your hours, and bid the job accordingly. Clients love flat fees because they know exactly what they will pay. You have an incentive to get it done faster (your flat fee will still be the same) and you do not have to spend all that time adding up every quarter hour you spent on a project.

Step two: Give clients reasonable notice. Whether you intend to raise your rates $10 an hour, or 25 percent, or whatever, you need to give your clients advance warning so that it is not a shock and is something for which they can plan.

When you tell them, be businesslike. Do not apologize, and don't explain. Confidence is key. People raise their rates; that is a fact of business. You are good at what you do, and you deserve to raise your rates, too. Be sure that you tell clients your new rates are in line with the norm in the industry. If you do feel the urge to explain the rate hike, you can always say, for instance, "My fees are still reasonable, and I have not raised them in years. I have to keep up with my overhead," or "I decided that I need to raise my rates 10 percent every other year."

Step three: Test (optional). If raising your rates makes you nervous and concerned that you will lose clients, consider trying it out on a few clients for starters. Discover their reaction. If it works, then roll out fee increases across the board. If not, retreat!

Step four: Handle resistance. Clients who voice their displeasure will need a little extra TLC. Explain how much you do for them and how much extra you do that is gratis. Make sure they understand that your new fees are not out of line, and anyway, if they switched to someone new it would require time and training, and that would eat up any savings they might get. Reiterate all that you do. Explain that you dislike raising your rates but really have no choice and that based on your longstanding working relationship, you hope they will understand. If they still balk, consider giving them a perk, maybe another 60 days at the old price. That might work.

PART VIII

Business on a Shoestring

CHAPTER **34**

The Shoestring Entrepreneur

I am an optimist. It does not seem too much use being
anything else.

—WINSTON CHURCHILL

Although starting and growing a business on a shoestring is not the
optimal choice, if you are an entrepreneur at heart, it still beats
working for The Man. Indeed, starting on a shoestring puts you in
good company. Certainly most startups begin without as much
money as the owners would have liked, but they were started anyway.
But understand this, too: While starting and growing a business on a
tight budget is possible, it is not easy. To do it successfully requires
several things: the right attitude, OPM (other people's money), and
frugality.

THE RIGHT STUFF

While many startups do not have optimum funding, a shoestring
startup is a different animal. Starting on a shoestring usually means
that, rather than less than optimum funding, you have little if any funding at all. It means really starting from scratch, but you can do it.
Countless others have.

Begin your bootstrap entrepreneurial journey with a grounded understanding of what it will take. There are five rules of the road to follow:

1. *Know that fortunes have been made on minuscule beginnings.* Lillian Vernon started what would become a multimillion dollar mail order business with $2,000, using her kitchen table as her first office. Peter Hodgson borrowed $137 to buy the goo he would rename Silly Putty. Arnold Goldstein, author of *Starting on a Shoestring* (John Wiley & Sons, 4th ed., 2002), began his first retail discount store, containing roughly $100,000 of merchandise, using only $2,600 of his own money. Real estate is one way you could start on a shoestring right now. By obtaining a three percent FHA loan, you could buy a $150,000 duplex for $4,500 down. That is amazing. Even without 97 percent of the money needed, you could start a real estate business. There are ways to do it. If others did it, you can, too.

2. *Understand the difference between good debt and bad debt.* When you do not have enough money, you usually have to go into debt to get started or grow the business. However, not all debt is bad debt. Bad debt is unmanageable. Credit card bills that you cannot pay off are bad debt. But debt that helps you to get ahead in life—start a business, buy a home, or finance college—is good debt. Most millionaires started out in debt, but it was good debt. Although it is not ideal, if you have a plan to pay it back, startup debt can be good debt for you, too.

3. *Serve the market.* Every successful business must serve a market need. Whatever your shoestring idea is, it better be a darned good one because shoestring entrepreneurs do not often get second chances. Tapping friends and family to help finance your dream can happen about, well, once. Invest in only your best, most commercial idea or suffer the consequences.

4. *Shoestring businesses require creativity.* Improvising, making do, juggling, and borrowing from Peter to pay Paul will be required if you have to start, or want to grow, a business on a limited budget. Hire students. Buy some software and learn how to design your own web site. Ask for free help. You will have to be highly energetic and very creative if you are going to succeed in this sort of endeavor.

5. *You gotta believe.*   Northwestern University once conducted a survey of successful shoestring entrepreneurs and discovered that most of them had never owned a business before, had little business education, and even though they had not had enough money, had started a business anyway. Essentially, they did know enough to realize that they should have been afraid. You have to have the same chutzpah. To be successful, be out there, raising money, selling, projecting a confident image. If you are afraid or unsure, stop right there and make a U-turn. Do not pass Go and do not collect $200. Shoestring entrepreneurship is for the hearty alone.

OTHER PEOPLE'S MONEY (OPM)

There are two types of shoestring operations. The first is started without borrowing any money at all. Maybe you have $500 or $1,000 or $2,500 and want to start a business on your own and not take on any debt. Usually, such ventures begin as part-time home-based businesses that grow incrementally. Yes, it is possible to make a go of it, but the margin for error is so slim that it makes the possibility of succeeding very difficult. Nevertheless, that sort of shoestring entrepreneur will find some useful tips later in this chapter, and especially in the next chapter.

The second sort of shoestring entrepreneur is the one who wants to

Jay had a great idea for a business. He would create the world's most unique treasure hunt. In this James Bond adventure, Jay would hide some diamonds somewhere in his city, create clues as to where they were located, write a background storyline for participants, and hire actors to play parts in the scenario. Jay figured people would pay a lot of money for the chance to find diamonds and act out their movie star fantasies. The only problem was that Jay had little money. Undaunted, he wrote the script, asked some friends to play the parts, spent what money he did have creating a nice brochure . . . and then ran out of money. He finally put a little classified ad in the paper, hoping that a few people would sign up, and he would then use that money to buy the diamonds. One person called.

start a business without much of their own money, or who wants to grow his existing business but lacks the funds to do so. These entrepreneurs will have to use other people's money. The challenge is finding that other person with the money.

Finding that money is a two-step process. First, you will need a solid business plan. No investor will put money into your idea based on the idea alone. You will need facts and figures to back up rosy rhetoric.

Then you go out and start knocking on doors. Funding a startup without your own money is a numbers game. You will likely need to talk to *a lot* of people before getting the money you need. Chapter 8, *The Money Hunt*, explains how to approach friends, family, business associates, and professional colleagues. That is the place to start. Most of these people will want to see that you are investing in the business, too, figuring that if you are unwilling to take a financial risk, why should they? If you have no money to put into the business, be up front about that. Explain that your time, effort, and expertise will be your investment, and that is worth a lot. If you do have some money to invest, do so. Even a little can impress. Try not to get discouraged. Remember it is a numbers game.

Understand that armed with a business plan, a good idea, a winning smile, and little else, you represent both peril and promise for any would-be investor. The peril is that you could take their money and lose it on some untried scam. The promise is that you could take their money and make them wealthy with your great idea. Your challenge is to prove that the latter is far more likely to occur than the former.

> The key to winning over any investor is to look like a pro. Talking big without backup facts will make you look foolish. Be a businessperson. Draft a real business plan. Have your elevator pitch ready. Know your market. Know your numbers inside out. Know thy competition. Be able to defend your plan of action. Explain with conviction why your plan is a great opportunity for the investor.

The friends and family plan works sometimes and sometimes does not. If it does not work for you, here are a few other viable shoestring entrepreneur funding sources.

Locate a Partner

Not a few partnerships have begun because one person had the idea, skills, experience, or opportunity while the other had the money. If you have the desire and passion to start a business or need to grow your present business but lack the funding to do so, then teaming up with the right partner, one who has the money, represents a very real way to fund the plan. Of course you will have to give up half your equity, but that is a little price to pay to get to live the dream.

Here is an example: Chester Carlson was an inventor by nature. When he landed a job in a patent office that required him to duplicate detailed patent applications by hand, he decided that there had to be a better way to re-create them. So at his workshop at home at night after work Carlson began to tinker and fiddle. He eventually figured out a process that would allow him to reproduce documents electronically. Carlson then spent the next few years trying to sell his invention to companies like GE, RCA, and IBM. He had no success. He was an inventor, not a salesman.

Then a man named Joe Wilson heard about Carlson's invention. The president of a small photographic company called Haloid, Wilson went to see Carlson, was given a demonstration of the process, and said, "Of course it's got a million miles to go before it will be marketable. But when it does become marketable, we've got to be in the picture!" Wilson and Carlson decided to become partners; Carlson had the invention and Wilson had the money. Haloid eventually pumped $100 million into Carlson's invention before taking it to market and naming the machine, and the company, Xerox.

The question you probably have is, where to find that magic partner? There are several sources:

- Start by networking. Speak with your lawyer, accountant, and other business associates. Talk to friends, family, colleagues, and people where you worship. Get the word out. Networking works.
- Speak with suppliers and distributors, as they may know people in the field who are looking for an opportunity. Speak with people in your line of work who have retired. They may want to either get back in the saddle or become a passive investor/partner.

- Conduct an Internet search.
- Put an ad in the paper under the section Capital Needed. Scour the Capital Available section as well.

The Web is a fine place to find a business partner. Try these sites:

- www.businesspartners.com
- www.entremate.com
- www.findyouridealbusinesspartner.com

When speaking with potential partners, you will get the money you want *only if* the partner gets what he or she wants. Maybe he wants a say in day-to-day operations. Maybe he just wants a monthly cut of the profits. Here, then, is another winning concept from the desk of the successful small businessperson: *Ask them what they want and give them what they want.* Your partner might want to be a 50–50 partner like Joe Wilson and Chester Carlson were, or he might want to be a silent partner who merely wants to invest in return for a share of the company. You will get what you want if he gets what he wants.

Supplier and Distributor Financing

Distributors and suppliers want your business, and they know that by offering you some financial assistance, they just may turn you into a long-term, repeat customer. Your job, therefore, is to show them that if they lend you some money to get started, they will get your continued business. This happens more often than you might think.

Suppliers or distributors will want to learn about you, visit your business (if you have one), and check on your references. Like any other lender or investor, they need to be convinced that you will be able to pay them back. The key to success is preparation. You need a solid plan showing how helping you will help their bottom line.

Franchisor Financing

There are many franchisors who offer some degree of financing. While financing 100 percent of a franchise is not unheard of, 50 percent or so is more typical. According to the International Franchising Association, roughly 33 percent of all franchisors offer some type of financing. Some offer interest-only loans, others offer loans that require no payment for the first year, some finance everything, and others finance the franchise fee only. It all depends upon you and the franchisor. Ask.

It is also true that most franchisors have relationships with various lenders, so that may be another possibility. Other alternatives include franchisor loan guarantees or working capital loans. Finally, many franchisors usually have relationships with leasing companies who might be able to finance the equipment needed to run the franchise. Since this can be a major expense, do not overlook this possibility.

Other Options

Venture capital firms and angel investors may also be possibilities, and do not forget SBA guaranteed loans.

The Deal

When structuring any finance deal with a potential investor for your shoestring business, work to make the deal a win-win. When structuring a loan or investment deal, keep these points in mind:

- Ask for more money than you need. If they balk and negotiate down, it will not be a crisis, and if they don't, you will have more than enough.
- Make sure that your company takes out the loan. You incorporated, right?
- Get the interest rate as low as possible. Everything is negotiable.
- Work to get as much time as possible to repay the loan, with no pre-payment penalty.

GRAND OPENING

Shoestring entrepreneurship extends well beyond financing. Be vigilant about keeping your expenses to a minimum, in every area.

Rent

Rent is one of the biggest expenses a business has, so minimizing your rent is imperative. Avoid the high profile location and its high profile rent. Instead, think like a shoestring businessperson: Rent a smaller space than you would like, in an out-of-the-way location. Start a home-based business if you must, but just do not blow your dough on rent.

Business Incubators

Another low-cost option is to start your business in a business incubator, public or private nonprofit partnerships that work to promote entrepreneurship and small business growth. They do this by providing inexpensive space from which new businesses can be launched. Incubators usually also offer free (or very inexpensive) administrative service assistance, legal help, business planning, financial advice, and so forth. As the name indicates, they are places that nurture, or incubate, a business while it begins to spread its wings and fly.

Although all business incubators work to launch successful businesses, each is unique. In the Silicon Valley, for example, many business incubators foster computer-oriented startups, while in Wisconsin, the incubator may foster dairy and farming-related businesses. It depends upon the region and the incubator.

Many benefits are derived from starting your business in a business incubator:

- Reduced rent
- Financial and business assistance and expertise
- Shared services
- Contacts

You can find out what types of incubators are in your area by contacting the National Business Incubation Association at 614-593-4331, or by going to www.nbia.org.

Equipment

Shoestring entrepreneurs are always looking for a bargain. They buy furniture, equipment, and fixtures used, and if you are shoestringing, you should, too. The Yellow Pages are a good place to start. The Internet is a bargain hunter's paradise; eBay is but one of many places to look. Newspaper and magazine classified ads are great.

If you cannot find what you need used, many manufacturers finance up to 90 percent of your new purchase, which preserves your precious capital. Consider the option of leasing any fixtures or equipment you might need.

INVENTORY

Stocking the shelves of your store when you have a small budget is also possible. How do you do that, you ask? It is similar to a method mentioned earlier: Find suppliers who will give you their goods on credit. Thousands of wholesale product manufacturers, suppliers, and distributors are looking for business. One way for them to get it is to stock your shelves without requiring an upfront payment for the goods. They are paid when the goods sell.

Start by preparing a powerful package proving your pluck and thereby inducing them to want to work with you. It should contain your business plan, your stationery, letters of reference, the names of your lawyer and banker, and so on. Anything that gives you legitimacy helps your cause. Explain how much inventory you need, the terms you propose, and how and when you will pay it back. You need to convince the supplier that you are likely to become a new client who will be buying their goods for many years. That is what works.

After you have the package ready, contact the sales rep from the supplier/manufacturer/wholesaler whose products you want. Present the package to each and ask for an appointment with the company's credit manager or regional sales manager. You stand a pretty good chance of success if you have a good package, a decent credit rating, and some trade references.

If they agree to stock your shelves for no money down, agree to continue to buy from them for the term of the loan. Also agree to grant them a "security interest" in the merchandise, meaning that if you default or go bankrupt, they get their merchandise back.

> When negotiating the terms of the deal, *do not* agree to buy from this one manufacturer exclusively. For you, that should probably be a deal breaker.

You may get most of the product you need from one supplier, or it might take many suppliers lending you small amounts. Either way, you get the shelves stocked without investing a lot of your capital up front. When you are doing business on a shoestring, you do whatever it takes.

BUYING A BUSINESS WITH NO MONEY DOWN

Buying a business with little money of your own is akin to buying a small piece of real estate without a lot of money. Remember that $150,000 duplex, mentioned earlier? Using an FHA three percent loan, you need only $4,500 to buy it; the bank secures the loan with a lien against the property and loans you the rest. That is called "leverage." With the asset securing the loan, you can leverage a small amount of money into a large purchase. Well, leverage can be applied to the acquisition of a business, too. The secret is to find a willing seller who is open to some creative financing.

If you can get a conventional bank loan, great. Existing businesses have track records and assets (accounts receivable, autos, machinery, and so forth), so getting a bank loan is certainly possible. However, if you cannot get a bank loan, you still might be able to buy the business using seller financing. Sellers are often willing to finance some or all of the purchase.

Sellers need buyers, and if your purchase is made contingent on seller financing, they just might do it. Buyers are not always easy to find. Of course the seller will want to secure his loan with the ability to "foreclose" on the business and take it back if you default. If you agree to that (and you should), then getting them to finance your purchase is very realistic. The optimum plan would be to combine bank and seller financing. Say, for instance, that you want to buy a furniture store worth $100,000. Maybe the bank will finance half if the seller finances half, and away you go!

But what if the seller is willing to finance, say, 40 percent, and the bank will only match that? What if you need additional creative financing options to swing the deal? Where do you find that $20,000? There are several choices:

- *Debt financing.* Business sellers include in the asking price the amount they need to pay off their business debts. If you agree to assume those debts, you can reduce your down payment by that amount. Are you willing to assume $20,000 of the seller's debt?
- *Inventory financing.* When you buy a business, you also buy its inventory. If you are short $20,000, see whether the owner would agree to liquidate $20,000 in inventory. Then reduce the purchase price by that amount. Similarly, he could sell a business asset worth $20,000—a truck, machinery, real estate, even.
- *Broker financing.* The majority of all business sales are done through a broker. See whether the broker would be willing to reduce his or her commission to keep the deal alive.
- *Supplier financing.* Check with the business' suppliers. They may agree to loan you the $20,000 if it means they will continue to have a major account.

There are many ways to finance a business purchase with no money down. Creativity and a willing seller are all that is required.

CHAPTER 35

Marketing on a Shoestring

Sell to their needs, not yours.

—EARL G. GRAVES

There is no doubt that big corporations have resources and abilities not shared by their small business brethren. They have budgets we only dream about, experts to do their bidding, even managers to manage their managers. Likewise, we have attributes they do not. Small businesses are far less bureaucratic. We are resourceful, nimble and quick. I would venture to say that the only area where small businesses actually envy big businesses is with regard to their budgets. One ad in the *Wall Street Journal* might cost a Fortune 500 company $100,000. What kind of marketing could you do with $100,000? But fear not. Marketing need not cost a fortune. There are scores of way to market on the cheap, look big in the process, and even the playing field.

THE SHOESTRING RULES

Marketing need not cost a fortune to reap tremendous rewards, but first, you have to know the four ground rules.

1. *Shoestring marketing takes commitment.* If you are like most other small businesses, you have a few tried-and-true marketing

349

methods. But shoestring marketing means that you will try, and eventually adopt, several more methods. If three methods allow you to net $150,000 a year, what might you make with six methods? Therefore, you will try out many methods, test them, see which ones work best, and then add the winners to your marketing repertoire. This will take time as you must run an ad or test a marketing method several times before learning whether it is effective. Furthermore, a marketing campaign generally can take three to six months, so commitment is required.

2. *Shoestring marketing requires consistency.* To build a brand, you must send a consistent message repeatedly. Eventually, people will know that you are The King of Big Screens or that You Won't Be Undersold! or whatever is your promise to your customers. But to create that image, your marketing—shoestring and otherwise—must be consistent.

Consider the electronics store that spent a ton of money on a television campaign that lasted a week. The owner got results for about two weeks. He then tried a small, inexpensive ad *every week* in the Sunday entertainment section. It became his bread and butter. It created the profits. Consistency is key.

3. *Shoestring marketing requires creativity.* In the next section, you will find many different, inexpensive ways to market your business. Again, for this plan to work, you will need to try several and see which ones generate the best results. Try some that are foreign to you. Be creative.

4. *Shoestring marketing must be measured.* The only way to know whether your shoestring marketing campaign is working is if you are able to measure the results, so create ways to measure your campaigns. Your benchmark might be sales during the same month last year or the number of calls you receive from a flyer. Whatever the case, create a starting spot so that you can decide which methods garner the best results.

So this is the plan: Read through the many methods listed next and decide which ones might work best in your business. Set some benchmarks to test them against, and then try some out. Then try out some more. Be patient, be creative. Watch the bottom line, and then decide which methods should become additional tools in your marketing tool chest.

MAJOR MEDIA METHODS

There are many shoestring methods that allow you to advertise on television, radio, or in newspapers or magazines at a great discount.

Co-Op Advertising

Co-op advertising is a cost-sharing arrangement between a manufacturer and a retailer wherein the retailer places an ad that is *partially or fully paid for by the manufacturer.* The catch? The manufacturer's product or name must be mentioned in the ad. For example, my father had an expensive, prominent billboard on the San Diego Freeway in Los Angeles that said in big type "Carpet World . . . Elegance Underfoot." And then, at the bottom of the billboard, in much smaller print, it said "Featuring Ban-Lon Carpets." Ban-Lon paid for most of that ad. That is co-op advertising. Similarly, when a convenience store advertises a certain product, you can bet that company helped pay for the ad.

Collectively, manufacturers earmark approximately $30 billion annually to help small businesses stretch their advertising dollars, yet surprisingly much of that money goes unused. So an obvious way to stretch your advertising dollar is seeing whether any of your suppliers offer co-op funds. Having your suppliers pay for your advertising is an excellent way to grow your business without spending much more money.

> To learn more, pick up a copy of the *Co-Op Advertising Programs Sourcebook* or the *Co-Op Source Directory* .

Buy Remnant Space

Near press time, magazines and newspapers may have unsold advertising space, called remnant space. If you are flexible, willing, and able to buy at the last moment, you can pick up remnant space for a song. The same principle applies to unsold radio and television time. You can call your local media outlets and ask about remnant space possibilities on your own, or you can contact Media Networks to locate and purchase remnant space: call 800-225-3457.

Per Inquiry (PI) and Per Order (PO) Deals

Similar to barter, a PI or PO deal works when stations have unsold time. Say that you sell widgets. With this sort of deal you would cut a deal with a station in which they would, without any upfront costs to you, run your commercial selling your widgets. You then pay the station a percentage of whatever business you derive from that ad, based upon the number of orders (PO) or inquiries (PI) you received. Typically, the station might take 40 percent of whatever revenue the ad generated.

Overnight Radio

One inexpensive way to build your business is to use overnight radio advertising. In major media markets, advertising during drive time (7 A.M. to 9 A.M. and 4 P.M. to 7 P.M.) can run anywhere from $250 a minute to a whopping $1,000 a minute. At those prices, the necessary repetition you need to create a successful campaign may be unaffordable. But overnight ads, while certainly reaching a far smaller audience, cost much, much less, and still can be very effective.

Kristy Hicks is a radio account executive who explains that many large news talk stations have nighttime/overnight ratings that rival the ratings of many smaller stations during their drive time, but are sold at a fraction of the cost. For a recent client, for example, she was able to get overnight 60-second spots at a major station for $10 a minute in a major market and the audience size rivaled smaller stations' drive time audience. This is typical. Overnight spots usually undersold at most stations can usually be had at a great discount.

Kristy Hicks says that an effective overnight radio campaign requires three elements:

1. *A compelling message.* You have to be selling something people want to buy.
2. *Frequency.* Repetition is the key.
3. *Consistency.* Hicks points out that we all know the famous radio tag line "We'll leave the light on for you!" because Motel 6 never fails to use it. That is the power of consistency.

Cable Television

Whereas broadcast television is often cost prohibitive, cable TV, especially late at night, is not. And the great thing about cable is that you can target your market very specifically by advertising on the exact stations that your market watches. An overnight cable television ad might run as little as $25 a spot.

Newspapers

Advertising in the newspaper can be expensive, but here are a few ways to reduce your costs:

- Cut the size of your ad size in half, and save 50 percent. Double the size of your headline. If you then buy a premium placement (about 15 percent extra), you still save 35 percent and have an ad that might really get noticed.
- Consider advertising only in the neighborhoods that purchase your goods. You do not have to buy the whole region. You will save 50 percent or more.

Classified Ads

Both magazines and newspapers have classified ads and the best thing is that they reach people who are shopping and are ready to buy. If you test an ad and it works, ask for a frequency discount when buying in bulk. You can have as much success with a classified as you do with a display ad at a fraction of the cost. Tip: Have a snappy headline!

> When media reps quote you their rates, they quote from their *rate card*. Remember the rule that everything is negotiable. The rate card *is* negotiable.

The Yellow Pages

There are several ways to spend less on your Yellow Pages marketing. First time advertisers should get as much as a 40 percent discount their first year. I have a friend who advertises in the Yellow Pages for a year, drops out for a year, and then goes back. Each time he returns, he gets the newcomer discount. Also, consider advertising in the phone book that is not associated with the local phone company. Finally, find out about advertising in the online version of the book only.

Create an In-House Ad Agency

Media sources give discounts and breaks to "insiders"—PR agencies, ad buyers, people in the industry. So wouldn't it help you if they thought you were an insider? Well, you can be. Create an "in-house" ad agency. If you create one, and thereafter buy your ad time/space through your internal ad agency, you automatically get a 15 percent discount.

In-house ad agencies are amazingly easy to set up. Usually, all you need to show the media outlet is a checking account and stationery in the name of the in-house or internal ad agency. JJ's Stereos can create JJ's Stereos Advertising in an afternoon. Once you create one, and tell the advertising medium about it, you begin to save.

> Toll-free "800" phone numbers (also 888 and other exchanges) increase your response rate by 30 to 700 percent and are very affordable.

Publicity

It does not take much money to get some free publicity, but what it does take is a great press release or press kit. If you can convince a radio or television station, or a magazine or newspaper, that your business is newsworthy, and then get them to do a story about it, bingo! That free publicity is worth its weight in gold. Parlay it into more business, and reproduce that story for years to come, building credibility in the process.

PRINT TECHNIQUES

There are various other ways to market your business with little money, yet get big results using the printed word.

e-Newsletters

e-newsletters demonstrate how much you know about your field, and do so in a low-key, informative way. Then, when a recipient needs someone with your expertise or products, he thinks of you. While online newsletters are all the rage, physical newsletters should not be forgotten either.

Testimonials

Satisfied customers can be one of your best sales tools. Ask them to write you a testimonial on their letterhead, and then include these letters in your marketing materials and promotions. Testimonials lend credibility to your advertising offer and are great to use in sales presentations. My standard speaking contract states that if the meeting planner was happy with my speech, he or she will write me a letter of recommendation within two weeks after the event. I thereafter send these letters to prospective speaking clients.

> Ask happy current clients if they would mind if potential clients could call them regarding your products and services. This shows that you have built strong relationships with your clients and customers and are confident in the quality of your work.

Flyers

Hire a student to put flyers on cars downtown (5,000 flyers times 3 cents = $150). A good flyer offers cheap prices and emphasizes benefits, benefits, benefits!

Coupons

Most coupons are never redeemed, yet even so, creating a coupon costs almost nothing, and if your brand stresses low costs, coupons, even unredeemed, build your brand. If they are redeemed, you have driven some more business your way. To be effective, coupons must offer at least a 15 percent discount.

> Try adding a coupon to your invoices to sell more product to existing customers.

Gang Run

Some printers wait to do all of their large printing jobs at once. This is called a "gang run." If you can wait a while to get your marketing materials printed, contact some local printers and see when their gang run is scheduled. Tell them that you would like to buy the unused, extra space if they have any—they usually do. If you are patient, you can get printing at a fraction of the cost by buying their unwanted, unused, remnant space.

Personal Letters

George H.W. Bush is said to have written more than 10,000 thank-you letters and has credited that, at least partially, with getting elected president. In this era of instant communication, people really remember an actual letter. Consider writing a letter to your current customers, offering them a special discount, or sale, or something else as a way to thank them for their business. Then hire some students to address the letters by hand.

ACTIONS

There are plenty of other low-cost marketing tricks you can try.

Barter

There are two forms of barter, the traditional method where you and another vendor agree to trade goods or services, or more often these days, through a barter exchange, which acts as a middle-man. The exchange issues "barter bucks" to you when you do something for someone else in the group. You can then use those bucks to purchase the goods or services from anyone else in the group. The Internet has changed barter, too. Online barter exchanges have cropped up across the Net and are great places for small businesses to get started. A good virtual barter exchange should keep track of transactions, act as an intermediary, issue the currency, handle paperwork, and keep its fees to a minimum.

> According to the International Reciprocal Trade Association (IRTA) almost half a million small businesses use commercial barter exchanges every year, generating more than $10 billion in sales.

Barter offers several benefits:

1. *You can get rid of excess assets.* Store owners have excess inventory, restaurants have empty tables, chiropractors have free hours, and so on. Barter allows you to move assets and products that are not being used.
2. *You create new customers.* Barter exposes new people to your business. By joining a barter group, you may find that people who bartered for your goods or services may become regular clients.
3. *Barter saves money.* When you use your time rather than your money, you save money.

Contests

A contest can generate interest and free publicity for your business. For example, a restaurant might have a yearly contest to see which customer can eat the most of its famous Flaming Chicken Wings. Not only would this generate interest among its clientele, but a local newspaper might pick up the contest as a fun human interest story.

Networking

Having a good elevator pitch can create opportunities out of humdrum encounters.

Demonstrations

Demonstrating your product at a mall, trade show, or other high profile location usually leads to sales. Infomercials are nothing but 30-minute demonstrations.

Samples

When the car dealer lets you take the car you are considering buying home for the night, what is that? It is a free sample. Gourmet grocers set out free food all day, as does Costco. Why? Free samples are inexpensive loss leaders that create sales. What can you offer for free?

Seminars

Seminars are a good way for service businesses to introduce themselves to potential customers, build rapport, and entice people to want to know more. Seminars are used by many professionals; doctors offering Lasik eye surgery or lawyers who create living trusts are common. Though not the most inexpensive option, seminars can be a very lucrative marketing mechanism.

Become the Expert

When you become known as an expert in your field, whatever your field, you will find that the world will beat a path to your door. Consider that by being the expert:

- You immediately distinguish yourself from the competition.
- You immediately offer your clients something of value that competitors cannot, and do not, offer.
- You can charge more for your services.
- You become the first choice.

How do you come to be known as an expert? Pick something that you know or do, something you are passionate about, and begin to devote more energy to it. Then, share your analysis, ideas, and insights with colleagues and the public.

> Mark Paul spent 20 years at various levels and types of businesses. From Ford and Northrop to getting a patent and consulting, Paul gathered a wealth of valuable business knowledge throughout his career. When he decided that he wanted to focus on business startups, he knew that he needed to package his skills in a unique way to attract the right opportunity. So he wrote and self-published a book. *The Entrepreneur's Survival Guide: Tips and Tricks to Help You Start and Build Your Company* became Mark Paul's calling card. Now when he talks to people about business, he can refer them to *the book he wrote*. Talk about getting their attention! Go to www.synergy-usa.com.

How else can you become known as an expert? Draft a press release and get a television or radio segment done about you, or a newspaper article written about you. Write an article for the local paper, or for a trade journal. Advertise as "specializing in . . ." like the car dealer whose ad reads "Specializing in customers with credit problems."

Befriend a Concierge

The job of the concierge at a hotel or office building is to offer services to guests. Get on their list, and they become your marketing arm.

Offer Free Consultations

Free consultations usually lead to paying clients.

Be a Good Citizen

By sponsoring a youth sports team, coaching the team, or donating your services to charity, you begin to create a positive reputation in the community. What about sponsoring a segment on your local public broadcasting television or radio station? That certainly can be a chic method. All of this will (eventually) lead to more sales.

EXAMPLES

The many options previously listed are intended to whet your appetite. There are simply so many ways to market your business, many of which are underutilized by most small businesses, that it would be a shame if you stubbornly stuck to your same few techniques. Try a few of these out and see if you do not experience increased sales as a result.

Seasons Travel

Gross sales per month: $4,000

Marketing budget: 7.5 percent of gross—$300/mo

Monthly Shoestring Marketing Plan

Method	Cost	Analysis
Personal letters	Effectively $0	Only takes time
Brochures	$600 yearly—$50/mo	Always on hand
Classified ads	$20	One newspaper, once a week

Yellow Pages	$20	Small listing
Newspaper display ads	$100	One paper, once a week
Direct mail	$10	Postage
Public relations	$50	Cost of materials
Circulars	$50	Cost of materials and payment to son to put on cars
Total	**$300**	**Consistency is key**

Larry Allen and Associates, Attorneys at Law

Gross sales per month: $20,000

Marketing budget: 15 percent of gross—$3,000/mo

Monthly Shoestring Marketing Plan

Method	Cost	Analysis
Yellow Pages	$500	One large ad
Newspaper display ads	$1,000	Two medium weekly ads
Radio	$750	Always heard on the news talk station
Direct mail	$250	Three mailings a year
Free seminars	$450	Four times a year, amortized
Web site	$50	Design and promotion, amortized
Total	**$3,000**	**High profile**

PART IX

Small Business Success Strategies

CHAPTER **36**

Small Business
Success Secrets I: Money

I think it is an immutable law in business that words are
words, explanations are explanations, promises are
promises—but only performance is reality.

—HAROLD S. GENEEN

What counts is what works. Small businesses come in all shapes and
sizes. Some are good and some are not. Some make a lot of money
and some do not. Some foster happy, productive, meaningful workplaces and others do not. So what separates them? In these last two
chapters, the distinguishing characteristics of the best small businesses are explored.

MULTIPLE PROFIT CENTERS

According to the *New York Times* (Feb. 15, 2004), at a time when
Michael Jackson was facing many legal problems, he was also suffering from a potential cash crunch. The *Times* explained that Jackson
had a $70 million loan coming due. Although sources believed that
Jackson was going to have a hard time repaying it, Jackson was not
worried, because, according to the *Times*, "One adviser said that Mr.

365

Jackson had about a half-dozen sources of income, including royalties . . . his most valuable asset by far is the Beatles catalog of about 250 songs, which Mr. Jackson and Sony Music Entertainment own jointly . . . with an estimated value of $800 million to $900 million. The catalog of Mr. Jackson's own music . . . has an estimated value of $75 million to $90 million."

You would not be too worried, either, if you owned the rights to "Yesterday." So what is the point? Namely this: Michael Jackson felt safe financially because he does not rely on only one source of income. He has diversified his income sources (six, according to the article). So should you. The great small businesses know that all businesses have cycles, just as the economy has cycles. If you depend on only one or two sources of income, you can bet that there will be up times, *and there will be down times*. Cycles, after all, are cyclical.

> Diversifying your income is the same strategy investors use in the stock market. They know not to buy stock in just one company or sector, as that stock or sector might go up or it might go down. Diversifying their portfolio is a hedge against the down times.

The secret to beating the dreaded, inevitable business cycle is to have multiple profit centers. That way, when one part of your business is down, other parts are up, and vice versa. When "Thriller" is not selling because you have legal troubles, you can still count on "Sgt. Pepper."

If you are a photographer specializing in weddings, consider adding portraits or high school graduations to your portfolio. If you manufacture a wholesale product, what about adding some retail outlets, or vice versa? By creating multiple profit centers, you can ensure that, well, all your troubles will seem so far away.

SWIMMING WITH THE BIG FISH

It is easy to fall into a rut, especially when it is a comfortable rut. If your business earns a nice profit and is a good place to work, everyone might easily settle into a routine where growth is less important than maintaining the status quo. You know what you know, and what you know works. Why upset the apple cart?

But if you want to take your business to the next level, you will need to (1) break the routine, and (2) begin to associate with people who can help generate more business and revenue. Tried and true is nice if that is what you want. Superior small businesses, though, work to get to the next level.

A Board of Advisors

Bob Vukovich is an entrepreneur who has started two very successful businesses, is a mentor to many aspiring entrepreneurs, and is a judge at Moot Corporation (an internationally acclaimed business plan competition hosted by the University of Texas). Vukovich knows a thing or two about small business success. He says, "The worst thing you can do as an entrepreneur is to think you know everything. When I need advice, which is very often of a general nature rather than technical, it's very important to have a great board to turn to."

> In 1992, Allegheny College received the largest gift in its almost-200-year history: $22 million from Bob Vukovich and his wife, Laura.

The "great board" Vukovich is referring to could mean either your board of directors if you are incorporated, or if not, then a less formal board of advisors. This is something from which all small businesses could benefit. A board of advisors is a group whose purpose is to help you guide and grow your business. A great board is one that can offer you advice, feedback, expertise, perspective, and contacts.

"Contacts" are especially important. When you are a small businessperson, you can have only so many contacts and colleagues. More-over, if it is true that "it is not what you know, but who you know" (and it is), then a board of advisors helps you know more people. There is no telling what opportunities, contracts, or other sales might come from having the right board member.

But even beyond this, a good board is an important sounding board. By recruiting various experts and colleagues, you expand your small business' business IQ. So when looking for board members (five is a good number), look for potential members who:

- *Have experience.* You want to stock your board with business-savvy individuals. Putting your brother-in-law on your board negates its purpose, unless he offers something unique. The more heavyweights you get, the better. Not only will this vastly increase your small business acumen, but these are the kind of players who can steer business your way. Good board members will have contacts whom they can reach out to: investors, strategic partners, even potential customers. An experienced board also impresses the outside world, if you need a loan for example, or if you are trying to nab that big contract.
- *Have diverse skills.* None of us have all the necessary knowledge, experience, or skills required to run every aspect of our business (though we might like to think we do!). There are so many different facets of a small business—sales, finance, marketing, legal—that having board members with a variety of business skills ensures that you will have someone around who can answer questions and help solve problems when they arise.
- *Are independent.* You want people willing to be the devil's advocate, who will give you their honest feedback.

Board members are often compensated for their time, either with money or stock, although some are willing to assist for free. The opportunity to be involved in an interesting business, plus teaching what they know, may be satisfaction enough.

Contracts

Another way to start playing a bigger game is to go after bigger customers. Relying on the same customer base is a prescription for redundancy. If you continue to do the same thing, you will continue to get the same results. Instead, target larger potential customers for your goods or services. They are out there; you just need to know where to look.

A Unique Opportunity. The federal government contracts out $240 billion of business to private business every year, and by law, 23 percent of those contracts must go to small businesses. This means there is roughly *$60 billion* in government contracts available to small businesses every year. You have no idea how to even start finding, let alone bidding on, those contracts? You are not alone. Most small businesses have no idea, either, but Hector Barreto and Hewlett-Packard are here to help.

Hector Barreto is the head of the U.S. Small Business Administration. When he was first appointed to run the SBA, he quickly realized a fundamental truth: "What small business wants is the same as what big business wants—more business!" The question was, how could he help facilitate that?

According to Mr. Barreto, although the 23 percent, $60 billion set-aside seemed like a great opportunity to help small businesses get more business, most of these contracts went to small businesses "inside the Beltway." He thought that small businesses throughout the United States should have an equal opportunity to bid on, and get, these contracts. "They have the know-how," he told me, "but not the know who."

Business Matchmaking. To fix that, the SBA and Hewlett-Packard teamed up in 2002 to create a program called Business Matchmaking (www.businessmatchmaking.com). Business Matchmaking is a program that matches small businesses with government and private procurement officers looking to buy what the small businesses have

In 2002, Robyn West, HP's charming Vice President of Small and Medium Business and her team were looking for different ways to help small businesses succeed. They decided to contact the SBA, right when Hector Barreto was looking for a partner for Business Matchmaking. It was fortuitous. The SBA and HP teamed up, and a great new program was born.

to offer. As Mr. Barreto puts it, the program "matches small companies with federal, state, and local government agencies, and large corporations that have actual contract opportunities for products and services."

In order to facilitate this matchmaking, the SBA and HP have created a traveling program that goes to different cities around the country bringing together those looking to buy goods and services with local small businesses looking to sell such goods and services. Whereas it began as a program to help spread the 23 percent government contract set-aside wealth, Business Matchmaking now includes many large private businesses that also need and use small business vendors.

According to Administrator Barreto (that is his actual title), these events have been an unqualified hit, both in terms of the number of participants and the billions of dollars of contracts that have resulted. "In one or two days at one of these events, a small business can see more contractors with real contracts than they could in a year on their own," Barreto says. "It's better than a trade show because at our events, buyers who are ready to buy are meeting small businesses ready to sell. We are matching supply with demand."

Who is looking to buy from small businesses at these Business Matchmaking events? Recent participants include the Air Force, the Department of the Interior, the Department of the Treasury, the State Department, the Department of Veterans Affairs, General Dynamics, GlaxoSmithKline, Hewlett-Packard, Honeywell, Office Depot, Raytheon, the State of Florida, Boeing, the General Services Administration, Walt Disney World, and Xerox.

So if you have a product or service that you think might be useful to a government or large corporation, then go to businessmatchmaking.com and sign up. What you will find when you attend your event is what Mr. Barreto calls "a meaningful opportunity."

THE SYSTEM

In order to make more money and be even more successful, the successful small business should be organized in such a way that the owner or owners are free: free to spend time networking and marketing, free to go after big contracts, and free to spend time on those parts of the business they enjoy and less time on those parts they do not.

One would think that would be the case. After all, a very big reason why entrepreneurs create their businesses in the first place is for the freedom—freedom from the boss, from the grind, from being an employee. But if you have owned a business for any length of time, you may not be all that free. The demands on your time are great; indeed, that is probably the chief complaint among small business owners. If you are like them, you likely spend so much time handling issues and putting out fires that time to think and plan is lost. It is a paradox: Because you may have busted out of one work prison only to create another, you are likely not as free as you would have hoped.

Is there a solution? You bet, and it is a solution that, if implemented, will mean you will enjoy your business more and make more money. In his great book, *The E-Myth: Why Most Small Businesses Don't Work and What to Do About It*, author Michael Gerber explains that most small businesses can be divided into two parts. First, there is the "technical" part of the business: the baker bakes the bread, the web designer designs the web sites. Second, there is everything else associated with running a business: advertising, payroll, money—you know the program. The problem is that knowing how to make a great croissant or web site does not mean that you know how to run a great business. Therefore, the second part of the business is often the trouble spot for many small businesspeople, taking up far too much time and energy and preventing them from growing their business.

Gerber says that the solution to this too-common dilemma lies in one of the most successful businesses of all time—McDonald's. Whether you go into a McDonald's in Moscow, Russia, or Moscow, Idaho, you can expect the same thing. The restaurants are clean, affordable, and the food tastes the same wherever you go because founder

Ray Kroc created a system. Any franchisee who follows the system should get the same result, profits and all.

In *The E-Myth*, Gerber suggests that by creating a similar system (as opposed to haphazard individual efforts and decisions), your small business can become a machine that can run itself. If you systematize it, a bit or a lot, you better enable your employees to do their job, thereby freeing you to do yours. Gerber says that you will know if the system you create works "if it works without you to work it." Does that not sound nice?

Take a look at your business. What works? How could it be more efficient? Think of your business as a prototype for 100 more that will be just like it. What would those other businesses need to know, and what processes will they need to have, to create optimum results? Who needs to do what, and when? How can their work be made predictable and accountable? How can you get employees to take pride in the results? Answering these sorts of questions will help you start creating a system.

> "Does it work? [The] answer is a resounding 'Yes!' it does work. Every time it is applied. And it will work for you. It works because it requires the full engagement of the people working it. It can't be done half-heartedly. It can't be done frenetically. It can only be done intelligently, systematically, and compassionately."
> —Michael Gerber

If you can create a step-by-step guide to running your business, much as any franchisor would, a guide that will allow others to deal with details, then you, the owner, will be able to concentrate on those things you most enjoy, think strategically, and have far more free time. Or consider: If you are really good at creating a system, you could hire a manager and employees to run the business for you altogether. You could become an absentee owner who collects the profits and pays for labor. Many small business owners do just that, their businesses being turnkey operations that simply make them money while they do other things.

Here is the seven-step process:

Step 1: Create your primary aim.   No, not your aim for your business, but your aim for yourself. How do you want your life to look? What do you really want to do on a daily basis? Gerber says until you know what you want your perfect life to be like, you cannot figure out how your business should be organized.

Step 2: Create your strategic objective.   "Your strategic objective is a very clear statement of what your business has to ultimately do for you to achieve your Primary Aim," says the author. What is your vision for your business? Who are your customers, how much money would the business make, and what is its purpose?

Step 3: Create your organizational strategy.   Based upon your answers to steps one and two, how would you need to organize your business? What would your business look like if you were not forced to handle every little thing? Would you need to add or delete staff? What job descriptions and training would they need? How could you turn your business into a turnkey operation?

> "The path you're now on, this entrepreneurial path, winds around corners that will amaze you at times, and even shock you at others. That's why it's so exciting! It's the path of surprise. It's the path of constant engagement. And because it's all of those things, it's truly the path of life, or, as Rollo May puts it, 'the path of freedom.' "   —Michael Gerber

Step 4: Create your management strategy.   In the best franchises they say, "The system is the solution." You need to create that system for every part of your business. A great system is essentially a multiple series of checklists. Anyone should be able to look at their checklist and know what to do. It should be the same thing as creating the same French fries time and again.

Step 5: Create your people strategy.   The danger of creating this system is that employees may feel like they are nothing but a cog in the machine. A people strategy prevents this, so your people strategy is what you want your business culture to be and how you plan to implement it. Your way of doing business becomes part of your operations manual, and system.

Step 6: Create your marketing strategy. Your marketing strategy examines who your customers are and how they fit in with your new business model.

Step 7: Create your systems strategy. You have three systems: Hard systems (computers, cash registers), soft systems (people), and information systems (inventory control, sales, and so forth). Your business process needs to integrate all three systems.

For more information, pick up a copy of *The E-Myth,* by Michael Gerber.

By systematizing your business you will be freed up to make more money and have your business live up to its full potential.

CHAPTER **37**

Small Business Success Secrets II: Vision

What you can do, or dream you can, begin it.
Boldness has genius, power, and magic in it.

—GOETHE

Owning a small business has much more to do with vision and boldness than it does with profits and losses, which are a means to an end. In fact, the business itself is a means to an end. We start a business because we have a dream, a destiny fulfilled by creating a sustainable, beautiful business we love. No, we are not always successful, but it is this vision of creating something special, of making the world and our world better, that drives us. Which begs the question: How can we better realize this passion? Are there business traits that the best of the best can teach the rest? Indeed there are. The best businesses are beacons illuminating the path so that as we continue our entrepreneurial journey, there is light showing us which way to go.

THE BEST BUSINESSES

In their excellent book, *Built to Last* (HarperBusiness, 2002), authors James C. Collins and Jerry I. Porras seek to answer the question, "What makes the truly exceptional companies different from other companies?" The results of their exhaustive research and analysis is fascinating and applicable to businesses both small and large. More than a desire for profits, or a plan to produce pleasing products, the best businesses are founded on, and driven by, vision.

It helps to remember that every amazingly huge, Fortune 500, Nasdaq-traded, stock-splitting, name branded, well-known company you see once started out as a small business. Yet by adhering to their vision they were able to grow beyond their humble roots and become something special. And when I say special, I am not talking about money or profits, though they are nice. I am talking about a business that makes a difference for its shareholders and owners, for its employees, and for its customers. A special business, a great business, solves problems, creates value, is enviable.

The Business Is the Thing

To have a successful business you need not be a genius, you do not have to invent the Next Big Thing, and you do not have to start out with a Big Idea. Wal-Mart began as a single five-and-dime store in Arkansas. Founder Sam Walton told the *New York Times*, "I had no vision of the scope of what I would start, but I always had confidence that as long as we did our work well and were good to our customers, there would be no limit." His big idea, to create a chain of rural discount stores, did not arrive for quite some time: "Like most overnight successes [Wal-Mart] was about 20 years in the making."

Slow starts are okay. Bill Boeing's first plane was such a failure that his aircraft company sold furniture for a few years. Microsoft lost money its first two years. Walt Disney went bankrupt before coming out with *Steamboat Willie*.

P.T. Barnum filed bankruptcy before he started his circus. Henry John Heinz's company filed for bankruptcy in 1875. The next year, he introduced a new condiment called tomato ketchup. Henry Ford's first two car companies failed, the first filing for bankruptcy and the second by agreement. In 1903, at the age of 40, he started the Ford Motor Company.

So if it is not the great idea that gets their motor running, what is it that sustains the small business in the early years? It is the dream, the business itself. As Collins and Porras put it in *Built to Last*, "Never, never, never give up. Be prepared to kill, revise, or evolve an idea, but never give up on the company." They cite HP as a classic example. "Bill Hewitt and Dave Packard kept tinkering, persisting, trying, and experimenting until they figured out how to build an innovative company that would express their core values."

So it is not your great idea that will sustain your business; it is your great business that will sustain the idea. The business is the thing. A slow start can be handled as long as a strong foundation is being laid. Create an organization with values that matter and processes that last. A visionary organization creates visionary products and profits, not the other way around.

There Is More to Business than Profits

You are idealistic; if you were not, then fear, criticism, the unknown, or the naysayers would have stopped you. So we know you are idealistic. The trick to sustained business greatness, then, is to transform that idealism into a set of core business values. The best small businesses have core values and live by them. These values guide owners and employees alike in their everyday activities.

In 1945, Japan was a country in ruins. Devastated by war and two nuclear bombs, Japan had a long, long way to go. It was then, in the remnants of Tokyo, that Masaru Ibuka decided to start a new company he would call Sony. Begun in a bombed-out, deserted department store, Sony was started with the last $1,600 of Ibuka's personal savings. Aside from initially creating some forgettable products (for example, sweet bean-paste soup), Ibuka quickly created a code for his nascent new company, including:

- "A place of work where engineers can feel the joy of technological innovation."
- "To pursue dynamic activities . . . for the reconstruction of Japan."
- "We shall welcome technical difficulties."
- "We shall eliminate any unfair profit seeking."

That last point is critical and illustrative. Everyone loves profits, but evidence indicates that the best businesses mix profits into the values bag, treating them equally with other important business attributes.

> Henry Ford is widely credited with helping to create the middle class by introducing both the five-day work week and the $5 day (roughly double the prevailing wage). The *Wall Street Journal* denounced this last action, stating that Ford had "injected spiritual principles into a field where they do not belong."

Great companies value values. They are not just enterprises created to make a buck. These businesses have a core ideology of which profit is but one ideal. As pointed out in *Built to Last*, in 1960 David Packard of HP gave a lecture to a group of employees. There he said:

> I want to discuss *why* a company exists in the first place. Many people assume wrongly that a company exists simply to make money. . . . As we investigate this, we inevitably come to the conclusion that a group of people get together and exist as an institution that we call a company so that they are able to accomplish something collectively that they could not accomplish separately—they make contributions to society.

Each small business must decide for itself what its core values are. They should be simple, guiding principles upon which to build. You do not need a reason and do not need to justify them. They are *your* core values. Figure out what they are and live by them.

A correlation to this is that the visionary small business should recruit people who can buy into the value system; discuss this during the interview process. Real values, to mean something, must be lived, and if an employee is unwilling to adopt your way, then theirs should be the highway.

When he died, Joe Wilson, founder of Xerox, was found with a small blue index card he apparently kept in his wallet. It said, in part, "To attain serenity through the leadership of a business which brings happiness to its workers, serves its customers, and brings prosperity to its owners."

Think Big

The most successful small businesses create clear, specific, big goals and then organize to achieve them. The goal serves as a focal point for the efforts of the participants. When Ruth Handler decided that her small toy company would create a doll that was a shapely woman, not a baby, as all girls' dolls had been up to that point, the goal was huge. The company had to invent new processes to manufacture the doll, and it took eight years. It changed the entire direction of her business. But her business—Mattel—and her invention—Barbie—transformed an industry. Setting the bar high raises expectations—of yourself, your staff, and of your business itself. A great, big audacious goal can get everyone excited. It crystallizes efforts.

However, a goal alone is not enough. Your business has to be committed, financially and emotionally, to achieving the goal. Goals without commitment is like a basketball without air. It's empty. Set goals for your company, commit to them, enroll your team in them, achieve them, and then set more.

Experiment

Before inventing Tupperware, Earl Tupper created a variety of forgettable products: knitting needles, egg peelers, compact mirrors, and flour sifters to name just a few. He just kept plugging along until he finally hit on a product that worked in the marketplace. This is true for many successful small businesses. Grand visions and strategic plans are wonderful, but it often takes plain old trial and error and plenty of experimentation before the magic combination hits.

Failures happen, but you have to keep throwing stuff against the wall to see what sticks. R.W. Johnson Jr. of Johnson & Johnson famously said, "Failure is our most important product." He knew that failure meant not only his company might learn something new, but that it should also prod them in the proper direction. If you continue to experiment and try new things, opportunities will eventually avail themselves.

In 1938, a DuPont scientist named Roy Plunkett was going to do some experiments of a substance known as TFE, and so stored a canister of the material in some dry ice at the end of the day to preserve it. The next day, the canister was seemingly empty. When he cut it open, he discovered the TFE had transformed into a silky substance that lined the inside of the canister. Plunkett had inadvertently created Teflon. Yet despite a few efforts to commercialize the product, DuPont found only industrial uses for Teflon. It took a Frenchman named Marc Gregoire, who had heard of the material and experimented mightily, to finally figure out how to stick the world's greatest nonstick substance to frying pans. The company he created to sell the pans, Tefal, is still the standard in the industry.

The Competitor Is You

Sure, capitalism is cutthroat, but the best small companies do not necessarily look to their competition to figure out what to do. Instead, they look to their own values and successes and try to top those. It is like the sports team, playing for the championship, who says, "We do not care what our opponent is going to do, what their defensive scheme is, or what plays they will run. This is not about them; it is about us. Are we up to it? How well will we carry out our plan? Will we be our best? If we are our best, no one can beat us."

Be your best. Have a vision. Dare to dream big dreams and have big goals. Commit to them and then chase them. Enroll your team in your cause. Try something new, then try something else. Make sure your small business means something; if it personifies your highest values, you will have created a business of which to be proud.

Be bold, for boldness has genius, magic, and power in it.

Appendix:
Sample Business Plan

THE DAILY PERC
BUSINESS PLAN

Contents

1.0 EXECUTIVE SUMMARY

The Daily Perc (TDP) is a specialty beverage retailer. TDP uses a system that is new to the beverage and food service industry to provide hot and cold beverages in a convenient and time-efficient way. TDP provides its customers the ability to drive up and order (from a trained Barista) their choice of a custom-blended espresso drink, freshly brewed coffee, or other beverage. TDP is offering a high-quality option to the fast-food, gas station, or institutional coffee.

The Daily Perc offers its patrons the finest hot and cold beverages, specializing in specialty coffees, blended teas, and other custom drinks. In addition, TDP will offer soft drinks, fresh-baked pastries, and other confections. Seasonally, TDP will add beverages such as hot apple cider, hot chocolate, frozen coffees, and more.

The Daily Perc will focus on two markets:

The Daily Commuter—someone traveling to/from work, out shopping, delivering goods or services, or just out for a drive.

The Captive Consumer—someone who is in a restricted environment that does not allow convenient departure and return while searching for refreshments, or where refreshment stands are an integral part of the environment.

The Daily Perc will penetrate the commuter and captive consumer markets by deploying Drive-thru facilities and Mobile Cafes in the most logical and accessible locations. The Drive-thru facilities are designed to handle two-sided traffic and dispense customer-designed, specially ordered cups of premium coffees in less time than required for a visit to the locally owned cafe or one of the national chains.

In addition to providing a quality product and an extensive menu of delicious items, to ensure customer awareness and loyalty, as well as good publicity coverage and media support, we will be donating up to 7.5% of revenue to local charities based upon customer choices.

The Daily Perc's financial picture is quite promising. Since TDP is operating a cash business, the initial cost is significantly less than many startups these days. The process is labor intensive and TDP recognizes that a higher level of talent is required. The financial investment in its employees will be one of the greatest differentiators between it and TDP's competition. For the purpose of this pro-forma plan, the capital expenditures of facilities and equipment are financed. There will be minimum inventory on hand so as to keep the product fresh and to take advantage of price drops, when and if they should occur.

The Daily Perc anticipates the initial combination of investments and long term financing of $425,000 to carry it without the need for any additional equity or debt investment, beyond the purchase of equipment or facilities. This will mean growing a bit more slowly than might be otherwise possible, but it will be a solid, financially-sound growth based on customer request and product demand.

The Daily Perc chooses to become the Drive-thru version of Starbucks between the mountains, obtaining several million dollars through an initial public or private offering that would allow the company to open twenty to thirty facilities per year in all metropolitan communities in the North, Midwest, and South with a population of over 150,000. This is the preferred Exit Strategy of the Management Team. The danger in this is that competitors would rise up and establish a foothold on a community before—or in the midst of—the arrival of The Daily Perc, causing a potential for a drain on revenues and a dramatic increase in advertising expenditures to maintain market share. Knowing these risks—and planning for them—gives TDP the edge needed to make this scenario work.

The balance sheet estimates a Net Worth of $1,075,969 for the third year, cash balances of $773,623 and earnings of $860,428, based on 13 Drive-thrus and four Mobile Cafes, it is not unrealistic to put a market value of between $4 and $9 million on the company. At present, such companies are trading in multiples of four to 10 times earnings, and it is simple mathematics to multiply the success of TDP by the number of major and smaller metropolitan areas between the mountain ranges of the United States.

Highlights (Planned)

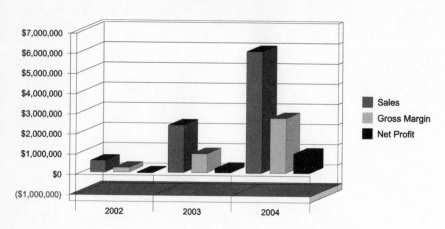

1.1 Objectives

The Daily Perc has established three firm objectives it wishes to achieve in the next three years:

1. Thirteen Drive-thru locations and four fully booked Mobile Cafes by the end of the third year.
2. Gross Margin of 45% or more.
3. Net After-tax Profit above 15% of Sales.

1.2 Mission

The Daily Perc Mission is three-fold, with each being as integral to our success as the next.

- **Product Mission**—Provide customers the finest quality beverage in the most efficient time.
- **Community Mission**—Provide community support through customer involvement.
- **Economic Mission**—Operate and grow at a profitable rate through sound economic decisions.

1.3 Keys to Success

There are four keys to success in this business, three of which are virtually the same as any foodservice business. It is our fourth key—the Community Mission—that will give us that extra measure of respect in the public eye.

1. The greatest locations—visibility, high traffic pattern, convenient access.
2. The best products—freshest coffee beans, cleanest equipment, premium serving containers, consistent flavor.
3. The friendliest servers—cheerful, skilled, professional, articulate.
4. The finest reputation—word-of-mouth advertising, promotion of our community mission of charitable giving.

2.0 COMPANY SUMMARY

The Daily Perc is a specialty beverage retailer. TDP uses a system that is new to the beverage and food service industry to provide hot and cold beverages in a convenient and time-efficient way. TDP provides its customers the ability to drive up and order from a trained Barista their choice of a custom blended espresso drink, freshly brewed coffee, or other beverage. TDP is offering a high quality option to the fast-food, gas station, and institutional coffee.

2.1 Company Ownership

The Daily Perc is a Limited Liability Corporation. All membership shares are currently owned by Bart and Teresa Fisher, with the intent of using a portion of the shares to raise capital.

The plan calls for the sale of 100 membership units in the company to family members, friends, and Angel Investors. Each membership unit in the company is priced at $4,250, with a minimum of five units per membership certificate, or a minimum investment of $21,250 per investor.

If all funds are raised, based on the pricing established in the financial section of this plan, Bart and Terri Fisher will maintain ownership of no less than 51% of the company.

2.2 Startup Summary

The Daily Perc's startup expenses total just $370,170. The majority of these funds—roughly $300,000—will be used to build the first facility, pay deposits, and provide capital for six months of operating expenses. Another $35,000 will be used for the initial inventory and other one-time expenses. The Daily Perc anticipates the need for roughly $30,000 in operating capital for the first few months of operation.

Startup Requirements

Startup Expenses

Legal	$3,500
Office Equipment	$4,950
Drive-thru Labor (6 months)	$65,000
Drive-thru Finance Payment (6 months)	$12,300
Drive-thru Expenses (6 months)	$8,520
Land Lease (6 months)	$7,200
Vehicle Finance (6 months)	$3,700
Administration Labor (6 months)	$54,000
Web Site Development & Hosting	$5,600
Identity/Logos/Stationery	$4,000
Other	$5,000
Total Startup Expenses	$173,770

Startup Assets Needed

Cash Balance on Starting Date	$25,500
Startup Inventory	$35,000

Other Short-term Assets	$0
Total Short-term Assets	$60,500
Long-term Assets	$131,400
Total Assets	$191,900
Total Requirements	$365,670

Funding Investment

Partner 1	$10,000
Partner 2	$10,000
Partner 3	$10,000
Partner 4	$10,000
Partner 5	$11,500
Partner 6	$10,000
Partner 7	$11,500
Partner 8	$10,000
Partner 9	$11,500
Partner 10	$10,000
Partner 11	$11,500
Partner 12	$11,500
Other	$97,770
Total Investment	$225,270

Short-term Liabilities

Accounts Payable	$0
Current Borrowing	$9,000
Other Short-term Liabilities	$0
Subtotal Short-term Liabilities	$9,000
Long-term Liabilities	$131,400
Total Liabilities	$140,400
Loss at Startup	($173,770)
Total Capital	$51,500
Total Capital and Liabilities	$191,900

Start-up

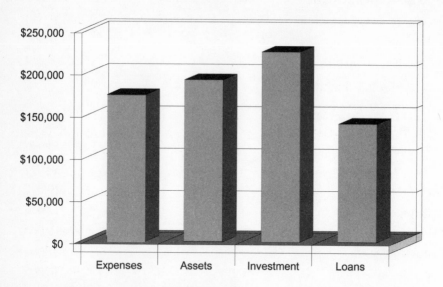

2.3 Company Locations and Facilities

The Daily Perc will open its first drive-thru facility on Manchester Road in the Colonial Square Shopping Center. Twelve more drive-thru facilities will be placed throughout the metropolitan area over the next three years. The drive-thru in the Colonial Square Shopping Center will serve as the commissary for the first mobile unit.

The demographic and physical requirements for a Drive-thru location are:

- Traffic of 40,000+ on store side.
- Visible from roadway.
- Easy entry with light if less than 30,000 cars.
- Established retail shops in area.

3.0 PRODUCTS

The Daily Perc provides its patrons the finest hot and cold beverages, specializing in specialty coffees and custom blended teas. In addition, TDP will offer select domestic soft drinks, Italian sodas, fresh-baked pastries, and other confections. Seasonally, TDP will add beverages such as hot apple cider, hot chocolate, frozen coffees, and more.

3.1 Product Description

TDP provides its customers, whether at a Drive-thru facility or one of the Mobile Cafes, the ability to custom order a coffee beverage that will be blended to their exact specifications. Each of TDP's Baristas will be trained in the fine art of brewing, blending, and serving the highest quality hot and cold beverages, with exceptional attention to detail.

Besides coffees, The Daily Perc will offer teas, domestic and Italian sodas, frozen coffee beverages, seasonal specialty drinks, pastries, and other baked goods. Through the web site and certain locations, TDP will market premium items such as coffee mugs, T-shirts and sweatshirts, ball caps, and more.

3.2 Competitive Comparison

The Daily Perc considers itself to be a player in the retail coffee house industry. However, it knows that competition for its products range from soft drinks to milkshakes to adult beverages.

The Daily Perc's primary competition will come from three sources:

1. National coffee houses such as Starbucks and Panera.
2. Locally owned and operated cafes.
3. Fast food chains and convenience stores.

What will make The Daily Perc stand out from all its competitors are two things:

The Daily Perc will be providing products in the most convenient and efficient way available—either at one of the two-sided Drive-thru shops, or at one of the Mobile Cafes. This separates TDP from the competition in that its customers won't need to find a parking place, wait in a long line, jockey for a seat, and clean up the mess left by a previous patron. TDP customers can drive or walk up, order their beverage, receive and pay for the beverage, and drive off.

The second differentiator is The Daily Perc's focus on providing a significant benefit to the community through a possible 7.5% contribution to customer-identified charities, schools, or other institutions.

3.3 Sourcing

The Daily Perc purchases its coffees from PJ's Coffee. TDP also has wholesale purchasing agreements for other products with Major Brands, Coca-Cola, Big Train, Al's Famous Filled Bagels, L&N Products, and Royal Distribution.

The Drive-thru facilities are manufactured by City Stations and the Mobile Cafes are manufactured by Tow Tech Industries.

Fulfillment equipment suppliers include PJ's Coffee, City Stations, Talbert Ford, and Retail Image Programs. The Daily Perc's computer equipment and Internet connectivity is provided by NSI Communications.

3.4 Technology

The Daily Perc's delivery system is based on its technology. TDP is using state-of-the-art, two-sided, Drive-thru facilities to provide convenience and efficiency for its clientele. An architectural exterior diagram of the Drive Thru building can be found on the following page. (All diagrams have been removed from this plan.)

The Daily Perc has also designed state-of-the-art Mobile Cafes that will be deployed from time to time on high school and college campuses, corporate campuses, and at special events.

3.5 Future Products

As seasons change, The Daily Perc will be offering products that will enhance sales and satisfy its customers' desires. During summer months, TDP will subsidize lower hot beverage sales with frozen coffee drinks, as well as soft drinks, and other cold beverages. TDP will also have special beverages during holiday seasons, such as Egg Nog during the Christmas season and Hot Apple Cider in the Fall.

The Daily Perc's primary desire will be to listen to its customers to ascertain what they are looking for most, and provide it.

4.0 MARKET ANALYSIS SUMMARY

The Daily Perc will focus on two markets:

1. **The Daily Commuter**—someone traveling to or from work, out shopping, delivering goods or services, or just out for a drive.
2. **The Captive Consumer**—someone who is in a restricted environment that does not allow convenient departure and return while searching for refreshments, or where refreshment stands are an integral part of the environment.

4.1 Market Segmentation

The Daily Perc will focus on two different market segments: Commuters and Captive Consumers. To access both of these markets, TDP has two different delivery systems. For the commuters, TDP has the Drive-thru coffee house. For the captive consumer, TDP has the Mobile Cafe.

Commuters are defined as any one or more individuals in a motorized vehicle traveling from point "A" to point "B." The Daily Perc's greatest concentration will be on commuters heading to or from work, or those out on their lunch break.

Captive Consumers would include those who are tethered to a campus environment, or in a restricted entry environment that does not allow free movement to and from. Examples would include high school and college campuses, where there is limited time between classes, and corporate campuses where the same time constraints are involved, but regarding meetings and project deadlines, and special events—such as carnivals, fairs or festivals—where there is an admission price to enter the gate, but exiting would mean another admission fee, or where refreshments are an integral part of the festivities.

The following chart and table reflect the potential numbers of venues available for the Mobile Cafes and what growth could be expected in those markets over the next five years. For a conservative estimate of the number of Captive Consumers this represents, multiply the total number of venues in the year by 1,000. As an example, in the first year, The Daily Perc is showing that there are a total of 2,582 venues at which we might position a Mobile Cafe. That would equate to a Captive Consumer potential of 2,582,000.

Similarly, there are well over 2,500,000 commuters in the metropolitan area, as well as visitors, vacationers, and others. It can also be assumed that these commuters do not make only one purchase in a day, but in many cases, two and even three beverage purchases.

The chart reflects college and high school campuses, special events, hospital campuses, and various charitable organizations. A segment that is not reflected in the chart (since it would skew the chart so greatly) is the number of corporate campuses in the metropolitan area. There are over 1,700 corporate facilities that house more than 500 employees, giving us an additional 1,700,000 prospective customers, or a total of 2,582 locations at which we could place a Mobile Cafe.

Market Analysis (Pie)

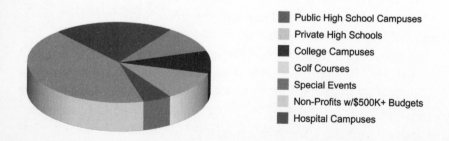

- Public High School Campuses
- Private High Schools
- College Campuses
- Golf Courses
- Special Events
- Non-Profits w/$500K+ Budgets
- Hospital Campuses

Market Analysis

Potential Customers	Growth	2001	2002	2003	2004	2005	CAGR
Public High School Campuses	1%	80	81	82	83	84	1.23%
Private High Schools	0%	88	88	88	88	88	0.00%
College Campuses	0%	77	77	77	77	77	0.00%
Golf Courses	0%	99	99	99	99	99	0.00%
Special Events	3%	43	44	45	46	47	2.25%
Non-Profits w/$500k+ Budgets	2%	362	369	376	384	392	2.01%
Hospital Campuses	0%	100	100	100	100	100	0.00%
Total	1.10%	849	858	867	877	887	1.10%

4.2 Target Market Segment Strategy

TDP's target market is the mobile individual who has more money than time, and excellent taste in a choice of beverage, but no time to linger in a cafe. By locating the Drive-Thrus in high traffic/high visibility areas, this unique—and abundant—consumer will seek The Daily Perc out and become a regular guest.

To penetrate the target market for the Mobile Cafes, these units will do what they were designed to do. The Daily Perc will take the cafe to the customer! By using the community support program TDP is instituting, arrangements will be made to visit a high school, college campus, or a corporate campus once or twice a month (Even visit these facilities for special games, tournaments, recruiting events, or corporate open houses). And, for every cup or baked good sold, a portion is returned to the high school or college. It becomes a tremendous, painless way for the institution to gain a financial reward while providing a pleasant and fulfilling benefit to their students or employees.

4.2.1 Market Needs. The United States is a very mobile society. With the introduction of the automobile, we became a nation that thrived on the further freedom of going where we wanted when we wanted. It has only gotten worse. There are over 250 million men, women and children in America, half of whom are too old, too young, or too poor to drive an automobile. Yet, there are more licensed vehicles in the country than people. And that mobility has created a unique need in our society.

Our market is made up of consumers who have busy schedules, a desire for quality, and disposable income. As much as they would like the opportunity to sit in an upscale coffee house and sip a uniquely blended coffee beverage and read the morning paper, they don't have the time. However, they still have the desire for the uniquely blended beverage as they hurry through their busy lives.

4.2.2 Market Trends. Nearly twenty years ago, a trend towards more unique coffees began to develop in the U.S. There had always been specialty coffee stores, such as Gloria Jeans and others, but people began to buy espresso machines for their homes and offices, and people began to have coffee tastings. Then espresso bars began to appear and, inevitably, along came Starbucks—the quintessential bastion of the upwardly mobile professional who wanted to take control over how their beverage would taste and smell.

However, we have also become more rushed for time during that same period. Those same consumers who helped push Starbucks to $2.2 billion in global sales are now rushing kids to soccer and basketball games, running to the grocery and trying to get to work on time and back home in time for dinner—or to get to the next soccer game. Yet, they still have the desire for that refreshing, specially blended coffee each morning.

Lately, we've seen the introduction of beverage dispensers at convenience stores that spit out overly-sweet, poorly blended cappuccinos in flavors such as french vanilla or mocha, and consumers are paying as much as $3.00 for these sub-standard beverages.

The market is primed for the introduction of a company that offers a superior quality, specially blended product in a convenient, drive-thru environment at a price that is competitive to the national coffee houses.

4.2.3 Market Growth. According to industry statistics, the consumption of coffee and flavored coffee products is growing rapidly. The largest national brand for retail coffee outlets achieved $2.2 billion in sales in 2000 with 3,000 retail outlets. They are anticipating opening 7,000 more outlets in the next five years and increasing revenues to over $6 billion.

That is the coffee consumer market. The segment of that market we are targeting is the commuter and that number is increasing. In the metropolitan area, as with many metropolitan areas in the country, there is a migration away from the cities.

It is estimated that there are well over 2.5 million commuters driving to and from work each day in our market. Statistically, at least 50% of those are coffee drinkers. That gives The Daily Perc a significant daily target for its products. Those numbers are growing by 6% per year.

4.3 Industry Analysis

The coffee industry has grown by tremendous amounts in the U.S. over the past five years. Starbucks, the national leader, had revenues in fiscal 2000 of $2.2 billion. That is an increase of 32% over fiscal 1999. Starbucks plans to increase revenues to over $6.6 billion from 10,000 retail outlets by 2005.

Even general coffee sales have increased with international brands such as Folgers, Maxwell House, and Safari coffee reporting higher sales and greater profits.

America is definitely a coffee country and the coffee industry is reaping the rewards.

4.3.1 Industry Participants. There is only one national Drive-thru coffee franchise operation in the U.S. with any legs, and that is a subsidiary of Chock Full o' Nuts called Quikava. Quikava operates predominantly on the East Coast and in the Upper Great Lakes. The East and West coasts, and even some Mountain and Midwest states, have smaller local drive-thru chains such as Caffino, Java Espress, Crane Coffee, Java Drive, Sunrise Coffee, and Caffe Diva. However, other players in the premium coffee service industry would include Starbucks, Gloria Jean's, Caribou Coffee, Panera and locally owned and operated coffee shops or "cafes."

4.3.2 Distribution Patterns. The cafe experience comes from the Italian origins of espresso. The customer comes in to a beautifully decorated facility, surrounded by wondrous aromas and finds himself involved in a sensory experience that, more often than not, masks an average product at a premium price. However, the proliferation of cafes in the United States proves the viability of the market. It is a duplication of the same delivery process as currently exists in Europe.

4.3.3 Competition and Buying Patterns. There are four general competitors in The Daily Perc's drive-thru market. They are the national specialty beverage chains, such as Starbucks and Panera, local coffee houses—or cafes—with an established clientele and a quality product, fast food restaurants, and convenience stores. There is a dramatic distinction among the patrons of each of these outlets.

Patrons to a Starbucks, or to one of the local cafes, are looking for the "experience" of the coffee house. They want the ability to "design" their coffee, smell the fresh pastry, listen to the soothing Italian music, and read the local paper or visit with an acquaintance. It is a relaxing, slow paced environment.

Patrons of the fast food restaurants or the convenience stores are just the opposite. They have no time for idle chatter and are willing to over-pay for whatever beverage the machine can spit out, as long as it's quick. They pay for their gas and they are back on the road to work. Although they have the desire and good taste to know good from bad, time is more valuable to them.

Competitors to the Mobile Cafes on campuses would include fast food restaurants—assuming they are close enough to the consumer that they can get there and back in the minimal allotted time, vending machines, and company or school cafeterias. The consumers in this environment are looking for a quick, convenient, fairly priced, quality refreshment that will allow them to purchase the product and return to work, class, or other activity.

Competitors to the Mobile Cafes at events such as festivals and fairs would include all the other vendors who are licensed to sell refreshments. Attendees to such events expect to pay a premium price for a quality product.

4.3.4 Main Competitors. When measuring head-to-head, direct competitors, we have found that there are none in the metropolitan area. The Daily Perc will be the first double-sided, drive-thru coffee house in the metropolitan area. However, there is still significant competition from traditional coffee houses and other retailers.

National Chains: Starbucks, the national leader, had revenues in fiscal year 2000 of $2.2 billion. That is an increase of 32% over fiscal year 1999. Starbucks plans to increase revenues to over $6.6 billion from 10,000 retail outlets by 2005.

Panera had revenues of $151 million from corporate owned stores and $350 million from franchised locations in fiscal year 2000. This fiscal year revenue was an increase of 28.9% on a per store basis versus fiscal year 1999.

The Daily Perc believes it has a significant competitive advantage over these chains because of the following benefits:

- Drive-thru Service
- More Substantial Customer Service
- Community Benefit
- Mobile Cafes
- Selection
- Higher Product Quality

Local Cafes: The toughest competitor for The Daily Perc is the established locally owned cafe. TDP knows the quality and pride that the local cafe has in the product purchased by their customers. Any local cafe has a customer base that is dedicated and highly educated. The quality of beverages served at an established cafe will surpass any of the regional or national chains.

The competitive edge The Daily Perc has on the local cafes is based on the attributes of:

- Drive-thru Service
- Supply Discounts
- Mobile Cafe
- Consistent Menu
- Community Benefit
- Quality Product

Drive-thru Coffee Houses: There is not a drive-thru specialty beverage retailer with significant market presence in the central United States. The only company with similar depth to that of The Daily Perc is Quikava, a wholly owned subsidiary of Chock Full o' Nuts. However, Quikava has limited its corporate footprint to the East Coast and the Great Lakes Region.

In the drive-thru specialty beverage market, The Daily Perc has a competitive edge over the smaller retailers, and even Quikava, due to:

- Mobile Cafes
- Consistent Menu
- Community Benefit
- Quality Product
- Supply Discounts
- Valued Image
- Greater Product Selection

Fast Food and Convenience Stores: These are two industries where The Daily Perc will experience a certain level of competition. The national fast food chains and national convenience store chains already serve coffee, soda, and some breakfast foods. The national fast food chains obviously know the benefits and value to customers of drive-thru. TDP knows that within the specialty coffee and tea market, the quality of the products sold will be much greater than what can currently be purchased at fast food and convenience stores. The addition of domestic soda sales for these stores is a large part of revenue. TDP knows the quality of our products, along with the addition of domestic soda and the ease of drive-thru, gives it a competitive edge over fast food and convenience stores.

Other Competition: The Daily Perc knows that once it has entered the market and established a presence, others will try to follow. However, TDP believes that the corporate missions and even the organizational design will be imitated, but never duplicated. TDP will constantly evaluate its products, locations, service, and corporate missions to ensure that it remains a leader in the specialty beverage industry.

5.0 STRATEGY AND IMPLEMENTATION SUMMARY

The Daily Perc will penetrate the commuter and captive consumer markets by deploying Drive-thru facilities and Mobile Cafes in the most logical and accessible locations. The Drive-thrus are designed to handle two-sided traffic and dispense customer-designed, specially ordered cups of specialty beverages in less time than required for a visit to the locally owned cafe or one of the national chains.

The Daily Perc has identified its market as busy, mobile people whose time is already at a premium, but desire a refreshing, high quality beverage or baked item while commuting to or from work or school.

In addition to providing a quality product and an extensive menu of delicious items, to ensure customer awareness and loyalty, as well as positive public and media support, The Daily Perc could be donating up to 7.5% of revenue from each cup sold in individual Drive-thrus to the charities of the customers' choice.

5.1 Strategy Pyramids

The Daily Perc's strategy is to show people that TDP has an excellent product, convenient accessibility, and with a community benefit. To execute this strategy, TDP is placing the Drive-thrus and Mobile Cafes at easily accessible locations throughout the metropolitan area. TDP is pricing its product competitively and training the production staff to be among the best Baristas in the country. Then, through coupons and display ads at the locations, TDP will involve the customers in community support efforts by explaining that a portion of their purchase price will be donated to a charity of their choosing.

In so doing, TDP has:

- Provided a customer with a quality product at a competitive price.
- Provided the customer with a more convenient method for obtaining their desired product.
- Demonstrated how TDP appreciates their loyalty and patronage by donating money to their personal cause.

5.2 Value Proposition

The Drive-thru facilities provide a substantial value proposition in that the customer does not have to find a parking place, exit the vehicle, stand in line to order, wait for the beverages ahead of him to be produced, pay a premium price for average product, find a place to sit, clean up the previous patron's mess, then enjoy their coffee—assuming they have sufficient time to linger over the cup.

The Daily Perc concept is that the customer drives up, places the order, receives a high quality product at a competitive price, and drives away, having wasted little time in the process.

The Daily Perc is also providing a significant community value to patronizing TDP. For every purchase a customer makes from us, TDP will donate up to 7.5% of the sale to the local charity selected by the customer.

5.3 Competitive Edge

The Daily Perc's competitive edge is simple. TDP provides a high quality product at a competitive price in a Drive-thru environment that saves time.

5.4 Marketing Strategy

First and foremost, The Daily Perc will be placing its Drive-thru facilities in locations of very high visibility and great ease of access. They will be located on high traffic commuter routes and close to shopping facilities in order to catch customers going to or from work, or while they are out for lunch, or on a shopping expedition. The Drive-thrus are very unique and eye-catching, which will be a branding feature of its own.

The Daily Perc will be implementing a low cost advertising/promotion campaign which could involve drive-time radio, but not much more.

The Daily Perc will rely on building relationships with schools, charities and corporations to provide significant free publicity because of its community support program. By giving charitable contributions to these institutions, they will get the word out to their students/faculty/employees/partners about TDP. Word of mouth has always proven to be the greatest advertising program a company can instill. In addition, the media will be more than willing to promote the charitable aspects of TDP and provide the opportunity for more exposure every time TDP writes a check to another organization.

5.4.1 Positioning Statements. For busy, mobile people whose time is already at a premium, but desire a refreshing, high quality beverage or baked item while commuting to or from work or school.

5.4.2 Pricing Strategy. The Daily Perc pricing will be comparable to the competition, but with the value-added feature of immediate, drive-thru service and convenience. The following table illustrates our competitive pricing structure. (Table removed for confidentiality.)

5.4.3 Promotion Strategy. The long-range goal is to gain enough visibility to leverage the product line into other regions and generate inquiries from potential inventors. To do that, The Daily Perc needs:

Public relations services at $1,000 per month for the next year intended to generate awareness of editors and product information insertions, reviews, etc. It is anticipated that the school fundraising program will generate a fair amount of publicity on its own and will, perhaps, minimize—or even eliminate—the need for a publicist.

Advertising at $1,000 per month concentrating on drive time radio. The Daily Perc will experiment with different stations, keeping careful track of results. As with the school fundraising program, TDP expects the facilities and signage to be a substantial portion of our advertising. However, in the startup phase, TDP needs to let people know where to look for the facilities.

5.4.4 Distribution Strategy. The Daily Perc will locate Drive-thru facilities in high traffic areas of the city where it knows working commuters will be passing.

The Daily Perc will also make arrangements for the Mobile Cafes to be at as many schools, businesses, and events as possible every year, so that new customers, those who come in from areas where TDP may not have a Drive-thru facility, can be reached and those who didn't have the time to stop off that morning at their favorite Daily Perc.

5.4.5 Marketing Programs.

Distinctive Logo: "Papo" is a very happy and conspicuous sun. The sun is one of infinite mental pictures. The sun touches every human being every day. Obviously, TDP wants to touch every customer every day. That is why the use of the sun lends itself to being the corporate identifier. Papo is already an award winning logo. Papo won in the New Artist Category of the 2001 Not Just Another Art Director's Club (NJAADC).

Distinctive Buildings: TDP is using diner style buildings for its Drive-thru facilities. TDP has worked closely with the manufacturer to make the building distinctive, so that it is easy to recognize, and functional.

The Fund-Raising and Catering Trailer: The Mobile Cafe will be a key marketing tool. The similarities between the Mobile Cafes and the Drive-thru facilities will be unmistakable. The exposure these units will provide cannot be measured in dollars. The Daily

Perc will negotiate visits with the Mobile Units at schools, hospitals, corporations and other entities. In the case of schools and certain corporations, a portion of all sales made while on their campus could go to a program of their choice. The organization would promote its presence to their constituency and encourage them to frequent the Drive-thru establishments so that their charitable cause is nurtured. This will give those patrons an opportunity to taste the products and become a regular customer of the Drive-thru facilities. The Mobile Cafes will also be appearing at community events such as fairs, festivals, and other charitable events.

Advertising and Promotion: In the first year, The Daily Perc plans to spend $18,000 on advertising and promotion, with the program beginning in September, after the opening of the first Drive-thru. This would not be considered a serious advertising budget for any business, but TDP feels the exposure will come from publicity and promotion, so most of the funds will be spent on a good publicist who will get the word out about the charitable contribution program and how it works in conjunction with the web site. TDP also believes that word-of-mouth advertising and free beverage coupons will be better ways to drive people to the first and second locations.

In the second year, The Daily Perc is increasing the budget to $36,000, since it will need to promote several locations, with particular emphasis on announcing these openings and all the other locations. TDP will continue to use publicity as a key component of the marketing program, since TDP could be contributing over $70,000 to local schools and charities.

In the third year, The Daily Perc will increase its advertising and promotion budget to $72,000, with the majority of the advertising budget being spent on drive time radio. As in the previous years, TDP will get substantial publicity from the donation of nearly $200,000 to local schools and charities.

5.5 Sales Strategy

There will be several sales strategies put into place, including posting specials on high-profit items at the drive-up window. The Baristas will also hand out free drink coupons to those who have purchased a certain number of cups or something similar. TDP will also develop window sales techniques such as the Baristas asking if the customer would like a fresh-baked item with their coffee.

5.5.1 Sales Forecast. In the first year, The Daily Perc anticipates having two Drive-thru locations in operation. The first location will open in the third month of this plan and be fully operational beginning on the 1st day of September. The second Drive-thru will open six months later. TDP is building in a certain amount of ramp-up for each facility while commuters become familiar with its presence. The Drive-thrus will generate 288,000 tickets in the first year of operation, or approximately $558,000 in revenue.

In the second year, The Daily Perc will add two more Drive-thrus and, in the third year, TDP will add an additional nine Drive-thru facilities. The addition of these facilities will increase the revenue from Drive-thrus to a total of over 1,000,000 tickets or $2.35 million in the second year and 2,675,000 tickets or just over $6 million in the third.

In addition to the Drive-thrus, The Daily Perc will deploy one mobile unit in the fourth quarter of the first fiscal year. TDP expects this mobile unit to generate 10,000 tickets each, at an average ticket price of $2.45, which will generate gross revenues of approximately $24,500.

In the second quarter of the second fiscal year, The Daily Perc will deploy a second and third mobile unit. TDP expects all three mobile units to generate 150,000 tickets, or gross revenue of $375,00 in the second year. In the third fiscal year, with an additional fourth mobile unit deployed, TDP expects to see 264,000 mobile unit tickets, or $673,200 in gross revenue.

The Daily Perc is also showing revenue from the commerce portion of our web site, where it will sell "The Daily Perc" T-shirts, sweatshirts, insulated coffee mugs, pre-packaged coffee beans, and other premium items. TDP is not expecting this to be a significant profit center, but it is an integral part of the marketing plan—as a function of developing our brand and building product awareness. TDP expects revenues from this portion, to begin in the second fiscal year, to reach $26,000 initially, and $36,000 in the third fiscal year.

Sales Monthly (Planned)

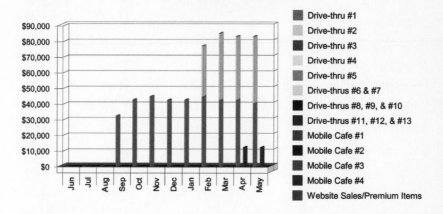

Total first year unit sales should reach 298,402, equating to revenues of $558,043. The second year will see unit sales increase to 1,177,400, or $2,348,900. The third year, with the addition of such a significant number of outlets, we will see unit sales increase to 2,992,000, equating to gross sales revenue of $6,022,950.

Sales Forecast

Unit Sales	2002	2003	2004
Drive-thru #1	202,913	300,000	325,000
Drive-thru #2	85,489	300,000	325,000
Drive-thru #3	0	275,000	325,000
Drive-thru #4	0	150,000	325,000
Drive-thru #5	0	0	300,000
Drive-thrus #6 & #7	0	0	450,000
Drive-thrus #8, #9, & #10	0	0	450,000
Drive-thrus #11, #12, & #13	0	0	225,000
Mobile Cafe #1	10,000	60,000	66,000
Mobile Cafe #2	0	45,000	66,000
Mobile Cafe #3	0	45,000	66,000
Mobile Cafe #4	0	0	66,000
Web Site Sales/Premium Items	0	2,400	3,000
Total Unit Sales	298,402	1,177,400	2,992,000

Unit Prices	2002	2003	2004
Drive-thru #1	$1.85	$1.90	$1.95
Drive-thru #2	$1.85	$1.90	$1.95
Drive-thru #3	$0.00	$1.90	$1.95
Drive-thru #4	$0.00	$1.90	$1.95
Drive-thru #5	$0.00	$1.90	$1.95
Drive-thrus #6 & #7	$0.00	$1.90	$1.95
Drive-thrus #8, #9, & #10	$0.00	$1.90	$1.95
Drive-thrus #11, #12, & #13	$0.00	$1.90	$1.95
Mobile Cafe #1	$2.45	$2.50	$2.55
Mobile Cafe #2	$0.00	$2.50	$2.55
Mobile Cafe #3	$0.00	$2.50	$2.55
Mobile Cafe #4	$0.00	$2.50	$2.55
Web Site Sales/Premium Items	$0.00	$11.00	$12.00
Sales			
Drive-thru #1	$375,389	$570,000	$633,750
Drive-thru #2	$158,154	$570,000	$633,750
Drive-thru #3	$0	$522,500	$633,750
Drive-thru #4	$0	$285,000	$633,750
Drive-thru #5	$0	$0	$585,000
Drive-thrus #6 & #7	$0	$0	$877,500
Drive-thrus #8, #9, & #10	$0	$0	$877,500
Drive-thrus #11, #12, & #13	$0	$0	$438,750
Mobile Cafe #1	$24,500	$150,000	$168,300
Mobile Cafe #2	$0	$112,500	$168,300
Mobile Cafe #3	$0	$112,500	$168,300
Mobile Cafe #4	$0	$0	$168,300
Web Site Sales/Premium Items	$0	$26,400	$36,000
Total Sales	$558,043	$2,348,900	$6,022,950
Direct Unit Costs	2002	2003	2004
Drive-thru #1	$0.64	$0.61	$0.59
Drive-thru #2	$0.64	$0.61	$0.59
Drive-thru #3	$0.00	$0.61	$0.59
Drive-thru #4	$0.00	$0.61	$0.59

Drive-thru #5	$0.00	$0.61	$0.59
Drive-thrus #6 & #7	$0.00	$0.61	$0.59
Drive-thrus #8, #9, & #10	$0.00	$0.61	$0.59
Drive-thrus #11, #12, & #13	$0.00	$0.61	$0.59
Mobile Cafe #1	$0.64	$0.61	$0.59
Mobile Cafe #2	$0.00	$0.61	$0.59
Mobile Cafe #3	$0.00	$0.61	$0.59
Mobile Cafe #4	$0.00	$0.61	$0.59
Web Site Sales/Premium Items	$0.00	$6.50	$6.50
Direct Cost of Sales	*2002*	*2003*	*2004*
Drive-thru #1	$129,864	$184,440	$192,920
Drive-thru #2	$54,713	$184,440	$192,920
Drive-thru #3	$0	$169,070	$192,920
Drive-thru #4	$0	$92,220	$192,920
Drive-thru #5	$0	$0	$178,080
Drive-thrus #6 & #7	$0	$0	$267,120
Drive-thrus #8, #9, & #10	$0	$0	$267,120
Drive-thrus #11, #12, & #13	$0	$0	$133,560
Mobile Cafe #1	$6,400	$36,888	$39,178
Mobile Cafe #2	$0	$27,666	$39,178
Mobile Cafe #3	$0	$27,666	$39,178
Mobile Cafe #4	$0	$0	$39,178
Web Site Sales/Premium Items	$0	$15,600	$19,500
Subtotal Direct Cost of Sales	$190,977	$737,990	$1,793,770

5.5.2 Sales Programs.

Corporate Tasting Events. TDP plans to host tasting events for customers on a quarterly basis. Each quarter, at the introduction of each season, TDP will be adjusting its menu to reflect the changes in the flavors served.

Drink Coupons. At fundraising events for schools and corporate events, we will be giving away drink coupons as door prizes or awards. This encourages the person to come in for their free beverage and bring a friend or buy a baked item or a package of our premium coffee. The Drive-thru units will also be distributing coupons for special menu items or new product introductions.

Chamber of Commerce and Professional Memberships. Because of the need to sell the Mobile Cafe services, TDP will be an active participant in the Regional Chamber, local Chambers of Commerce, Foodservice Associations, and Specialty Beverage Associations. The exposure and education that these organizations provide is outstanding, but equally important are the contacts and opportunities made available for deploying a Mobile Cafe—or even two—at a special event.

5.6 Strategic Alliances

The Daily Perc has and will continue to depend heavily on our alliance with PJ's Coffees, as well as our alliances with the Mobile Cafe and Drive-thru facility manufacturers and consumable products providers. However, we will always be looking for better quality products, more favorable pricing, or more timely delivery from other potential alliances.

We also consider the schools, non-profit organizations, and even corporations who host one of our Mobile Cafes as a strategic alliances, since they are providing exposure to our products and we are providing them a financial benefit.

5.7 Milestones

The Milestone table reflects critical dates for occupying headquarters, launching the first Drive-thru and subsequent Drive-thrus, as well as deployment of the mobile units. The Daily Perc also defines our break-even month, our web site launch and subsequent visitor interaction function, and other key markers that will help us measure our success in time and accomplishment.

Milestones (Planned)

Milestone	Start Date	End Date	Budget	Manager	Department
Light Website	6/1/01	8/15/01	$5,600	COO	Mktg.
Open First Drive-thru	7/15/01	8/31/01	$105,400	COO	Admin.

First Break-even Month	12/1/01	12/31/01	$0	COO	Finance
Open Second Drive-thru	12/15/01	2/1/02	$105,400	COO	Admin.
Receive First Mobile Unit	3/1/02	3/30/02	$86,450	COO	Admin.
Launch Website Voting	5/1/02	6/1/02	$12,500	COO	Mktg.
Open Third Drive-thru	4/15/02	6/1/02	$105,400	COO	Admin.
Receive Second and Third Mobile Units	7/15/02	9/1/02	$172,900	COO	Admin.
Open Fourth Drive-thru	12/15/02	2/1/03	$105,400	COO	Admin.
Install Point-of-Sale System	12/1/02	2/1/03	$21,000	CIO	MIS
Occupy Headquarters	4/1/03	5/15/03	$45,000	COO	Admin.
Open Fifth Drive-thru	4/15/03	6/1/03	$105,400	COO	Admin.
Receive Fourth Mobile Unit	4/15/03	6/1/03	$86,450	Equip.	Admin.
Open Drive-thrus 6 and 7	7/15/03	9/15/03	$210,800	COO/Dir.	Mgnt.
Open Drive-thrus 8, 9 and 10	10/15/03	12/15/03	$316,200	COO/Dir.	Mgnt.
Open Drive-thrus 11, 12, and 13	1/15/04	3/1/04	$316,200	COO	Admin.
Expand to Kansas City	1/15/04	6/1/04	$176,943	COO	Mgnt.
Open First Franchise	10/31/03	9/1/04	$45,000	CFO	Finance
Initiate Exit Strategy	10/1/04	1/1/05	$100,000	CFO	Mgnt.
Totals			$2,122,043		

6.0 MANAGEMENT SUMMARY

The Daily Perc is a relatively flat organization. Overhead for management will be kept to a minimum and all senior managers will be "hands-on" workers. There is no intention of having a top-heavy organization that drains profits and complicates decisions.

At the zenith of this three-year plan, there will be four "Executive" positions: chief operating officer, chief financial officer, chief information officer, and director of marketing. There will be other mid-management positions, such as district managers for every four Drive-thrus, and a facilities manager to oversee the maintenance and stocking of the Mobile Cafes, as well as overseeing the maintenance and replacement of equipment in the Drive-thru facilities.

6.1 Organizational Structure

The organization will be a relatively flat one, since the majority of personnel are involved in production and there will be a relatively low headcount in management.

There are three functioning groups within the company: Production, Sales and Marketing, and General and Administrative. For purposes of this plan—and to show the details of adding senior level management—The Daily Perc has broken management down as a separate segment, but it is an integral part of the General and Administrative function.

Production involves the Baristas, or Customer Service Specialists, who will be manning the Drive-thrus and Mobile Cafes and blending the beverages for the customers. Sales and Marketing will handle the promotion and scheduling of the Mobile Cafes, as well as the promotion of the Drive-thrus and the Community Contribution program. General and Administrative manage the facilities, equipment, inventory, payroll, and other basic, operational processes.

6.2 Management Team

The Daily Perc has selected Mr. Barton Fisher to perform the duties of chief operating officer. Bart has a highly entrepreneurial spirit and has already started a company from scratch (NetCom Services, Inc.) that ran in the black within three months of inception, and paid off all initial debt within six months. Upon leaving NSI in April 2001, the company had again paid off all debt and was running a profit monthly. Combine his experience, leadership, and desire with three years of research in specialty drinks and drive-thru service, and TDP knows that Bart is the individual who will get the company out of the gate and up to full speed for a long time to come.

Ms. Mary Jamison has been selected to fulfill the position of book-keeper and office manager. Mary has been the business administrator of Jones International, Inc. for the past four years. Jones is a $4 million company that retails vitamins and other betterment products. Over those four years, Mary has written numerous corporate policies and directed the financial reporting and reconciliation. The Daily Perc considers Mary to be a great addition to the team when she becomes available in November of 2001. Until that time, she will be working with Mr. Fisher on a part-time basis to help establish the corporate accounts and policies.

Mr. Tony Guy has been selected to perform the duties of corporate events coordinator on a part time basis. Mr. Guy has over five years in the business-to-business sales realm. Last year he was responsible for over $250,000 in sales of promotional material to corporate and educational clients.

Mr. Chuck McNulty has been selected to fulfill the position of warehouse/trailer manager. Chuck has been working for Nabisco, Inc. as a service representative for over ten years. His experience in account services, merchandising, and inventory control is a welcome addition to The Daily Perc team. Chuck will use his knowledge in conjunction with the rest of the team to establish inventory and warehouse policies. The warehouse manager is responsible for inventory of all products sold by The Daily Perc. Some merchandising experience is a welcome addition. Training in the First In First Out (FIFO) style of inventory control is a requirement. Also, knowledge of ergonomics and health issues would be important. Chuck's domain will be the headquarters, the trailers, and the drive-thrus—ensuring that minimum and maximum inventories are maintained. Working with the mobile and drive-thru Baristas will be integral to his task as well.

6.3 Management Team Gaps

The Daily Perc knows that it is going to require several quality management team members over the next three years, beginning with a district manager for every four Drive-thrus. This person will oversee the quality of product, the training of the Baristas, the inventory management, and customer satisfaction. Ideally, as The Daily Perc grows, it will be able to promote from within for this position. This individual will be responsible for the operation of up to four drive-thrus under his/her management. They will be required to visit between locations and possibly even join administrative personnel on training or marketing travel. Clearly, as the need arises, these individuals will ideally be selected from the Mobile Cafe or Drive-Thru team.

By the beginning of the third year, The Daily Perc will hire three key senior managers. They are: a chief financial officer, a chief information officer, and a director of marketing. The role of each of these individuals will be discussed in subsequent sections of this plan.

6.4 Personnel Plan

The Daily Perc expects the first year to be rather lean, since there will only be two locations and one mobile unit—none of which will be deployed for the entire year. The total headcount for the first year, including management, administrative support, and customer service (production), will be 15, with a total payroll of $242,374, a payroll burden of $36,356, and a total expenditure of $278,730.

The second year, with the addition of two Drive-thrus and two mobile units, The Daily Perc will add customer service personnel, as well as a district manager and some additional support staff at headquarters, including an Inventory Clerk, Equipment Technician, and administrative support. The headcount will increase by nearly 100% in the second year to 29, with a payroll of $846,050 and a payroll burden of $126,908.

The third year will see the most dramatic growth in headcount, due to the addition of nine Drive-thrus and another mobile unit. In the third year, there will also be an increase of 180% over the previous year. Total payroll for the third year will be $2,024,250, with a payroll burden of $303,638. There will be a significant increase in the senior management team, with the addition of a chief financial officer, a chief information officer, and a director of marketing. There will also be a second and third district manager, and a corporate events sales executive. Total personnel will reach 81.

The chief financial officer will be brought on to oversee the increase in numbers of retail outlets and to manage a dramatically more detailed P&L statement and to manage the Balance Sheet. The chief information officer will be brought in to help us with the deployment of a Point-of-Sale computerized cash register system that will make tracking and managing receipts and charitable contributions more robust. Ideally, this individual will have a large amount of point of sale and Internet experience. Specifically, how to tie in POS systems to the Internet and inventory controls. Also, knowledge in establishing technology guidelines for the company and franchisees in the future. This individual will also be added in fiscal year three.

The director of marketing will be charged with managing the relationships with advertising agencies, public relations firms, the media, and our website.

Personnel Plan

Production Personnel	2002	2003	2004
Drive-thru Team	$135,474	$439,250	$1,098,650
Mobile Cafe Team	$9,400	$172,800	$225,600
Equipment Care Specialist (Headquarters)	$0	$22,000	$77,000
Other	$0	$12,000	$24,000
Subtotal	$144,874	$646,050	$1,425,250
Sales and Marketing Personnel			
District Manager (Four Drive-thrus)	$0	$22,000	$77,000
Corporate Events Sales Exec	$0	$0	$36,000

Director of Marketing	$0	$0	$72,000
Other	$0	$0	$0
Subtotal	$0	$22,000	$185,000
General and Administrative Personnel			
Bookkeeper/Office Administrator	$24,500	$46,000	$54,000
Warehouse/Site Manager	$7,000	$42,000	$48,000
Inventory Clerk	$0	$12,000	$42,000
Other	$0	$6,000	$12,000
Subtotal	$31,500	$106,000	$156,000
Other Personnel			
Chief Operating Officer	$66,000	$72,000	$78,000
Chief Financial Officer	$0	$0	$96,000
Chief Information Officer	$0	$0	$84,000
Other	$0	$0	$0
Subtotal	$66,000	$72,000	$258,000
Total Headcount	15	29	81
Total Payroll	$242,374	$846,050	$2,024,250
Payroll Burden	$36,356	$126,908	$303,638
Total Payroll Expenditures	$278,730	$972,958	$2,327,888

7.0 FINANCIAL PLAN

The Daily Perc's financial picture is quite promising. Since TDP is operating a cash business, the initial cost is significantly less than many startups these days. The process is labor intensive and TDP recognizes that a higher level of talent is required. The financial investment in its employees will be one of the greatest differentiators between it and TDP's competition. For the purpose of this pro-forma plan, the facilities and equipment are financed. These items are capital expenditures and will be available for financing. There will be a minimum of inventory on hand so as to keep the product fresh and to take advantage of price drops, when and if they should occur.

The Daily Perc anticipates the initial combination of investments and long-term financing of $425,000 to carry it without the need for any additional equity or debt investment, beyond the purchase of equipment or facilities. This will mean growing a bit more slowly than might be otherwise possible, but it will be a solid, financially sound growth based on customer request and product demand.

7.1 Important Assumptions

The financial plan depends on important assumptions, most of which are shown in the following table. The key underlying assumptions are:

- The Daily Perc assumes a slow-growth economy, without major recession.
- The Daily Perc assumes of course that there are no unforeseen changes in public health perceptions of its general products.
- The Daily Perc assumes access to equity capital and financing sufficient to maintain its financial plan as shown in the tables.

General Assumptions

	2002	2003	2004
Short-term Interest Rate %	10.00%	10.00%	10.00%
Long-term Interest Rate %	9.00%	9.00%	9.00%
Tax Rate %	0.00%	0.00%	0.00%
Expenses in Cash %	10.00%	10.00%	10.00%
Personnel Burden %	15.00%	15.00%	15.00%

7.2 Key Financial Indicators

The following chart shows changes in key financial indicators: sales, gross margin, operating expenses, collection days, and inventory turnover. The growth in sales exceeds 250% each year. TDP expects to keep gross margin above the 38% projected for the first year, but it doesn't anticipate anything higher than 46%, since our payroll expenses will increase substantially as it grows into new areas and faces new competition.

The projections for inventory turnover show that TDP will maintain a relatively stable amount of inventory in its headquarters warehouse so that it has no less than two weeks of inventory on hand, but no more than three weeks, in order to keep products fresh. The only time it would consider holding larger stores of inventory is if there was some catastrophic event that could cause a dramatic rise in the price of its coffees or teas.

Benchmarks (Planned)

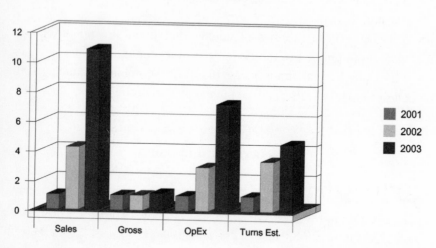

7.3 Break-even Analysis

To arrive at the average monthly fixed costs, The Daily Perc calculated the fixed costs for the Drive-thru to be $26,750. Using the average price per unit, less the average cost per unit, divided into the fixed costs of operation, TDP concludes that we will need at least 22,181 units per month to reach break-even at $41,034 per month.

Break-even Analysis

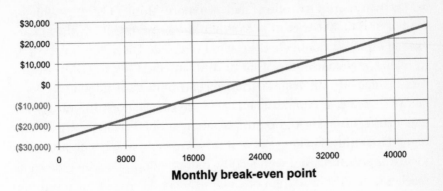

Monthly break-even point

Break-even point = where line intersects with 0

Break-even Analysis

Break-even Analysis:

Monthly Units Break-even	22,181
Monthly Sales Break-even	$41,034

Assumptions:

Average Per-Unit Revenue	$1.85
Average Per-Unit Variable Cost	$0.64
Estimated Monthly Fixed Cost	$26,750

7.4 Projected Profit and Loss

The Daily Perc is expecting some dramatic growth in the next three years, reaching $558,043 in sales and a 39.56% Gross Profit Margin by the end of the first year. Expenses during the first year will be roughly $233,483, leaving a Net After-tax loss of $20,541, or 3.68%. This loss will provide TDP with a tax loss carry-forward for the second year of $30,936.

Aside from production costs of 60%, which include actual production of product and commissions for sales efforts, the single largest expenditures in the first year are in the general and administrative (G&A) area, totaling 23% of sales. G&A includes expenses for rents, equipment leases, utilities, and the payroll burden for all employees.

Sales increase by nearly 400% in the second year, due to the addition of two more Drive-thrus and two more Mobile Cafes, reaching a total of $2,348,900, with a Gross Profit Margin of 39.58%. Although operating expenses double in the second year, The Daily Perc will be able to realize a Net After-tax profit of $190,467 or 6.79% of sales. In that same year, TDP will make charitable contributions of $70,000.

The third year is when The Daily Perc has the opportunity to break into markets outside the metropolitan area. TDP will see nine additional Drive-thru facilities open in the third year, which will drive sales to $6,022,950 and, even with a 200% increase in production costs, help reach a Gross Profit Margin of 45.05%. Several expenses take substantial jumps this year—advertising increasing from $36,000 to $72,000 and donations increasing from $72,000 to $180,000—and TDP will be adding several key management team members. These increases, as well as those for increased equipment leases and rents, raise our operating expenses to $1,673,431, leaving a Net After-tax profit of $860,428, or 11.96% of sales. The single largest expense sector in the third year, outside of production, is still G&A costs, but it is down from 23% in the first year and 18.5% in the second year to just 15.02%.

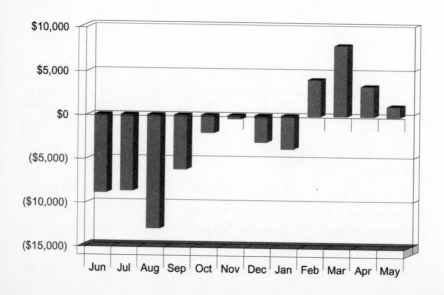

Profit Monthly (Planned)

Pro Forma Profit and Loss

	2002	2003	2004
Sales	$558,043	$2,348,900	$6,022,950
Direct Cost of Sales	$190,977	$737,990	$1,793,770
Production Payroll	$144,874	$646,050	$1,425,250
Sales Commissions	$1,416	$35,234	$90,344
Total Cost of Sales	$337,267	$1,419,274	$3,309,365
Gross Margin	$220,776	$929,627	$2,713,585
Gross Margin %	39.56%	39.58%	45.05%

Operating Expenses:

Sales and Marketing Expenses:

	2002	2003	2004
Sales and Marketing Payroll	$0	$22,000	$185,000
Advertising/Promotion	$18,000	$36,000	$72,000
Web Site	$1,000	$15,000	$22,000
Travel	$4,000	$7,500	$15,000
Donations	$3,332	$70,467	$180,689
Total Sales and Marketing Expenses	$26,332	$150,967	$474,689
Sales and Marketing %	4.72%	6.43%	7.88%

General and Administrative Expenses:

	2002	2003	2004
General and Administrative Payroll	$31,500	$106,000	$156,000
Payroll Burden	$36,356	$126,908	$303,638
Depreciation	$21,785	$92,910	$196,095
Leased Offices and Equipment	$0	$6,000	$18,000
Utilities	$9,640	$19,800	$41,100
Insurance	$12,570	$32,620	$63,910
Rent	$16,800	$50,400	$126,000
Total General and Administrative Expenses	$128,651	$434,638	$904,743
General and Administrative %	23.05%	18.50%	15.02%

Other Expenses:

Other Payroll	$66,000	$72,000	$258,000
Legal/Accounting/Consultants	$12,500	$24,000	$36,000
Total Other Expenses	$78,500	$96,000	$294,000
Other %	14.07%	4.09%	4.88%
Total Operating Expenses	$233,483	$681,605	$1,673,431
Profit Before Interest and Taxes	($12,707)	$248,022	$1,040,154
Interest Expense Short-term	$883	$750	$750
Interest Expense Long-term	$15,282	$37,204	$81,482
Taxes Incurred	$0	$0	$0
Extraordinary Items	$0	$0	$0
Net Profit	($28,872)	$210,068	$957,922
Net Profit/Sales	–5.17%	8.94%	15.90%

7.5 Projected Cash Flow

Cash flow will have to be carefully monitored, as in any business, but The Daily Perc is also the beneficiary of operating a cash business. After the initial investment and startup costs are covered, the business will become relatively self-sustaining with the exception of seasonal dips, which TDP has attempted to account for, through changes in the menu items.

Assuming an initial investment and financing of $415,000, which would include $30,000 of operating capital, The Daily Perc anticipates no cash flow shortfalls for the first year or beyond. March and May are the greatest cash drains, since TDP will be experiencing the cost of second drive-thru and mobile unit startup. Again, TDP sees heavier than normal drains of cash in December and January, as there will be certain accounts payable coming due.

Cash (Planned)

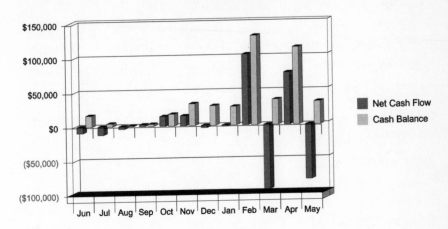

Cash Flow (Planned)

Pro Forma Cash Flow	2002	2003	2004
Cash Received			
Cash from Operations:			
Cash Sales	$558,043	$2,348,900	$6,022,950
From Receivables	$0	$0	$0
Subtotal Cash from Operations	$558,043	$2,348,900	$6,022,950
Additional Cash Received			
Extraordinary Items	$0	$0	$0
Sales Tax, VAT, HST/GST Received	$0	$0	$0
New Current Borrowing	$0	$0	$0
New Other Liabilities (interest-free)	$0	$0	$0
New Long-term Liabilities	$181,463	$253,970	$729,992
Sales of Other Short-term Assets	$0	$0	$0
Sales of Long-term Assets	$0	$0	$0
Capital Input	$0	$0	$0
Subtotal Cash Received	$739,506	$2,602,870	$6,752,942

Expenditures	*2002*	*2003*	*2004*
Expenditures from Operations:			
Cash Spent on Costs and Expenses	$46,456	$156,861	$405,542
Wages, Salaries, Payroll Taxes, etc.	$278,730	$972,958	$2,327,888
Payment of Accounts Payable	$378,280	$1,288,311	$3,283,708
Subtotal Spent on Operations	$703,466	$2,418,130	$6,017,137
Additional Cash Spent			
Sales Tax, VAT, HST/GST Paid Out	$0	$0	$0
Principal Repayment of Current Borrowing	$1,500	$0	$0
Other Liabilities Principal Repayment	$0	$0	$0
Long-term Liabilities Principal Repayment	$26,469	$0	$0
Purchase Other Short-term Assets	$0	$0	$0
Purchase Long-term Assets	$191,850	$429,700	$1,356,993
Dividends	$0	$0	$0
Adjustment for Assets Purchased on Credit	($191,850)	($429,700)	($1,356,993)
Subtotal Cash Spent	$731,435	$2,418,130	$6,017,137
Net Cash Flow	$8,071	$184,740	$735,805
Cash Balance	$33,571	$218,312	$954,116

7.6 Projected Balance Sheet

The Daily Perc's projected balance sheet shows an increase in net worth to just over $1 million in 2004, at which point it expects to be making 11.96% after-tax profit on sales of $6.02 million. With the present financial projections, TDP expects to build a company with strong profit potential, and a solid balance sheet that will be asset heavy and flush with cash at the end of the third year. The Daily Perc has no intention of paying out dividends before the end of the third year, using the excess cash for continued growth.

Pro Forma Balance Sheet

Assets

Short-term Assets	2002	2003	2004
Cash	$33,571	$218,312	$954,116
Inventory	$16,392	$42,762	$64,191
Other Short-term Assets	$0	$0	$0
Total Short-term Assets	$49,963	$261,074	$1,018,307
Long-term Assets	$323,250	$752,950	$2,109,943
Accumulated Depreciation	$21,785	$114,695	$310,790
Total Long-term Assets	$301,465	$638,255	$1,799,153
Total Assets	$351,428	$899,329	$2,817,460

Liabilities and Capital

	2002	2003	2004
Accounts Payable	$39,823	$163,266	$529,433
Current Borrowing	$7,500	$7,500	$7,500
Other Short-term Liabilities	$0	$0	$0
Subtotal Short-term Liabilities	$47,323	$170,766	$536,933
Long-term Liabilities	$286,394	$540,364	$1,270,356
Total Liabilities	$333,717	$711,130	$1,807,289
Paid-in Capital	$225,270	$225,270	$225,270
Retained Earnings	($173,770)	($202,642)	$7,426
Earnings	($28,872)	$210,068	$957,922
Total Capital	$22,628	$232,696	$1,190,618
Total Liabilities and Capital	$356,345	$943,825	$2,997,907
Net Worth	$17,711	$188,199	$1,010,171

7.7 Business Ratios

Standard business ratios are included in the following table. The ratios show a plan for balanced, healthy growth. The Daily Perc's position within the industry is typical for a heavy growth startup company. Industry profile ratios based on the Standard Industrial Classification (SIC) code 5812, Eating Places, are shown for comparison. Comparing the ratios in the third year with the industry, this pro-forma plan appears to be within an acceptable difference margin.

TDP's return on net worth and net worth number differ from the Industry Profile due to the lack of overhead when compared to a typical walk-in cafe. The Drive-Thru and Mobile business model is lean, thus allowing for increased return ratio and providing a lower Net Worth.

Ratio Analysis

	2002	2003	2004	Industry Profile
Sales Growth	0.00%	320.92%	156.42%	7.60%
Percent of Total Assets				
Accounts Receivable	0.00%	0.00%	0.00%	4.50%
Inventory	4.66%	4.75%	2.28%	3.60%
Other Short-term Assets	0.00%	0.00%	0.00%	35.60%
Total Short-term Assets	14.22%	29.03%	36.14%	43.70%
Long-term Assets	85.78%	70.97%	63.86%	56.30%
Total Assets	100.00%	100.00%	100.00%	100.00%
Other Short-term Liabilities	0.00%	0.00%	0.00%	32.70%
Subtotal Short-term Liabilities	13.47%	18.99%	19.06%	23.10%
Long-term Liabilities	81.49%	60.09%	45.09%	28.50%
Total Liabilities	94.96%	79.07%	64.15%	51.60%
Net Worth	5.04%	20.93%	35.85%	48.40%
Percent of Sales				
Sales	100.00%	100.00%	100.00%	100.00%
Gross Margin	39.56%	39.58%	45.05%	60.50%

Selling, General & Administrative Expenses	44.74%	30.63%	29.15%	39.80%
Advertising Expenses	3.23%	1.53%	1.20%	3.20%
Profit Before Interest and Taxes	−2.28%	10.56%	17.27%	0.70%
Main Ratios				
Current	1.06	1.53	1.90	0.98
Quick	0.71	1.28	1.78	0.65
Total Debt to Total Assets	94.96%	79.07%	64.15%	61.20%
Pre-tax Return on Net Worth	19.53%	151.95%	111.11%	1.70%
Pre-tax Return on Assets	0.98%	31.80%	39.84%	4.30%
Business Vitality Profile	*2001*	*2002*	*2003*	*Industry*
Sales per Employee	$37,203	$82,418	$74,819	$0
Survival Rate				0.00%
Additional Ratios	*2002*	*2003*	*2004*	
Net Profit Margin	−5.17%	8.94%	15.90%	n.a.
Return on Equity	−163.02%	111.62%	94.83%	n.a.
Activity Ratios				
Accounts Receivable Turnover	0.00	0.00	0.00	n.a.
Collection Days	0	0	0	n.a.
Inventory Turnover	7.43	24.95	33.54	n.a.
Accounts Payable Turnover	10.50	8.65	6.89	n.a.
Total Asset Turnover	1.59	2.61	2.14	n.a.
Debt Ratios				
Debt to Net Worth	18.84	3.78	1.79	n.a.
Short-term Liab. to Liab.	0.14	0.24	0.30	n.a.
Liquidity Ratios				
Net Working Capital	$2,620	$90,308	$481,374	n.a.
Interest Coverage	−0.79	6.53	12.65	n.a.

Additional Ratios

Assets to Sales	0.63	0.38	0.47	n.a.
Current Debt/ Total Assets	13%	19%	19%	n.a.
Acid Test	0.71	1.28	1.78	n.a.
Sales/Net Worth	31.51	12.48	5.96	n.a.
Dividend Payout	$0	0.00	0.00	n.a.

7.8 Exit Strategy

There are three scenarios for the investors and management to recover their investment—two with significant returns on each dollar invested.

Scenario One. The Daily Perc becomes extremely successful and has requests from other communities for Daily Perc operations to be opened there. This opens the door for franchising opportunity. When one looks at the wealth that has been created by the likes of McDonald's, Wendy's, Kentucky Fried Chicken, Burger King, and Taco Bell, the value of franchising a great idea cannot be dismissed. However, developing a franchise can be extremely costly, take years to develop, and be destroyed by one or two franchisees who fail to deliver the consistency or value on which the founding company had built its reputation.

Scenario Two. The Daily Perc chooses to become the Drive-thru version of Starbucks, obtaining several million dollars through an initial public or private offering that would allow the company to open twenty to thirty facilities per year in the region of the country between the mountain ranges, in both major and small metropolitan communities. This is the preferred Exit Strategy of the Management Team. The danger in this is that competitors would rise up and establish a foothold on a community before—or in the midst of—the arrival of The Daily Perc, causing a potential for a drain on revenues and a dramatic increase in advertising expenditures to maintain market share. Knowing these risks—and planning for them—gives TDP the edge needed to make this scenario work.

Scenario Three. By the third year, the growth and community support for The Daily Perc will have made the news in more than just the metropolitan area. It can be assumed that competitors, such as Starbucks or Quikava, will have seen the press and realized the value proposition in The Daily Perc's business plan. This will make TDP an attractive target for buyout. The company could be purchased by a much larger competitive concern by the end of the third year.

Taking a conservative approach to valuation and estimating that The Daily Perc would be valued at $7.5 million, and assuming that all 250 units of ownership in TDP are distributed to investors, a cash purchase of TDP would net each unit $30,000. With each unit selling at $4,250, that constitutes a Return on Investment of 705% over the three years. However, any buyout will most likely involve a cash/stock combination. A cash/stock buyout would be favorable, since the buying company would pay a higher price and the transaction would not have such severe tax consequences to the sellers.

Conclusion. Of the three scenarios, the management team prefers Scenario #2. The same numbers would relate to a public or private offering as are used in Scenario #3, but to make an offering available, there would be a dilution of shares that would provide additional shares for sale to the new investors.

Assuming the capital acquisition described in this plan is completed, there will be 250 units of the company in the hands of investors, constituting 100% of the authorized and issued units. For purposes of future fundraising, it will be necessary to authorize a stock split of, perhaps 5,000 to one, turning the current 250 units into 1,250,000 units.

Using the balance sheet for the third year, which estimates a Net Worth of just over $1.45 million, cash balances of $1.29 million and earnings of $1.06 million, based on 13 Drive-thrus and four Mobile Cafes, it is not unrealistic to put a market value of $15 million to $25 million on the company. At present, such companies are trading in multiples of 20 to 30 times earnings, and it is simple mathematics to multiply the success of TDP by the number of commuter heavy metropolitan areas in the United States.

With a corporate valuation of $7,500,000, each of the new units would have a market value of $6/unit. By authorizing an additional 750,000 units, there would be a total of 2,000,000 units with a market value of $3.75 per share. By offering the 750,000 shares at the price of $3.75 per unit, TDP would raise an additional $2,812,500 in expansion capital, which would be sufficient to open locations in an additional three to five cities.

References

Books

American Bar Association Guide to Small Business. ABA Press, 1998.

Brandt, Steven C. and Stafford Frey Cooper. *Stay Out of Court and in Business: Every Businessperson's Guide to Minimizing Legal Troubles*. Archipelago Publishing, 1997.

Branson, Richard. *Losing My Virginity*. Random House, 1998.

Coffman, Steve, Cindy Kehoe, and Pat Wiedensohler (editors). *The Internet-Plus Directory of Express Library Services: Research and Document Delivery for Hire*. American Library Association, 1998.

Collins, James C. and Jerry I. Porras. *Built to Last: Successful Habits of Visionary Companies* (Harper Business Essentials). HarperBusiness, 2002.

Easton, Jaclyn. *Striking It Rich.com*. McGraw-Hill, 2000.

Edwards, Paul and Sarah Edwards. *Working from Home: Everything You Need to Know About Living and Working Under the Same Roof*. Jeremy Tarcher, 1999.

Gerber, Michael E. *The E-Myth Revisited: Why Most Small Businesses Don't Work and What to Do About It*. HarperBusiness, 1995.

Goldstein, Arnold S. *How to Buy a Great Business With No Cash Down*. Wiley, 1989.

———. *Starting on a Shoestring: Building a Business Without a Bankroll*. Wiley, 2002.

Harroch, Richard D. *Small Business Kit for Dummies*. For Dummies, 1998.

Lesonsky, Rieva. *Start Your Own Business: The Only Start-Up Book You'll Ever Need*. Inc Entrepreneur Media. McGraw-Hill, 2001.

Levinson, Jay Conrad. *Guerrilla Marketing: Secrets for Making Big Profits from Your Small Business* (Guerrilla Marketing). Houghton Mifflin, 1998.

Mancuso, Anthony. *Nolo's Quick LLC: All You Need to Know About Limited Liability Companies.* Nolo.com, 2003.

Seid, Michael and Dave Thomas. *Franchising for Dummies.* For Dummies, 2000.

Strauss, Steven D. *The Big Idea: How Business Innovators Get Great Ideas to Market.* Dearborn, 2001.

———. *The Business Startup Kit.* Dearborn, 2003.

Winter, Barbara. *Making a Living Without a Job: Winning Ways For Creating Work That You Love.* Bantam, 1993.

Web Sites

www.Inc.com
www.Entrepreneur.com
www.SBA.gov
www.USATODAY.com/money/smallbusiness.front
www.MrAllBiz.com

Index

About the Author

Steven D. Strauss is the country's leading small business expert. An internationally recognized lawyer, business columnist, and speaker, Steve is also the author of a dozen books. Steve's business column, Ask an Expert, appears weekly at USATODAY.com and is one of the most highly syndicated small business columns in the world. You can read his column every week at www.MrAllBiz.com/columns.

A highly sought-after commentator and media guest, Steve has been featured on CNN, CNBC, Bloomberg Television, *The O'Reilly Factor*, MSNBC, Court TV, the BBC, and ABC News. He has been seen in many magazines, including *Time, Inc.*, *New York*, and *Entrepreneur*. He has been featured in many newspapers, including *Investor's Business Daily*, *USA Today*, the *New York Daily News*, the *Los Angeles Times*, the *Detroit Free Press*, and the *Chicago Tribune*.

Steve speaks to business groups the world over, including a recent visit to the United Nations. He consistently receives rave reviews for his humor, friendliness, energy, insight, and delivery.

A small business owner himself, Steve is the president of The Strauss Group (Strauss Law Firm, Strauss Seminar Company, *Ask an Expert* column syndication, and MrAllBiz.com). He graduated from UCLA, the Claremont Graduate School, and the McGeorge School of Law. If you would like to receive Steve's free newsletter *Small Business Success Secrets*, have him speak to your organization, or otherwise get in contact with him, visit his web site, www.MrAllBiz.com.

www.MrAllBiz.com